Gustave Masson

Mediaeval France

Gustave Masson

Mediaeval France

ISBN/EAN: 9783348010207

Printed in Europe, USA, Canada, Australia, Japan

Cover: Foto ©ninafisch / pixelio.de

More available books at **www.hansebooks.com**

MEDIÆVAL FRANCE

FROM THE REIGN OF HUGUES CAPET
TO THE BEGINNING OI
SIXTEENTH CENTUl

BY

GUSTAVE MASSON, B.A.

UNIV. GALLIC., OFFICIER D'ACADÉMIE, MEMBER OF THE SOCIÉTÉ DE L'HISTOIRE
DE FRANCE, ASSISTANT MASTER AND LIBRARIAN OF HARROW SCHOOL

𝔏𝔬𝔫𝔡𝔬𝔫

T. FISHER UNWIN

PATERNOSTER SQUARE

NEW YORK: G. P. PUTNAM'S SONS

MDCCCXCVII

To

M. GUSTAVE RUAULT,

THE FOLLOWING VOLUME IS AFFECTIONATELY DEDICATED,

GUSTAVE MASSON.

PREFACE.

"THE story of a nation," we conceive, is read, not only in its political annals, in the records of the battle-field, and the details of treaties of peace; but in its social life, in the development of commerce, industry, literature, and the fine arts. Accordingly, whilst attempting throughout the following pages to give the history of Mediæval France, we have allowed a large share to what may be called the intellectual side of the subject, more especially to the formation and progress of national literature. Without pretending to exhaust the topic, we have illustrated it by extracts from several authors, accompanied, whenever necessary, by a translation in English. The reader will thus be able to follow at the same time the development of the language; and the glossary at the end of the volume will help him to understand the archaisms used in the original passages quoted in the text.

We have consulted the best sources for the preparation of this work, especially the histories of Messrs. Michelet, Duruy, Bordier and Charton, Demolins, and

Chéruel ("Dictionnaire des institutions, mœurs et coutumes de la France"), and we trust that it may not be found unworthy of the series of which it forms a part.

GUSTAVE MASSON.

CONTENTS.

V.

VI.

VII.

I *

LIST OF ILLUSTRATIONS.

CHRONOLOGICAL TABLE

POLITICAL EVENTS.	THE CHURCH.	SCIENCE AND LITERATURE.
987 Hugues Capet *k.*	987 Council at Reims.	
996 Hugues Capet *d.*	996 „ at Saint Denis.	
1031 Henry I. *k.*		
1095 Preaching of the Crusade.	1095 „ at Clermont.	
1097 Nicæa taken by the Crusaders.		
1098 Battle of Dorylæum.		
1099 The Crusaders take Jerusalem.		
1100 Godfrey of Boulogne *d.*		
1108 Philip I. *d.*		1108 Aimon, Abbot of Fleuri *d.*
1112 King Henry of England captures and puts to death Hélie, Count of Mans.		1112 Robert Wace *b.*
	1115 Peter the Hermit *d.* The Monastery of Clairvaux founded by St. Bernard.	
1119 Battle of Brenneville lost by Louis VI.		
1124 War between France and Germany.		
1137 Louis VII. *k.*		
	1140 Abbey of La Trappe founded in France.	
1143 The Town of Vitry burnt.		
1147 Second Crusade preached.		1147 Giraud le Roux, *troubadour, fl.*
1148 Siege of Damascus by the Crusaders.		
1149 Louis VII. returns to France.		
1150 Henry Plantagenet, Count of Anjou, Maine, and Touraine.		1150 Villehardouin *b.* Arnaud, Daniel, *troubadour, fl. cours d'amour.*

1152 Suger d.
1179 Louis VII. visits as a pilgrim the tomb of
       Thomas à Becket.
1180 Philip Augustus k.
1187 Saladin takes Jerusalem—formation of com-
       munes.
1188 Third Crusade. The tax called Saladin's
       tithe (dime Saladine) imposed.
1190 The Kings of France and England go to
       the Crusade. The walls and gates of
       Paris are built.
1191 Philip Augustus returns to France.
1196 Marriage of Philip Augustus and of Agnès
       de Méranie.
1201 War between England and France. Agnès
       de Méranie d.
1207 John, King of England, summoned to ap-
       pear before an assembly of the French
       peers. His estates in France confiscated.
1210 Crusade against the Albigenses.

1213 Battle of Muret, won by Simon de Montfort.
1214 Battle of Bouvines.
1215 Louis IX. k. of France b. Magna Charta.

1210 Otho IV. excommuni-
       cated by Innocent III.
       Council of Paris con-
       demns the metaphysi-
       cal works of Aristotle
       to be burnt.

1180 Robert Wace d.

1191 Chrestien de Troyes d.

1201 Thibaut de Champagne b.

1203 Bible Guiot de Provins pub-
       lished.

1213 Villehardouin d.

1215 Cathedral of Rheims consecrated.
       Paris. Statutes given

Political Events.	The Church.	Science and Literature.
1216 Invasion of England by Philip Augustus.	1216 The Order of the Dominicans approved by the Pope.	
1218 Simon de Montfort d.	1218 The study of Civil Law prohibited in the University of Paris—Canon Law alone allowed.	
		1222 Joinville b.
1222 Raymond VI., Count of Toulouse, d.	1226 National Council in Paris.	
1223 Louis VIII., King of France.		
1226 Louis IX. (Saint Louis) b. regency of Blanche of Castile.		
1234 Louis IX. marries Marguerite of Provence.	1237 The Carthusian Order of Monks in France.	
		1240 Adam de la Halle b.
1242 Battle of Taillebourg.		
1248 Louis IX. goes to the Crusade.		1250 Marcabrus, troubadour, fl.
1249 Damietta taken by the French.		
1250 Louis IX. defeated and taken prisoner at the Battle of Mansurah.		
1252 Death of Blanche of Castile.	1252 Foundation of the Monastic Order of Servites in France.	
1254 Louis IX. leaves Palestine.	1256 The Augustinian Order of Monks established in France.	
1258 Estienne Boileau, Provost of France.		1260 Guillaume de Lorris d.

1262 "*Jeu du mariage ou de la feuillie*," composed by Adam de la Halle.
1264 Vincent de Beauvais d.

1270 "*Établissements de Saint Louis*" published.

1284 "*Jeu de Robin et de Marion*," by Adam de la Halle.

1286 Adam de la Halle d.

1303 The Company (dramatic) of the *Basoche* established.

1286 Bull "*Clericis laicos.*"
1297 Pope Boniface VIII. excommunicates the Colonna family.
1300 The Celestine Order of Monks established in France.
1301 Bull "*Ausculta, fili.*"
1302 Bull "*Unam Sanctam.*"
1303 Arrestation and death of Pope Boniface VIII.
1304 Pope Benedict XI. d.

1314 Clement V. d.

1264 Battle of Lewes. The King of France arbitrates between Henry III. and the Barons.
1270 Louis IX. d.
1278 Pierre de la Brosse hanged in Paris.
1282 "The Sicilian Vespers."

1285 Philip IV. k.

1297 The French invade Flanders.

1301 Revolt at Bruges.
1302 Battle of Courtrai.
1303 Peace between the French and the Scotch.

1304 Battle of Mons-en-Puelle.
1308 The States-General at Tours approve the prosecution against the Templars.
1314 Jacques de Molay and a large number of Templars burnt alive in Paris (March).

POLITICAL EVENTS.	THE CHURCH.	SCIENCE AND LITERATURE.
1314 Philip the Fair *d.* States-General (August).		
1315 The serfs emancipated on the royal dominions. Enguerrand de Marigny *d.*		
	1317 The Benedictine abbeys of Saint Papoul Condom, Maillezais, Tulle, Sarlat, Montauban, Vabres, and Castress erected into bishoprics	
		1319 Joinville *d.*
1328 Battle of Cassel gained by Philip VI.		
1336 The Flemings supported against the French by Edward III.		1337 Froissart *b.*
1337 Beginning of the Hundred Years' War.		
1340 Naval battle near Sluys; the French defeated by the English. Truce of four years.		1341 Royal decree restraining the licentiousness of stage-players.
1341 War for the succession of Brittany.		
1344 Renewal of the war between France and England.		
1346 Battle of Cressy.		1347 William of Ockham *d.*
1347 Siege of Calais, and its surrender to the English.		
1348 The Black Plague. The Jews persecuted.		
1349 Vienness and Montpellier ceded to the French.		

1350 Philip VI. *d.*

1356 Battle of Poitiers. John, King of France, taken prisoner and sent to England. The *Jacquerie.*

1358 Treaty of Calais. Etienne Marcel.

1360 King John returns to France. Treaty of Brétigny.

1364 Battles of Cocherel (May 6) and of Auray (Sept. 29). Charles V. *k.*

1367 Battle of Navarette. Duguesclin made prisoner.

1376 Edward, Prince of Wales (the Black Prince) *d.*

1377 Edward III., King of England. Olivier de Clisson invades Brittany.

1380 Duguesclin *d.* Charles V. *d.*

1382 Battle of Roosebeke. The *Maillotins.*

1392 Murder of Olivier de Clisson.

1407 Murder of the Duke of Orléans.

1351 "*Mystère des enfants d'Aimeri de Narbonne,*" acted.

1352 "*Moralité du mauvais riche et du ladre,*" acted

1360 Buridan *d.*

1364 A university founded at Angers.

1378 "*Mystère de la prise de Jérusalem,*" acted.

1380 "*Mystère de la Passion,*" acted.

1382 Nicolas Oresme *d.*

1390 "*Jeu des sept vertus,*" acted.

1392 Earliest composition of the "*Farce de Patelin.*"

1395 "*Mystère de Griselidis,*" royal decree against stage-players.

POLITICAL EVENTS.	THE CHURCH.	SCIENCE AND LITERATURE.
1408 Valentine of Milan *d.* Peace of Chartres.	1408 The Pope excommunicates the King of France.	
1410 Civil War in France. The *Bourguignons* and the *Armagnacs*.		
1415 Battle of Azincourt (October 23).		
1418 The *Armagnacs* massacred in Paris.		
1419 The Duke of Burgundy murdered at Montereau.		
1420 Treaty of Troyes.		
1421 Battle of Baugé.		
1422 Henry V. *k.* of England, *d.* at Vincennes, near Paris, Charles VI.		
1423 Battle of Crevant.		
1428 The French defeated at Verneuil (Aug. 16) by the Duke of Bedford.		
1429 Battle of the Herrings. Joan of Arc obliges the English to raise the siege of Orléans.		
1431 Trial and death of Joan of Arc.		
1435 Treaty of Arras.		
1436 Paris recovered by the French.		
1437 Siege of Montereau. Charles VII. enters Paris.		
1440 The *Praguerie*.		1440 Arnoul and Simon Gréban *fl.*
1444 Truce of Tours between France & England.		
1449 Renewal of hostilities.		1449 Pierre Blanchet *b.*
1450 Battle of Formigny—the English defeated. Agnès Sorel *d.*		1450 "*Mystère des actes des apôtres,*" Gréban. acted.

1451 The English evacuate part of France. Campaign in Guienne.
1456 Jacques Cœur d.

1461 Louis XI. b.
1464 "Ligue du bien public" against Louis XI.
1465 Treaties of Conflans and of Saint Maur.
1467 Philip the Good, Duke of Burgundy, d.
1468 Revolt of inhabitants of Liège. Louis XI. at Péronne.

1475 The sees of Marseilles, Saint Pol, Toulon, and Orange form the ecclesiastical province of Avignon.

1476 Battle of Granson. Charles the Bold defeated.
1477 The Duke of Burgundy slain at Nancy.
1479 Battle of Guinegate.
1483 Louis XI d.
1484 The States-General assemble at Tours.
1488 Battle of Saint Aubin du Cormier.

1492 Britany united to the French Crown.
1494 Italian Campaign by Charles VIII.
1495 Battle of Fornovo between Charles VIII. and the Venetians.
1498 Charles VIII. d.
1499 Milaness invaded by the French.

1459 "*Mystère de la destruction de Troie*," by Jacques Millet.

1476 The *Basochians* allowed to resume their performances.

1483 Rabelais b.

1491 Mellin de Saint Gelais b.
1492 Marguerite de Valois b.

1495 Clément Marot b.

POLITICAL EVENTS.	THE CHURCH.	SCIENCE AND LITERATURE.
1500 Insurrection of Milan.		
1501 The kingdom of Naples invaded by the French and Spaniards.		
1503 Battles of Cerignola, Seminara, and Garigliano. The French driven from Italy.	1503 Pope Alexander VI. *d.*	1503 Michel de l'Hospital *b.*
1504 Truce between France and Spain.		
		1507 The " *Mystère de la Passion*," printed in Paris.
1508 Treaty of Cambrai.		1509 Calvin *b.* Etienne Dolet *b.*
1509 Battle of Agnadello.		Martial d'Auvergne *d.* Philippe
1510 Cardinal d'Amboise *d.*		de Commines *d*
1512 Battle of Ravenna. Gaston de Foix *d.*		1513 Jacques Amyot *b.*
1513 The Swiss defeat the French at Novarra.	1513 Pope Julius II. *d.*	
1514 Anne of Brittany *d.*		

SOURCES TO CONSULT ON THE HISTORY OF FRANCE FROM HUGUES CAPET TO LOUIS XII.

THE CAPETIANS.

1 Glaber (Raoul), *d.* about 1046. His chronicle extends from 900 to 1044.

1 Richer, 10th century. " Richeri Historiarum," IV. libri, 888—995. Invaluable for the history of that time.

1 Helgaud, *d.* 1048? "Epitome vitæ Roberti regis," 997—1031. Written in a detestable style, and too much as a panegyric ; but interesting.

1 Adalbéron, Bishop of Laon, *d.* 1030? 1031? Satirical poem inscribed to the king.

1 Eudes, monk of the Abbey of St. Maur des Fossés. Life of Bouchard (Burckhardt), Count of Melun and Corbeil, 950—1058.

1 Hugues de Sainte Marie, monk of Fleury (St. Benoît-sur-Loire), 11th century. " Chronicon Floriacense," —1108.

1 Hugues de Poitiers, 12th century. " Histoire du Monastère de Vézelai," Books ii.—iv., 1140—1167. Interesting details.

1 Guibert de Nogent, 1053—1124. "Gesta Dei per Francos " (History of the First Crusade) ; " de vitâ suâ." One of the best of mediæval chronicles.

1 Guillaume de St. Thierry.
1 Arnaud de Bonneval. } Life of St. Bernard, abbot of Clairvaux, 1091—1153.
1 Geoffroi de Clairvaux.

1 Rigord, *d.* 1207? "Life of Philip Augustus," 1165—1208. For the history of the first thirty years of the reign this work is incomparably the best.

1 Guillaume le Breton (*Gulielmus Brito*), 1150?—1226. Continuation of the previous work, 1208—1223, " Philippidos," libri xii., an historical poem of great interest.

1 Nicolas de Bray, 1160 ?—1230 ? " Gesta Ludovici VIII." Historical poem.

1,2 Guillaume de Nangis. "Chronicon," from the creation of the world to 1301, continued by other monks of Saint Denis to 1368.

1 Pierre de Vaulx-Cernay, 13th century. Chronicle of the war against the Albigenses.

1 Guillaume de Puy Laurens, 1210?—1295. Chronicle of the war against the Albigenses.

1 Simon de Montfort. Under that name a chronicle exists called "Des gestes glorieux des Français," 1202—1311.

1 Guillaume de Tyr, 1130?—1190? "Historie des Croisades," 1095—1184. Most interesting.

1,2 Ernoul and Bernard le trésorier. Chronicle, 1201—1231.

1 Albert (or Albéric) d'Aix, 12th century. "Chronicon Hieroso-lymitanum," 1095—1120.

1 Raimond d'Agiles. Interesting account of the First Crusade, 1096 —1100.

1 Jacques de Vitry, *d.* 1240. "Historia Orientalis, Historia Occidentalis."

1 Raoul de Caën, 12th century. "Gesta Tancredi," —1105. (First Crusade.)

1 Robert le Moine, 1055—1122. "Historia Hierosolymitana." (First Crusade.)

1 Foulcher de Chartres. "History of the Crusades," 1095—1127.

1 Odon de Dueil, *d.* 1162. Wrote a history of the expedition of Louis VII. in Palestine, 1146—1148.

1,2 Orderic Vital, 1075—1142. His ecclesiastical history abounds in interesting details on the state of society in the 11th and 12th centuries.

1 Guillaume de Jumièges, 11th century. "Historia Norman-norum," 850—1137.

1 Guillaume de Poitiers, 11th century. "Gesta Gulielmei Ducis" (William the Conqueror), —1070.

3 Guillaume Anelier. History of the war in Navarre, 1276. 77.

Published separately. } "Grandes Chroniques de France," 376—1381.

2,4,5,6 Geoffroi de Villehardouin, 1155?—1213. "La Conqueste de Constantinoble." The earliest chronicle written in French, 1198—1207.

4,6 Henry de Valenciennes. Continues Villehardouin's chronicle.

3 Cuvelier, 14th century. A metrical history of Duguesclin.

6 "Chronique Métrique de Saint Magloire, 1223—1292.

6 "Chronique Métrique d'Adam de la Halle," 1282?

6 Guillaume Guiard, 13th century. "La Branche des royaux Lignages." A rhymed chronicle, 1165—1306.

6 Godefroi de Paris. "Chronique Métrique de Philippe le Bel," 1300—1316.

c,4,5 Le Sire de Joinville, 1224—1319. "Vie de Saint Louis." Charming by its style, its grace, and its simplicity.

2,6 Jean Froissart, 1337—1410.   Chronique, 1326—1400.   The chronicler *par excellence*.

THE VALOIS.

2,4,5 Christine de Pisan, 1363?—1431.   "Le Livre des faits et bonnes mœurs du sage roy Charles (V.)."   Authentic and interesting, but too pompous in style, 1336—1380.

2 "La Chronique du bon Duc Louis de Bourbon," 1360—1410.

4,5 "Le livre des faicts du bon Messire Jean le Maingre, dit Mareschal de Boucicaut," 1368—1421.

3 "Chronique du Religieux de Saint Denis," 1380—1422.

4 Jean-Juvénal des Ursins, 1388—1473.   "Histoire de Charles VI., roi de France," 1380—1422.

2,6 Enguerrand de Monstrelet, 1390?—1453. Chronique, 1400—1444. Tedious when compared to Froissart, but valuable for its accuracy and completeness.

2,6 Lefèvre de Saint Rémy, 1394—1468.   Mémoires, 1407—1435.

2,4,5 Pierre de Fénins.   Mémoires, 1408—1425.

4 "Journal d'un bourgeois de Paris sous le règne de Charles VI," 1408—1422.

7 Guillaume Cousinot.   "Chronique de la Pucelle," 1422—1429.

7 Pierre Cochon, —1443.   "Chronique Normande," 1118—1430.

7 Jean Chartier, —1462.   "Chronique de Charles VII.", 1422—1461.

4,5 Th. Godefroi.   "Histoire d'Artus III., Duc de Bretaigne, Comte de Richemont, et connétable de France," 1413—1457.

4,5 Th. Godefroi.   "Mémoires relatifs à Florent, Sire d'Illiers."

4,6 "Journal d'un bourgeois de Paris sous le règne de Charles VII," 1422—1449.

4,5 Olivier de la Marche, 1426—1502.   Mémoires, 1er et 2nd livres, 1435—1488.

4,5 Olivier de la Marche.   "S'ensuyt l'état de la maison du Duc Charles de Bourgogne, dit le Hardi, 1474.

4,5,6 Jacques du Clercq, 1420—, seigneur de Beauvoir en Ternois. Mémoires, 1448—1467.

2,6 Mathieu d'Escouchy (or de Courcy).   Chronique, 1444—1461. Continuator of Monstrelet.

2,4,5 Philippe de Commines, 1443—1509.   Mémoires, 1464—1498. The first French author who has written history with the depth and sagacity of a man accustomed to political life.

4,5 "Chronique Scandaleuse," 1460—1483.   On the life of Louis XI. Does not deserve the title under which it is known.

2 Thomas Basin, 1412—1491.   "Histoire de Charles VII., et de Louis XI."   Written in Latin ; most valuable.

c

3 Jean Masselin, —1500. "Journal des états généraux de 1484."

4,5 Guillaume de Villeneuve. Mémoires, 1494—1497. Very curious memoirs.

4,5 Jean Boucher, 1476—1550? "Panégyrique du Chevalier sans reproche," 1460—1525.

2,4 "Le Loyal Serviteur." Très joyeuse, plaisante, et récréative histoire du bon chevalier sans paour et sans reproche, 1476—1520. A masterpiece.

6 George Chastellain, 1403—1475. "Chronique du bon chevalier Jacques de Lalaing," 1430—1453.

6 George Chastellain. "Déclaration de tous les hautz faitz et glorieuses adventures du duc Philippe de Bourgogne," 1464—1470.

5 Jean Molinet, —1507. Chronique, 1470—1506.

THE VALOIS-ORLÉANS.

4,5 Robert de la Marck, seigneur de Fleuranges, 1491—1537. "Histoire des choses mémorables adventures du reigne de Louis XII. et François I.," 1499—1521. Interesting memoirs, but written too much in a *fanfaron* style.

The foregoing list comprises the *principal* chronicles and memoirs published in the collections edited by :—1. M. Guizot. 2. *Le Société de l'histoire de France.* 3 The French Government ("Documents inédits"). 4 MM. Michaud and Poujoulat. 5 MM. Petitot and Monmerqué. 6 M. Buchon. 7 M. Jannet ("Bibliothèque Elzévirienne").

CHRONOLOGICAL LIST OF ALL THE CHANCELLORS OF FRANCE FROM THE BEGINNING OF THE CAPETIAN DYNASTY TO THE REIGN OF LOUIS XII.

HUGUES CAPET. Adalbéron, Archbishop of Reims—Gerbert, Archbishop of Reims—Reginald, Bishop of Paris--Rotger, Bishop of Beauvais.

ROBERT. Abbo, Bishop—Francon, Bishop of Paris—Arnulphus, Archbishop of Reims—Baldwin—Fulbert of Chartres.

HENRY I. Gervais, Archbishop of Reims (1059, 1065)—Baldwin (1061—1067) — Peter, Abbot of Saint Germain (1067—71)—Guillaume (1073)—Godfrid (1075—92) —Roger of Beauvais (1070, 1080, 1105)—Ursion of Senlis (1090)—Hubert (1091, 92) — Hambaud (1095)—Arnulphus (1097)—Gislebert (1095, 1105) —Etienne (1106, 1108).

LOUIS THE FAT. Etienne (the same as above, 1108—1116—Etienne de Garlande (1116, 1125, 1133)—Fulchrade (1119)— Simon (1125, 1133)—Hugues (1129)—Algrin (1134, 37).

LOUIS THE YOUNG. Algrin (the same as above, 1150)—Noël, Abbot of Rebais (1139, 40)—Cadure (1140—1147)—Lideric (1142)—Barthélemy (1147) — Baudouin (1147)— Simon (1150, 1153)—Hugues de Champfueri, Bishop of Soissons (1150, 51, 69, 72)—Roger (1154)— Hugues de Puiseaux (1178, 79).

PHILIP AUGUSTUS. Hugues de Puiseaux (as above, to 1185)—Hugues de Béthisy (1185, 86).

LOUIS VIII. Guérin (1186—1226).

LOUIS IX. Guérin (abdicates in 1227, then a vacancy occurs— Philip d'Antogny—Jean Allegrin (1240? vacancy in 1248)—Nicolas de Canis (1249)—Gilles, Archbishop of Tyre (1258)—Jean le Court d'Aubergenville,

Bishop of Evreux (1258, 1260, vacancy in 1259)—Simon de Brie (Pope under the name of Martin IV, 1261)—Philippe de Cature (1269)—Mathieu de Vendôme, Abbot of Saint Denis—Simon de Clermont.

PHILIP III.   Pierre Barbet, Archbishop of Reims (1270, vacancy in 1271, 73, 74, 79)—Henry de Vézelay (1279)—Pierre de Challon (1281—83).

PHILIP IV.   Jean de Vassaigne (1292, died in 1300)—Etienne de Sousy (1292, 1302, 1304)—Guillaume de Crespy (1293, 96)—Pierre Flotte (1300—1302)—Pierre de Belle-Perche, Bishop of Auxerre (1306, 1307)—Pierre de Grès—Guillaume de Nogaret (1307)—Gilles Aycelin, Archbishop of Narbonne (1309—1313)—Pierre de Latilly (1313—14).

LOUIS LE HUTIN.   Etienne de Mornai (1314—16).

PHILIP V.   Pierre d'Arablai (1316, 17)—Pierre de Chappes (1321)—Jean de Cherchemont (1320).

CHARLES IV   Pierre Rodier (1320—23)—Jean de Cherchemont (1323—28).

PHILIP VI,   Mathieu Ferrand (1328)—Jean de Marigny, Archbishop of Rouen (1329)—Guillaume de Sainte Maure (1329—34)—Pierre Rogert (since Clement VI., 1334)—Guy Baudet, Bishop of Langres (1334—38)—Etienne de Vissac (1338)—Guillaume Flotte (1339—47)—Firmin Coquerel, Bishop of Noyon (1347)—Pierre de la Forêt, Cardinal (1349—57).

JOHN II.   Pierre de la Forêt (1359)—Fouquet Bardoul—Gilles Aycelin de Montagu (1357, 1360)—Jean de Dormans, Bishop of Beauvais (1361).

CHARLES V.   Jean de Dormans (till 1317)—Guillaume de Dormans (1371)—Pierre d'Orgemont (1380).

CHARLES VI.   Milon de Dormans, Bishop of Beauvais (1383)—Pierre de Giac (1388)—Arnaud de Corbie (dismissed in 1398, reinstated 1400—1405 ; dismissed again, reinstated, exercises 1409 ; abdicates in 1412)—Hier de Martreuil (?)—Nicolas du Bois, Bishop of Bayeux (1398—1400)—Jean de Montagu, Archbishop of Sens (1405—1409)—Henri de Laistre (1413, 1418—20)—Henri le Lorgne de Marle (1413—1418)—Jean le Clerc (1420—25).

CHARLES VII.   Louis de Luxembourg (1424—1435, *named by Henry VI. as well as the next*)—Thomas Hoo (1436—39)—Robert le Maçon (*named by the Dauphin*, 1418, 1419—21)—Martin Gouges de Charpaigne, Bishop of Clermont (1421—38)—Renaud de Chartres, Archbishop of Reims (March 28, August 6, 1424,

	1428—45)—Guillaume Juvénal des Ursins (1445—1461).
Louis XI.	Pierre de Morvillier (1461—1465)—Guillaume Juvénal de Ursins (1472)—Pierre d'Oriole (1483).
Charles VIII.	Guillaume de Rochefort (1492)—Adam Fumée (1494)—Robert Briçonnet, Archbishop of Reims (1495—97)—Gui de Rochefort.
Louis XII.	Gui de Rochefort (as above till 1507)—Jean de Gannay (1512)—Etienne Poncher (1515).

THE PARLIAMENT.

The Supreme Court of Law in France held its sittings, first at intervals, afterwards (reign of Charles V.) permanently ; was re-organized by Philip the Fair (edict of 1302), and subdivided according to the nature of the duties it had to discharge.

1. Political functions—belonged to the Council of State (*Conseil d'État, Grand Conseil, Conseil Étroit*).

2. Judicial functions — belonged to the Parliament proper, divided into three Courts
   - *a. Chambre des requêtes*, tried cases brought directly before the Parliament.
   - *b. Chambre des enquêtes*, tried cases about which appeal had been made to Parliament.
   - *c. Grand' Chambre* or *Chambre des plaidoiries*, decided cases examined in the first instance by the *Chambre des enquêtes*.

3. Financial functions—belonged to the *Chambre des comptes*.

Number of persons composing the Parliament under the reigns of Charles VII., Louis XI., Charles VIII., and Louis XII. : —

1. Twelve Peers of France.
2. Eight Masters (*Maîtres des requêtes*).
3. Eighty Councillors, both laymen and ecclesiastics.

PROVINCIAL PARLIAMENTS.

Toulouse	created in	1302		Dijon	created in	1477
Grenoble	,,	,, 1453		Rouen	,,	,, 1499
Bordeaux	,,	,, 1462		Aix	,,	,, 1501

GENEALOGY OF THE CAPETIAN KINGS OF FRANCE TO THE REIGN OF LOUIS XII.

(THE LETTERS *b. d. k.* STAND RESPECTIVELY FOR *born, died, king.*)

HUGUES LE GRAND, L'ABBÉ, Count of Paris and of Orléans, Duke of Neustria, Burgundy, Aquitaine, and France, *d.* 956.

HUGUES CAPET, *b.* (?) 941, Duke of France, Count of Paris and of Orléans, 960; *k.* 987; *d.* 996.

ROBERT II., *b.* 970; *k.* 996; *d.* 1031.

HENRY I., *b.* 1005; *k.* 1031; *d.* 1060.

HUGUES LE GRAND, *b.* 1027, Count of Vermandois (*stem of the second branch of the Counts of Vermandois*).

ROBERT, Count of Dreux, (*stem of the Counts of Dreux*).

HUGUES LE GRAND, *b.* 1007; *d.* 1025.

PHILIP I., *b.* 1053; *k.* 1060; *d.* 1108.

LOUIS VI., LE GROS, *b.* 1078; Count of Vexin 1092; *k.* 1108; *d.* 1137.

LOUIS VII., LE JEUNE, *b.* 1120; Duke of Aquitaine, *k.* 1137; *d.* 1180.

PHILIP II., AUGUSTUS, = (1) ISABELLA of Hainault, (2) INGELBURGE of Denmark, (3) AGNES DE MÉRANIE,
b. 1165; *k.* 1180; *d.* 1223.   *b.* 1170; *d.* 1190.   *d.* 1236.   *d.* 1201.
a

LOUIS VIII., LE LION, b. 1187; k. 1223; d. 1236. = BLANCHE of Castile, b. 1187; Regent 1226–1236, 1249; d. 1252.

- PHILIP HUREPEL, b. 1200; Count of Boulogne; d. 1234.
- CHARLES, Count of Anjou & Provence (*stem of the Counts of Anjou, Kings of Naples*).
- ALPHONSE, b. 1220; Count of Poitou & Auvergne, 1241; Count of Toulouse, 1249; d. 1271.
- ROBERT, Count d'Artois (*stem of the Counts d'Artois*).
- LOUIS IX. (Saint Louis), b. 1215; k. 1226; d. 1270. = MARGUERITE of Provence, b. 1219; d. 1245.

PHILIP III., LE HARDI, b. 1245; k. 1270; d. 1285. = (1) ISABELLA of Arragon, b. 1247; d. 1271. (2) MARY of Brabant, d. 1321.

- JEAN (Tristan), b. 1250; Count of Nevers 1265; Count of Valois 1268; d. 1270.
- ROBERT, Count of Clermont (*stem of the house of Bourbon*).

PHILIP IV., LE BEL, b. 1268; k. of France 1285; d. 1314. = JEANNE of Navarre b. 1268; k. of Navarre 1285; d. 1314.

- CHARLES, Count of Valois (*stem of the house of Valois*).
- LOUIS, Count of Evreux (*stem of the Counts of Evreux, Kings of Navarre*).

LOUIS X., LE HUTIN, b. 1289; k. of Navarre 1307; k. of France 1314; d. 1316. = (1) MARGARET of Burgundy, b. 1290; repudiated & d. 1315. (2) CLÉMENCE of Hungary, d. 1328.

PHILIP V., LE LONG, b. 1294; Count of Poitiers 1311; k. of Navarre 1318; d. 1322. = JEANNE of Burgundy, d. 1329.

CHARLES IV., LE BEL, b. 1293; k. of France & Navarre 1322; d. 1338. = (1) BLANCHE of Burgundy, repudiated 1322; d. 1326. (2) MARY of Luxenburg, b. 1305; d. 1324. (3) JEANNE D'EVREUX, d. 1371.

GENEALOGY OF THE CAPETIAN KINGS OF FRANCE.

(THE LETTERS *b. d. k.* STAND RESPECTIVELY FOR *born, died, king.*)

B. VALOIS BRANCH.

CHARLES DE VALOIS, son of Philip le Hardi and Isabel of Arragon, *b.* 1270; Count of Alençon and Valois, 1285; *d.* 1325.

PHILIP VI. DE VALOIS=(1) JEANNE of Burgundy, *d.* 1348.
b. 1293; Count of Valois, 1325; (2) BLANCHE of Navarre, *d.* 1398.
k. 1328; *d.* 1350.

CHARLES DE VALOIS, Count of Alençon (*stem of the Counts of Alençon*).

JEAN II. LE BON, *b.* 1319; Count of Anjou and Maine, Duke of=(1) BONNE of Luxemburg, *d.* 1349.
Normandy and Guienne, 1335; *k.* 1350; *d.* 1364. (2) JEANNE of Auvergne, 1360.

CHARLES V. LE SAGE=JEANNE de Bourbon, *b.* 1337; *b.* 1338; *k.* 1364; *d.* 1378. *d.* 1380.

LOUIS, Duke of Anjou (*stem of the second house of Anjou*).

JEAN=(1) JEANNE D'ARMAGNAC. *d.* 1387.
b. 1370; (2) JEANNE, Countess of Governor of Auvergne and of Paris, 1405; Boulogne, *d.* 1422. *d.* 1416.

PHILIP LE HARDI Duke of Burgundy (*stem of the second house of Burgundy*).

CHARLES VI. LE BIEN-AIMÉ=ISABEL of Bavaria, *b.* 1368; *k.* 1380; *d.* 1422. *b.* 1370; *d.* 1435.

LOUIS, Duke d'Orléans.

CHARLES DE BERRY, Count of Montpensier.

JEAN DE BERRY, Count of Montpensier.

LOUIS, Duke of Guienne and Dauphin, *b.* 1396; *d.* 1415.

JEAN, Duke of Touraine, *b.* 1398; *d.* 1417.

CHARLES VII. LE VICTORIEUX=MARIE of Anjou, *b.* 1403; Duke of Touraine, Anjou, 1416; Dauphin, 1417; Re- *b.* 1394; gent, 1418; *k.* 1422; *d.* 1461. *d.* 1463.

CATHERINE=(1) HENRY V., King of England, *b.* 1401; (2) OWEN TUDOR. *d.* 1438.

HENRY VI., King of England, d. 1473.

EDMUND TUDOR, Earl of Richmond, d. 1456.

HENRY VII., King of England, d. 1509.

CHARLES, b. 1446; Duke of Berry, 1461; of Normandy, 1465; of Guienne, 1469; d. 1472.

CATHERINE.=CHARLES of Burgundy, b. 1428; Count of Charolais. d. 1446.

JEANNE=LOUIS, Duke of Orléans (Louis XII.), who re- pudiated her in 1498. b. 1464; Duchess of Berry, 1498; d. 1505.

LOUIS XI.=(1) MARGARET of Scotland, b. 1418; d. 1444. (2) CHARLOTTE of Savoy, b. 1445; d. 1483. b. 1423; k. 1461; d. 1483.

ANNE=PIERRE II. of Bourbon, Lord of Beaujeu, d. 1503. b. 1462; Dame of Beaujeu, 1474: regent, 1483: d. 1522.

CHARLES VIII. L'AFFABLE=ANNE of Brittany, d. 1514. b. 1470; k. 1483; d. 1498.

C. BRANCH OF VALOIS—ORLÉANS.

LOUIS XII., LE PÈRE DU PEUPLE, Grandson of Charles V.=(1) JEANNE of France.
b. 1462; Duke of Orléans, 1466; Governor of Paris, 1483; (2) ANNE of Brittany, b. 1476; d. 1514.
and of Normandy, 1491; Duke of Milan, 1494; k. 1498; (3) MARY, daughter of Henry VII., King of England,
d. 1515. b. 1496; d. 1534.

DATE.	KING.	PLACE OF MEETING.	PRINCIPAL SUBJECTS DISCUSSED.
1420 (December 6—10)	Charles VI.	Paris.	The States-General, at the request of the king, sanctions the treaty of Troyes.
1423 (January)	Charles VII.	Bourges or Selles in Berry.	A grant of 1,000,000 francs made by the States.
1428 (October)	—	Chinon.	The States demand the reform of the *chambre des comptes* and of the inferior Law Courts, appeal to the patriotism of all the feudal lords, and grant a subsidy of 400,000 *livres*.
1434 (April)	—	Blois? Tours?	No details.
1435 (February)	—	?	This assembly seems to have consisted chiefly of deputies of the Langue d'oc. Subsidies voted.
1439 (October— November)	—	Orléans.	Negotiations with the English sanctioned. Funds granted for the re-organization of the army which was new modelled, and made permanent by an edict published on the 2nd of November.
1440 (September)	—:	Bourges.	The States-General discussed exclusively religious questions, and chiefly the Papal schism. They pronounced for Eugénie IV. against Felix V.
1468 (April)	Louis XI.	Tours.	On the necessity of putting down abuses and of maintaining the unity of the kingdom.
1484 (January)	Charles VIII.	Tours.	The votes are taken by *nations* (France, Burgundy, Normandy, Aquitaine, Langue d'oc, Langue d'oil). The regency is given to Madame de Beaujeu.
1501? 1502? (January)	Louis XII.	Blois.	No details.
1506 (May)	—	Tours.	The title, "Father of the People," voted to Louis XII. ; he is requested, and consents to give his only daughter Claude in marriage to Francis, Duke d'Angoulême, heir to the throne.

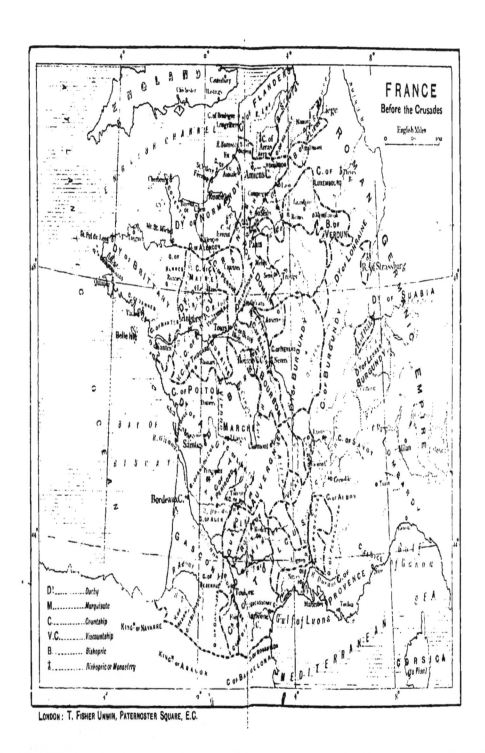

FRANCE

Before the Crusades

English Miles

MEDIÆVAL FRANCE.

I.

THE FIRST FOUR CAPETIAN KINGS.

(987–1108.)

THE story of ancient France can scarcely be said
to begin before Hugues Capet; during the Merovingian
dynasty it is the story of the Celts, the Romans, the
Greeks, and the Teutons ; under Charlemagne and his
successors it is closely interwoven with that of Germany. When, in 987, the Duke of France decided
upon assuming the title of king, the large and fertile
country included between the Rhine, the Pyrenees, and
the Atlantic Ocean could scarcely indeed be regarded as
forming one political community, but the various elements of which it consisted were gradually becoming
welded together, and all the inhabitants of that region,
whether north or south of the Loire, claimed the name
of *Frenchmen.* Let us take a glance at that series of
duchies, baronies, countships, and other quasi-indepen-
dent states of which Hugues Capet was the nominal
king. Brittany strikes us first as the district which

2

was the last to lose the originality of its laws, its customs, its language, and its literature ; as far back as
the fourth century the league or association of the
Armorican cities, governed by independent chieftains,
set at defiance both the Roman legions and the hordes
of Barbarians, who from the further side of the Rhine
overran the whole of Gaul.   They maintained their
freedom against the Northmen on the one side, and
the Angevins on the other.   After 982, however, they
ceased to form a separate state and became part of
France.   If we travel southwards, starting from the
banks of the Rhine, we find the provinces of Flanders,
Vermandois, Picardy ; and, going towards the east,
Lorraine.   Champagne owes its name (*Campania* in
Gregorius Turonensis) to the fertility of its soil, and
to its general appearance ; it was originally governed
by princes of the Vermandois family.   The Counts of
Anjou were undoubtedly the most powerful amongst the
vassals of Hugues Capet ; they played a conspicuous
part in the history of the Middle Ages, and were closely
mixed up with the political life, not only of France,
but of England.   Burgundy and Franche Comté must
not be forgotten, and in the course of this "story" we
shall often have the opportunity of recording the events
which brought the rulers of these provinces into col-
lision with the kings of France.   And now we come
to the banks of the Loire, on the southern side of which
the large districts of Septimania, Toulouse, Gascony,
Provence, and Guienne (corrupted from *Aquitania*) are
occupied by a population which still betrays its Latin
origin, and is decidedly the most intellectual and most
refined part of France.   There is the home of the

Troubadours; there flourishes the *Langue d'oc,* which has produced so many brilliant monuments of elegant literature.

We have thus given a short view of the principal territorial elements of which the French family consists ; we shall now describe as briefly, and yet as completely as we can, the constitution of the family itself and the political structure which prevailed during the period known as the Middle Ages.

Three different categories made up society in the Gaul of the sixth century ; namely, the Gallo-Roman, the Church, and the Barbarian. When Hugues Capet came to the throne, this threefold division still existed, but under different names : the lords held the position occupied previously by the Gallo-Romans, and whilst the Church retained its position, the serfs represented the lowest stratum of society, barbarians in point of fact, if not by express designation. The bonds which connected these three orders with each other may be said to have arisen from two edicts or enactments which consecrated a revolution of ancient date, and resulting from the very nature and constitution of society. In times of political disturbances, when the most elementary notions of order seem forgotten and cast aside, it is a matter of course that the weak should endeavour to secure the protection of the strong, and to obtain, if possible, the conditions of peaceful life and of undisturbed labour. Now, in 847 an edict given at Mersen contained the following clause : " Every free man shall be allowed to select for himself a lord, either the king or one of the king's vassals ; and no vassal of the crown shall be obliged to follow the king to war, except against foreign enemies." The force of this enactment will be obvious. We must bear in mind that at the time of his accession, Hugues Capet was no more than the equal of most of the lords between whom the territory of France was divided, and even inferior in power to some of them. Nor was this a solitary case, and as his subjects could thus make their obedience a matter of bargain, the sovereign would frequently find himself helpless in times of civil war, and being equally unable to enforce submission upon the lords, and to protect the common class of his subjects, these would naturally group themselves around the more powerful barons.

As the edict of Mersen affected the question of *security*, so that of Kiersy told upon the status of *property*. Under the Carlovingian dynasty property was of two kinds ; the holders of allodial lands (*allodial* from *all*, and the old Teutonic substantive *od*, goods, property) enjoyed them absolutely and independently. On the other hand, benefices or fiefs (from the Anglo-Saxon *feof*, cattle, money) were granted by a lord to a person who, in return for that grant, and for the protection it insured on the part of the baron, obliged himself to do military service, to render pecuniary assistance, &c. Now it would frequently happen that the owner of allodial property, isolated amongst all his independence, found it impossible to live securely and comfortably in the vicinity of barons stronger or more powerful than himself. He would then select one of these barons or feudal lords, *recommend* himself to him, as the saying was, make over to him by a kind of feigned cession his allodial property, and then receive it back again as a *benefice*, together with all the duties, obligations, and burdens belonging to it. As a matter of course, *beneficiary* property soon formed the rule, except south of the Loire, and there was no landed property which did not depend upon another property, no man who was not the vassal or dependant of another man. The hereditary transmission of landed property and of all charges, offices, and positions of trust was sanctioned by the edict of Kiersy (877).

We thus see that every great lord or landowner, enjoying the same rights and privileges as the king himself, there existed throughout the length and breadth of France as many sovereigns as there were dukes, counts, viscounts, &c. When Hugues Capet came to the throne, he found a hundred and fifty barons owning the right of legislating, coining, administering justice, making war, and concluding treaties with their neighbours. The king, therefore, had no real power *as such*, but only so far as he possessed some important fief, whether dukedom or countship. Before the accession of the Capetian dynasty the royal domain consisted of the city of Laon and a few insignificant villas ; after the year 987 it comprised the whole duchy of France, and Hugues Capet was thus, in point of real power, the equal of his vassals.

It should not be forgotten that a real hierarchy bound together all owners of fiefs, and in this complicated system the same individual could be at the same time suzerain and vassal. The King of France, for instance, was vassal of the Abbot of Saint Denis, and the Duke of Burgundy held the same position towards the

Bishop of Langres ; thirty-two knights-bannerets owed service and homage to the Viscount of Thouars, who, in his turn, was a vassal of the Count of Anjou, himself a vassal of the King of France. Our readers will see at once that every count was not necessarily superior to a viscount and inferior to a duke. The Count of Anjou, for example, had nothing to do, hierarchically, with the Duke of Burgundy, and the only point these two lords had in common was their position as vassals of the King of France.

Three principal ceremonies characterized the feudal relations between the lord and his vassal. The latter, when doing homage to the former, knelt before him, and placing his hand in that of his future suzerain, declared that he would become *his man*, and as such acknowledged himself bound to defend his life and his honour. He then took the oath of faith or fidelity, having previously removed his sword and his spurs. This was called *hommage-lige*, and bound the vassal to military service for an unlimited time, and on whatsoever territory the lord thought fit to lead his dependants. For circumstances and at epochs when war was permanent, or nearly so, the *hommage-lige* prevailed ; thus in the code of laws known by the name of "Assises de Jérusalem," drawn up after the taking of the Holy City by the Crusaders in 1099, it is regarded as *the* rule. The *hommage simple* or *franc* was of a less stringent character ; it implied military service only for the space of forty days yearly, within the limits of the fief, and with the permission of performing that service by deputy. The vassal did homage standing, wearing his sword and spurs, and placing one hand on a copy of the Gospels. The ceremony once over, the tie between the lord and his vassal is complete, and an interchange of duties, services, and obligations must be the necessary result. We can imagine the scene taking place in the hall of óne of those imposing castles, the ruins of which add even at the present time so much picturesqueness to the landscapes in France, Germany, England, Italy, and Spain.

Just as the republics of antiquity had their *forum* and their *agora*, just as the France of Louis XIV. boasted of its Versailles, just as modern England possessed its court of Parliament, so did the feudal system raise its castles and its strongholds as the centre of authority and the symbol and the abiding place of power. The edifice is generally built upon a height ; its architecture is massive, but without any particular beauty. A series of towers, either round or square, connected together by formidable walls, and pierced here and there with loop-holes form the structure. At Montlhéry there were no less than five concentric enclosures commanding each other, and giving additional security to the *château*. You arrive ; the entrance-gate, flanked by small towers and surmounted by a guard-room, presents itself before you. Three moats, three drawbridges must be crossed. At every step you take, a challenge meets you, and if admittance is granted, you find yourself before the keep (*donjon*), a strongly fortified building which contains the family records and the family treasure . The lodgings, farmhouses, stables, and other dependencies are scattered about to the right and to the left, and an underground passage leaves an

CHATEAU OF MONTLHÉRY.

exit from within to the plain or to the neighbouring forest.

There is not a single feature in these splendid castles which does not remind us that war is the constant occupation of those who dwell within, and that military service is the chief obligation which the vassal owes to his lord. We have said the *chief,* not the only one. The help of wise counsel and of wholesome advice is also frequently needed , it may likewise happen that the lord is retained prisoner in foreign lands ; the vassals must then club together to pay his ransom. When he gives his eldest daughter in marriage, when his eldest son is made knight, or is about to start for the Crusades, pecuniary aids are also expected as a matter of course. Estates might, and did often, change hands ; others were confiscated or left without owners, on account of the death of the heir: hence fresh and heavy duties paid over to the lord. If the vassal was a minor, the suzerain became his guardian, and as such received the income till his ward had attained his majority. The daughters of the vassal were obliged to receive husbands at the hand of the lord, unless they preferred forfeiting a considerable sum of money. .It will be easily imagined that under such a system fiefs were multiplied as much as possible, because every fief meant military service—a thing of the utmost importance in those days—and money, which at all times is a matter of great consequence. The right of hunting, of fishing, of crossing a river, of escorting merchants and other persons of the same description had to be purchased. The vassals were compelled to

A KNIGHT.

bake their bread in the seigniorial ovens, to grind their corn in the seigniorial mill, to make their wine in the seigniorial wine-press, paying certain sums for the use of conveniences which they were obliged to avail themselves of (*banalités*).

All the vassals of the same lord were considered as *pairs* or equals, and they formed in their capacity a kind of court of justice from which appeals were allowed to the lord himself. Whenever in discussions or differences agreement was impossible, the case was decided by a duel or appeal to arms. The right of private warfare was thus not only tolerated, but sanctioned as a matter of necessity. All lords had the right of pronouncing judicial sentences, but that right was not the same in all cases. Only barons enjoying the privilege of *high justice* (haute justice) could condemn to death, and accordingly erect the gallows in the neighbourhood of their castles. The *middle* and *low justice* (moyenne justice, basse justice) only applied to minor cases, which were punished by fines.

Lower than the vassals came the serfs who had no rights—a whole army of wretched creatures who, under their threefold designations of serfs properly so called, *mainmortables*, and *vilains*, *manants* . or *roturiers*, were more or less under the absolute dependence of the feudal baron. Of the serfs, an old legist has said that the baron might take from them whatever they had, and that he might either rightfully or wrongfully keep them in prison whenever and as long as he liked, being accountable to God alone. The *mainmortables* were better off; if they paid regularly their rents, dues, reliefs, &c., the lord could not

exact anything more from them, unless as a punishment for some misdeed ; but they could not marry
except with the permission of the lord, and, at their
death, all their property reverted to him.   The
manants or *roturiers* enjoyed their freedom, at any
rate, and could transmit their property to their
children, but still they had to put up with certain
obligations which often rendered their peace and their
condition, in general, extremely precarious.   The
vassals had, as we have seen, to pay to the baron
certain fines, reliefs, dues, &c. ; we need hardly say
that the serfs and vilains were treated in a far more
arbitrary fashion still.   Besides contributions in kind
and in money, they found themselves compelled to
give away their time and their labour without the
slightest compensation.   When a road had to be
made on the manorial estate, a building to be erected
or repaired, furniture or agricultural implements to be
provided, the serfs were set to work as part of the
obligations to which they were bound.   In fact, the
serfs were made to feel constantly that they had no
free action, and that they could dispose neither of.
their service nor of their labour.

What was the Church doing in the meanwhile, and
what part did it play in the general progress of social
institutions?   There is no doubt that the influence
exercised by it was a beneficial one as a whole, but it
had become part and parcel of the feudal system, and
the archbishops, bishops, and abbots exercised tem-
poral power as well as spiritual authority.   We are
at first inclined to wonder perhaps when we read that
during the Middle Ages the Church possessed, in

France as well as in England, more than one-fifth
of the whole territory ; but we must remember that
whilst, on the one hand, the threat of excommunication prevented many otherwise unscrupulous
persons from tampering with Church property, the zeal
and the piety of the great majority of the rich faithful
resulted, on the other, in grants of land and other
substantial donations to churches, abbeys, and monasteries. Despite the character which ordination had
stamped upon them, ecclesiastical dignitaries retained
much of those fighting qualities so essentially belonging to feudalism. In his history of France
(vol. ii.), Michelet mentions several amusing instances of this fact. As early as Charlemagne the
bishops are indignant when a peaceful mule is brought
round to them if they wish to ride; what they want
is a charger; they jump upon it unaided ; they hunt,
they fight ; the blows they deal with their swords are
their style of blessing ; the penances they impose are
the heavy and formidable strokes of their battle-axes.
We hear of a bishop deposed by the whole episcopal
bench as pacific and not sufficiently courageous ; the
barons became clergymen, the clergymen barons.

Such, in brief, was the state of French society when
Hugues Capet ascended the throne. And here the
question arises : Who was Hugues Capet ? What
do we know about his origin ? There exists a *chanson
de geste* (romance of chivalry) which bears the name
of that king, and where occurs the following passage :

> " Pour ce vous lyray la vie d'un guerrier
> De coy on doit l'istore et loer et prisier,
> Et le grant hardement que Dieux ly fist querquer

Pour soustenir droiture et honneur exauchier.
Ce fu Huez Capez c'on apelle bouchier :
Ce fu voirs, mais moult space en savoit du mestier. "

" Therefore I shall read you the life of a warrior,
Whose history should be praised and valued,
And the great courage which God led him to seek
To uphold right and exalt courage.
This was Hugues Capet, whom they called a butcher :
This was true, but he knew very little of the trade."

Hugues Capet, a butcher (the nephew of a butcher
as the song says elsewhere) ; this statement is odd
enough, but what is more singular still, the same origin
is ascribed to the first Capetian king by Dante
("Purgatorio"), the chronicler of Saint Bertin, Villon
("Ballade de l'appel"), and Cornelius Agrippa ("De
vanitate scientiarum"). We know, indeed, that the
great Italian poet was animated by a spirit of hostility
when he ascribed to Hugues Capet so low an origin ;
we are also aware that the author of the chronicle of
Saint Bertin quotes the legend only to contradict it ;
but what motive can Villon and others have had to
give it credence, if it was not the wish to flatter the
bourgeoisie by identifying with it a brave soldier, or,
on the other hand, to represent Hugues Capet as a
mere usurper?

By opposition to this hypothesis some chroniclers
have endeavoured, with more ingenuity than success,
to find a family connection between the Duke of
France and the Carlovingians, just as at an earlier
period a fanciful genealogical tree had been devised,
showing that Pepin the Short could trace back his
origin to the Merovingian dynasty. Be the result
what it may, Hugues Capet ruled over France for

the space of nine years, and died in 996, at the comparatively early age of fifty-four. When his son Robert ascended the throne, France, as well as the rest of Europe, was under the impression of extreme terror. It was a general belief that the end of the world would take place in the year 1000, and a society so disorganized as feudalism still was, could not but be much struck by that idea, unwarranted as it might be. One good result came out of it in the shape of great moral improvement ; and if the Church profited through the liberality of the faithful, in the shape of donations, legacies, &c., it is only fair to say that the ecclesiastical dignitaries, the clergy, both secular and regular, did their utmost to enforce discipline, to put down abuses, and to check the ambition and wanton disposition of the barons and lords. Robert has left behind him the reputation of one of the most pious kings who ever occupied the French throne. "More of a monk than of a sovereign," says some historian ; and the poets and chroniclers continually allude to the "times of good King Robert." He got into trouble with the Pope for having married a distant relative, Bertha, daughter of Conrad the Peaceful, King of Arles, and widow of Eudes I., Count of Blois. In spite of the threats of the Court of Rome, notwithstanding the express decision of a council, Robert persisted in retaining his wife, and it was only in 1006 that he repudiated her, and married Constance, daughter of William Taillefer, Count of Toulouse. The appearance of the Southerners in Paris seems to have created not only astonishment, but disgust. "Conceited men," says the chronicler,

Radulph Glaber, "of light character and dissolute, life ; their dress, the very trappings of their horses are odd and fantastic ; they are close-shaved like stage-performers, their hair is cut short, their buskins are absurdly long ; they jump rather than walk ; they have an utter disregard for their word, and no one dare trust them." The contrast between Robert's kindly disposition and the haughtiness of his queen is repeatedly dwelt upon by the historians, who illustrate it by characteristic anecdotes. "Constance never jokes," says the monk Helgaud. She incited to rebellion, first, Robert's eldest son, Hugues, who died in 1025 ; and, secondly, his third son, Henry. The peaceful reign of the second Capetian monarch was marked, however, by events of considerable importance. He was offered the crown of Italy and the dukedom of Lorraine ; conscious, no doubt, of his own weakness he refused both, and if he acted rightly in declining the former presentation, we must own that he was not well-advised when he refused the latter ; after a war which lasted sixteen years he obtained possession of the dukedom of Burgundy, which, however, was lost temporarily to the crown by Henry the next king.

Another important fact, which we must not leave unmentioned, is the insurrection of the Normandy peasants in 997. The insolence and tyranny of the barons was felt in that part of France more than anywhere else, for the simple reason that the serfs and the commoners constituted the chief part of the original population, whilst the aristocracy belonged to the invaders who had scarcely for a century settled down in Neustria. Why should authority be in the hands of comparative strangers, especially when it was so brutally misused ?

Fellowship in suffering knit together all the victims of feudal tyranny ; after the work of the day was over the inhabitants of the same neighbourhood used to assemble together, and discuss the long tale of their grievances, the duties they had to pay, the *corvées* to which they were subjected, the labour for which they received no compensation.

> " Les paysans et les vilains,
>   Ceux du bocage et ceux des plaines,
>   Par vingt, par trente, par centaines,
>   Ont tenu plusieurs parlemiints ;
>   Que jamais, par leur volonté
>   N'aront seingneur ni avoé."

> " The peasants and the vilains,
>   Those of the woods and those of the plains,
>   By twenties, by thirties, by hundreds,
>   Have held several parliaments
>   (To the effect) that never with their consent
>   Shall they have lord or champion."

The chronicler, William of Jumièges, gives us an interesting account of the origin and development of a vast association, having its ramifications throughout the length and breadth of the duchy, and the object of which was nothing else but the destruction of the feudal system. Unfortunately the plot was discovered, and the members of the central committee, if we may use such a name, were seized by a body of soldiers under the orders of the Count of Évreux, uncle of the then Duke of Normandy, Richard II. They were all frightfully maltreated, and those who survived were

3

sent back to their villages with the view of inspiring
terror and submission to the rest of the population.

A system of persecution organized against the
Jews must also be noted, the cause of this being, as
was then alleged, the destruction of the Church of the
Holy Sepulchre by the Fatimite Caliph of Egypt.
The first public execution of heretics likewise took
place about that time ; thirteen were burned at Orléans, in 1022; Toulouse and other places witnessed
similar executions.   One of the unfortunate persons
thus sentenced to death had been confessor to Queen
Constance ; as he passed by her side on his way to
the place of execution, she put out one of his eyes
with a wand she held in her right hand.

Death surprised Robert whilst he was busy copy-
ing the obituary register of the Church of Melun
(1031).   His third son, Henry I., succeeded him, the
first being dead, and the second incapacitated by
weakness of mind.   Constance would have wished
her fourth son, Robert, to obtain the crown ; but this
could not be, and Henry had to satisfy the ambition of Robert by giving over to him the duchy of
Burgundy.

During the early part of the Middle Ages several
cases took place of marriages annulled by the Pope, because they had been brought about between persons connected together by relationship, at degrees condemned
by the Church.   Henry I., determined to avoid such
a difficulty, sought and obtained the hand of Anne,
daughter of the Grand Duke of Russia.   It was
reported that she descended, on her mother's side,
from Philip, King of Macedon.

If the first Capetians were naturally of a timid disposition, and better fit for the quiet seclusion of a monastery than for the turmoil of political life, the surrounding lords, on the contrary, obtained an undesirable reputation by their crimes and their ambition. Robert, Duke of Normandy, was one of them; nicknamed *the Magnificent* by his barons, he appears to have rather deserved the sobriquet of *the Devil*, which the common people bestowed upon him. His first step in public life was a crime, for he usurped the Duchy of Normandy by poisoning the lawful ruler, Richard III., his brother, and the chief barons. He then interfered with all his neighbours, and, finally, having endeavoured to atone for his wickedness by a pilgrimage to Jerusalem, he died in Asia Minor on his way home. His son, who was destined to be so famous under the name of William the Conqueror, after having succeeded in reducing, with the help of the King of France, his turbulent vassals to obedience, ended by turning against Henry, and defeating the royal forces in several encounters, more particularly at Mortemer, in 1054.

Foulques Nerra (the black), Count of Anjou, was also a good specimen of the mediæval baron. When a man undertakes no less than three pilgrimage the Holy Land, we are justified in believing th catalogue of his sins was particularly heav was certainly the case with Foulques N stance, Robert's queen, was his niece plained to him one day of a favourite The Count of Anjou immediatel knights, and ordered them to

favourite, and stab him wherever they might find him.
Foulques Nerra had two wives ; according to one
version, he ordered the former one to be burned alive ;
according to another, he had her thrown down a
precipice, and as she contrived to escape, he stabbed
her himself. He ill-used his second wife so much
that she was obliged to retire to the Holy Land. We
are not much astonished at learning that, overcome
by remorse, Foulques Nerra caused himself to be
fastened to a hurdle, and thus dragged through the
streets of Jerusalem, whilst two of his servants
scourged him with all their might, and he kept repeating, "Have pity, O Lord, on the traitor, the perjured Foulques !" He died (1040) on his way home,
leaving the countship of Anjou to his son Geoffrey
Martel, as warlike as he had been himself, and who
was a powerful ally of the King of France against the
Duke of Normandy.

We thus see that the feudal system was bearing
already its fruit in a plentiful crop of acts characterized by cruelty, abuse of power, and unbridled
ambition. At this point (1041) the Church stepped
in, and resolved upon mitigating, if ever so little, the
distress from which the lower classes of society were
ering. Accordingly an edict was published,
ed pretty nearly in the following terms : " From
nesday evening to the Monday morning in
, on high festivals, and during the whole
d of Lent, all deeds of warfare are ex-
en. It shall be the truce of God.
s it shall compound for his life, or
country." As we may suppose,

whilst this new law gave the greatest satisfaction to the mass of the population, it was vigorously resisted by barons such as the Count of Anjou and the Duke of Normandy ; but they were finally obliged to acquiesce in a decision which was so beneficial to society at large.

Philip I. was only seven years old when he succeeded his father. Indolent and feeble, he saw the whole of Western Europe rushing in various directions, carried away by the love of adventure, without feeling the slightest desire to follow their example. Considering his inert disposition, it is a wonder that Philip, for the sake of joke, should have exposed himself to the fury of such a man as William the Conqueror. "When will that fat fellow be confined?" said he, alluding to the King of England's stoutness. "I shall go and be churched in Paris, with ten thousand lances instead of wax tapers." William nearly kept his word ; marched into the domains of the King of France, destroying everything, burning towns and villages, and putting the inhabitants to the sword. The city of Mantes was reduced to a heap of ruins, and only death arrested the progress of the infuriated William. He expired at Rouen from the results of a wound he had received at the sacking of Mantes.

Philip carried on, with the same indolence, against William Rufus the policy of antagonism which he had displayed in his relations with the Conqueror, and helped to swell the list of French monarchs excommunicated by the Pope for illegal marriage. He died in 1108.

II.

PILGRIMAGES TO THE HOLY LAND—THE CRUSADES—CHIVALRY.

AN old writer belonging to the seventh century, named Marculphus, has left under the title of *formulæ*, a series of enactments or decisions on points of law. Amongst these documents is the following curious piece of which we give a translation : "Be it known unto you, holy fathers, bishops, abbots and abbesses, dukes, counts, vicars, and all people believing in God and fearing Him, that the pilgrim ——, a native of ——, has come to us and asked our advice, because, incited by the great enemy of mankind, he has killed his own son —— or his nephew —— ; for this reason, and in accordance with custom and canon law, we have pronounced that the aforesaid —— should devote — years to a pilgrimage. When, therefore, —— presents himself before you, kindly give him lodging, accommodation, and fire, bread and water, and allow him to repair at once to the holy places." This kind of passport shows that even as far back as the Merovingian dynasty pilgrimages to Jerusalem and to the Holy Land in expiation of some notorious crime or act of wickedness were of frequent occurrence. The culprit had often to wear around his neck, his waist, and his wrists, chains forged out of his own armour, thus bearing about him both the memorials of his social position and their marks of his misdeeds. The pilgrims started on their long and dangerous voyage, and those of them who were fortunate enough to return home after a protracted absence, brought back marvellous tales respecting the sacred relics which the Holy City offered to the veneration of the faithful, and heart-rendering stories of the sufferings which the Europeans had to bear from the combined Jews and Mahometans.

It was natural that in course of time pilgrimages of this kind should lead to military interventions; the earliest appeal to arms proceeded from a Frenchman, Gerbert of Aurillac, who became Pope under the name of Sylvester II. (1002); and the powerful eloquence of another Frenchman, Peter the Hermit, a native of Picardy, led to the departure of the first Crusading army. Well might the Chronicler Guibert de Nogent speak of these expeditions as *Gesta Dei per Francos.*

A general council had been announced as about to meet at Clermont on the 18th of November, 1095. An immense concourse of people gathered together, and in their midst appeared a man, wretched to look at, small in stature, bare arms and bare feet; his dress was a species of woollen tunic and a cloak of coarse cloth. That was Peter the Hermit; his piercing eye seemed to penetrate into the hearer's heart, and no one could resist the earnestness of his preach-

ing ; he had just arrived from Italy where he had
persuaded Pope Urban II. to summon the people to
arms on behalf of the Christian faith.   The answer to
his discourse was unanimous : " Diex el volt ! Diex el
volt !" ("God wills it") resounded on all sides, and several
thousands of men, fastening to their garments, as a
rallying sign, a cross cut out of red cloth, expressed
their determination of starting at once for the Holy
Land.   The army was indeed a motley assemblage,
and the van-guard made up for their want of discipline by their enthusiasm and their simple faith.   A
nobleman from Burgundy bearing the significant
name of Gautier sans avoir (Walter the Penniless),
went first, leading a host of fifteen thousand men ;
then came Peter the Hermit at the head of one
hundred thousand pilgrims ; finally a German priest,
Gotteschalck, followed by fifteen thousand more,
formed the rear.   The disorders committed by all
that rabble were so great that the inhabitants of the
countries through which they passed rose up against
them, and made a fearful slaughter of them.   The
handful which succeeded in reaching the shores of
Asia Minor fell under the sword of the Turks in the
plains of Nicæa, all but three thousand men and
Peter the Hermit.

In the meanwhile the real warriors of the expedition were preparing and mustering to the number
of six hundred thousand foot soldiers and one hundred thousand cavalry.   They, too, formed three
divisions. The first, consisting of men from the
northern districts (Lorraine and the banks of the
Rhine), went through the basin of the Danube ; they

GODFREY OF BOULOGNE IN THE MOVING TOWER.

were commanded by Godefroi de Bouillon (Godfrey of
Boulogne), Duke of Lower Lorraine, a descendant of
Charlemagne, and particularly distinguished by his
courage, his loyalty, and his genuine piety. The
next corps, consisting of the Crusaders belonging to
the central provinces (Normandy, France, and Burgundy), under the orders of Hugues, Count of Vermandois, Robert, Duke of Normandy, and Stephen,
Count of Blois, went to embark in the seaports of the
kingdom of Naples. Raymond of Saint Gilles,
Count of Toulouse, and the Bishop of Le Puy, were
at the head of the third division, chiefly composed of
men from Southern France. They marched through
the Alps, and afterwards through Friuli and Dalmatia.
The general *rendezvous* was Constantinople.

The opposition of character between the Franks,
rough, warlike, and uncultivated on the one hand, and
the effeminate, astute, plausible and servile Byzantines
on the other, led to disagreeables and to collisions,
which it required all the diplomatic skill of the
Emperor Alexis to minimize and to smooth away.
He contrived to exact from the chiefs of the expedition the promise that they would do him homage for
whatever territories they might happen to conquer
in Asia Minor, and he felt considerable relief when
the last soldier of the army had left Europe. The
Crusaders started at the beginning of the spring of
1097, and on the 15th of May they laid siege to
Nicæa. There as well as at Dorylæum they signally
defeated the Turks, and arrived before Antioch on the
18th of October. By this time the invading army
was very much reduced, for on their way they were

naturally obliged to leave garrisons at all the points most liable to be attacked, without taking any account of the results of famine, sickness, and other such causes. The capture of Antioch after a siege of six months proved to be another serious calamity, inasmuch as the Crusaders, in order to indemnify themselves, so to say, for the hardships and toils of the journey, indulged in excesses which rendered them peculiarly liable to be attacked by pestilential diseases. The wisest course would have been to march straight towards Jerusalem, instead of which they lingered for six months in Antioch, and a considerable proportion of them were struck down by the plague. The remainder, fifty thousand in number, skirting as closely as possible the Mediterranean seashore in order to keep in communication with the Genoese, on whom they depended for provisions, arrived at last in view of the Holy City. The assault took place on the 14th of July, 1099, at break of day. Tancred de Hauteville and Godefroi de Bouillon were the first to penetrate into the city. The struggle was terrible ; the Mahometans occupied the mosque of Omar, where they vigorously defended themselves ; fighting went on from street to street ; one chronicler tells us that the horses waded in blood, and it is certain that acts of unparalleled cruelty were committed. When the work of actual conquest was over, and the next thing was to organize the new empire, the enthusiasm of the Crusaders sobered down, and the thoughts of many went homewards. Godefroi and Tancred gradually saw their companions forsake them and return to Europe ; only three hundred knights remained faithful to the cause which they had embraced. Fifty years elapsed before a fresh Crusade was attempted.

It is interesting to see the feudal system introduced in the East amongst Biblical associations ; fiefs were established on exactly the same plan as those in Europe ; the principalities of Antioch and of Edessa were governed respectively by Bohemond and Baldwin ; to them were added later on the countship of Tripoli and the marquisate of Tyre. There were lordships and feudal tenures at Tiberias, Ramlah, Jaffa. A code of laws was indispensable for the proper government of the European colony; Godefroi de Bouillon, now King of Jerusalem, caused it to be compiled under the title of "Assises de Jérusalem," "a precious monument," says Gibbon, "of feudal jurisprudence. The new code, attested by the seals of the King, the Patriarch, and the Viscount of Jerusalem, was deposited in the Holy Sepulchre, enriched with the improvements of succeeding times, and respectfully consulted as often as any question arose in the Tribunals of Palestine. With the kingdom and city all was lost ; the fragments of the written law were preserved by jealous traditions and variable practice till the middle of the thirteenth century ; the code was restored by the pen of John d'Ibelin, Count of Jaffa, one of the principal feudatories ; and the final revision was accomplished in the year 1369, for the use of the Latin kingdom of Cyprus."[1] Although the text of the *Assises* in the form we have it now is not by far of so old a date as was at first supposed, yet it is about

---

[1] Gibbon, " Decline and Fall," chap. lviii.

sixty years older than the *Coutumiers*, or law compila-
tions used in Europe, and has therefore considerable interest ; it is one of the fullest and most
trustworthy sources of information respecting the
feudal system. It is noteworthy that the *Assises*,
from the political point of view, establish the
sovereignty of the nation as represented by the
aristocracy and the *bourgeoisie*. " The justice and
freedom of the constitution," we still quote Gibbon,
" were maintained by two tribunals of unequal dignity. . . . The king, in person, presided in the upper
court, the court of the barons. Of these the four most
conspicuous were the Prince of Galilee, the Lord of
Sidon and Cæsarea, and the Counts of Jaffa and Tripoli, who, perhaps, with the constable and marshal, were
in a special manner the compeers and judges of each
other. But all the nobles who held their lands immediately of the crown were entitled and bound to
attend the king's court ; and each baron exercised a
similar jurisdiction in the subordinate assemblies of
his own feudatories. The connection of lord and
vassal was honourable and voluntary ; reverence was
due to the benefactor, protection to the dependant ; but
they mutually pledged their faith to each other, and
the obligation on either·side might be suspended by
neglect, or dissolved by injury." It is not too much
to say that, with the " Assises de Jérusalem " a model of
political liberty was introduced in Asia, the first and
indispensable condition of these laws being the assent
of those whose obedience they required, and for whose
benefit they were designed.

The share which the French took in the Crusades

makes of that event an important part in their national history. The first, as we have just seen, was nearly exclusively their work; they divided the second (1147) with the Germans, the third (1190) with the English, the fourth (1202) with the Venetians. The fifth (1217) and the sixth (1228) hardly deserve to be noticed; the seventh (1248) and the eighth (1270) were solely and entirely French. The movement of expansion which led, at an interval of fifteen centuries, the inhabitants of ancient Gaul to break through their frontiers and visit foreign climes is worth noting. They crossed the Pyrenees, as the Celtiberians had done; the British Channel, as the Belgæ and the Kymri; the Alps, as the Boii and the Insubres; the Rhine and the Danube, as those tribes who went to set Alexander at defiance, plundered Delphi, and struck Asia with fear. In all these cases the courage and daring displayed were the same, but in that of the Crusades the moving power was totally different. Formerly the French emigrated in quest of fortune and of material prosperity; when they took up the badge of the cross and marched towards Jerusalem, they were actuated by a moral principle which -doubled their energy and sanctified their actions. M. Cox ("Epochs of History") has summed up as follows the chief results of the Crusades :—

"We must not forget that by rolling back the tide of Mahometan conquest from Constantinople for upwards of four centuries, they probably saved Europe from horrors the recital of which might even now make our ears tingle; that by weakening the resources and power of the barons they strengthened the authority of the kings acting in alliance with the citizens of the great towns ; that this alliance broke up the feudal system, gradually abolished serfdom, and substituted the authority of a common law for the arbitrary will of chiefs, who for real or supposed affronts rushed to the arbitrament of private war. . . . These enterprises have affected the commonwealth of Europe in ways of which the promoters never dreamed. They left a wider gulf between the Greek and the Latin Churches, between the subjects of the Eastern Empire and the nations of Western Europe ; but by the mere fact of throwing East and West together they led gradually to that interchange of thought and that awakening of the human intellect to which we owe all that distinguishes our modern civilization from the religious and political systems of the Middle Ages." We must not forget trade, commerce, and manufactures, which received from the Crusades a wonderful development ; in the first place, the necessity of providing the armies of the Crusaders with arms, clothing, harness, horses, &c., led to an increase of industry which has never stopped since ; in the second place, the markets of Europe being now supplied with the produce of Asia, a new source of financial prosperity was opened, and soon became most popular.

The foundation of religious orders of knighthood was another result of the Crusades ; thus, in 1100, a Provençal gentleman, Gérard de Martigues formed the Order of the Knights Hospitallers, subsequently known as the Knights of Rhodes, and then as the Knights of Malta. The Knights of the Temple,

KING OF THE TENTH CENTURY.

established (1118) by the Frenchman Hugues des Payens, soon became formidable opponents of the *Hôpitallers*, and whilst carrying on against each other a very bitter feud, they were both equally suspected by the Church and dreaded by the kings of the various countries to which they belonged.

Chivalry is an institution which both affected the character of the Crusades, and received from them in return a powerful impulse ; it was another means by which the nobles separated themselves from the people, for no one might be a knight but a man of high birth. At the early age of seven he was re-moved from the care of women, and placed in the household of some lord or baron, who was supposed to give him the example of all chivalrous virtues. As page, varlet, or *damoiseau*, the lad accompanied the lord and lady of the manor on their rides, their excursions, their hawking parties, &c., and thus trained himself to the fatigues of war. At fifteen the page or varlet passed on to the higher rank of an *écuyer* (Squire) ; he might be an *écuyer d'honneur* or *écuyer de corps* in personal attendance upon his master or mistress ; as *écuyer tranchant* he carved for them in the dining-hall ; as *écuyer d'armes* he carried the baron's lance and the various parts of his armour, and whatever rank he occupied, he endeavoured, by some act of courage, to merit the coveted honour of re-ceiving, at the age of twenty-one, the order of knighthood.

"At last the day came which was to hold so im-portant a place in the young man's life. He prepared himself for the initiation by symbolic ceremonies. A

bath, signifying the purity both of the body and of
the soul, the night-watch, confession often made aloud,
the holy communion, preceded the reception of the
young knight.   Clothed in vestments of white linen,
another symbol of moral purity, he was led to the
altar by two discreet men of tried courage and experience, who acted as his military sponsors.   A priest

KNIGHT AND ARMS.

celebrated mass and consecrated the sword.   The
baron, whose business it was to arm the new champion, struck him on the shoulder with the sword-
blade, saying to him, 'I make thee a knight in the
name of the Father, and of the Son, and of the
Holy Ghost.'   He then bade him swear to em-
ploy his weapons in defence of the weak and the
oppressed, embraced him, and girt him with his sword.

The ceremony often concluded with a tournament. Chivalry conferred privileges and imposed duties. Formed in associations, and bound together by a sentiment of honour and of fraternity, the knights defended each other, and if one of them behaved in a disloyal or dishonourable manner, he was solemnly disgraced and condemned to death. Courtesy and respect for the weaker sex were virtues always expected from a knight."[1]

Chivalry was, to all intents and purposes, a kind of family, and as a natural result of that idea sprang up the science of heraldry and the habit of armorial bearings. The warriors of antiquity, it is true, caused to be painted on their shields their banners, and their arms, the devices, colours and emblems by which they might be distinguished from a distance ; but these symbols were essentially personal and peculiar to the individuals who wore them. Mediæval heraldry was a totally different thing ; armorial bearings formed a family distinction, the more important in proportion as it could be traced further back.

> " N'i a riche home ne Baron,
>   Ki n'ait lez li son gonfanon,
>   U gonfanon u altre enseigne."

> " There is no rich man nor Baron
>   Who has not his banner near him,
>   Either banner or other standard."

Thus says Robert Wace in his "Roman de Rou," and, of course, the standard or pennon was characterized by a distinctive cognizance of some kind. The habit

---

[1] Chéruel, " Dictionnaire des Institutions." &c.

soon spread of reproducing the armorial bearings, not
only on the shield, but on the helmet, the trappings of
the horses, the castle gates, the furniture, the dresses
of the ladies—on everything, in fact, which belonged
to the family. Colleges of heralds were instituted,
with laws, rules, and a procedure of their own ;
corporations, guilds, confraternities of every kind had
their devices, their mottoes, and their crests. Raymond
de Saint Gilles, Count of Toulouse (1047–1105), is
supposed to have been the first baron who boasted of
real armorial bearings, and the leopards which appear
on the royal standard of England are thought to
have originated from the animals painted in gold,
which ornamented the shield of Geoffrey Plantagenet
(about 1127).

To the creation of chivalry we must also ascribe
the origin of family names. Till then names had
merely been personal, each man only bearing the
one which he had received at his baptism ; this, however, was soon found insufficient ; some then added to
their own names that of their fathers ; others adopted
familiar sobriquets, such as *le Blanc, le Bon, Droiturier,
Tardif,* &c., or designations borrowed from their profession (*Le Maire, Prévôt, Le Bouteillier,* &c.), or trade
(*Boucher, Charpentier, Fléchier,* &c.). Many were
satisfied with adding the designation of their native
place, or some other local peculiarity, such as *Guillaume de Lorris, Bernard de Ventadour, Jean de la
Vigne,* &c.

As it might naturally be expected, the literature
and fine arts in France, as well as in all the countries
throughout Europe, were powerfully influenced by

TOURNAMENT.

the two movements we have just described—chivalry
and the Crusades.   Up to the eleventh century, the
Church had enjoyed, if we may so say, the monopoly
of intellectual culture, and illustrious as are Hincmar,
Roscelin, and Bérenger, we can hardly call them *French*
writers ; the earliest specimens of the national literature of France, with the exception of the famous
" Strasburg Oaths," belong to the tenth century ; they
are the *cantilène*, or song of Sainte Eulalie, a poem
on the Passion, a life of St. Léger, and a poem on
Boëthius.

The River Loire, which runs through France from
the south-east to the west, divides the country into
two unequal parts, each of which had during the
Middle Ages a legislation, a language, and a literature of its own.   South of the Loire was the country
of *Langue d'oc*, so called because the term indicating
affirmation in that language was *oc* (L. *hoc*).   This
region included necessarily a considerable number of
dialects which together with many grammatical
peculiarities had one common feature : " The general
language was distinguished from Northern French by
the survival to a greater degree of the vowel character of Latin.   The vocabulary was less dissolved
and corroded by foreign influence, and the inflections
remained more distinct.   The result, as in Spanish
and Italian, was a language more harmonious, softer,
and more cunningly cadenced than Northern French,
but endowed with far less vigour, variety, and
freshness." [1]

North of the Loire we find the *Langue d'oil* (L.

---

[1] Saintsbury, " History of French Literature."

Hoc illud), which, after a series of important modifica-
tions, was destined to survive its rival, and to become
the language of modern France.

Poetry was here, as in all countries, the earliest
form of literature, and when a twelfth-century poet
wanted to exercise his skill and his imaginative
powers on some subject or person worthy of being
celebrated, he had his choice out of three classes of
topics equally well calculated to interest his hearers :
(1) Classical antiquity offered to his genius or his
talent many a noble and inspiriting theme (Alexander the Great and his campaigns, the siege of Troy,
&c., &c.) ; (2) National history teemed with glorious
names which might well kindle enthusiasm within
the breast of a true poet (Charlemagne, Roland,
Doon of Mentz, Hugh Capet, &c.) ; (3) The wonderful exploits of King Arthur and the Knights of the
Round Table, the magic powers of Merlin the En-
,chanter, the Quest of the Holy Grail, were a source
of composition not less abundant, nor less interesting,
than the two others. A native of Arras, Jean Bodel,
himself the author of one of the chief mediæval epics,
" La Chanson des Saxons," has described with much
accuracy, in the following lines, the difference which
separates these three categories of poems from each
other—

" Ne sont que trois matières a nul home entandant :
    De France, et de Bretaigne, et de Rome la grant :
    Et de ces trois matières n'i a nule semblant (*resemblance*) ;
    Li conte de Bretaigne sont si vain (*frivolous*) et plaisant ;
    Cil (*those*) de Rome sont sage et de san (*sense, reason*) aprenant.
    Cil de France de voir (*truth*) chaque jor apparant."

"There are only three subjects for a clever man :
France, Brittany, and Rome the great :
And there is no similarity between these three subjects
The tales of Brittany are frivolous and pleasing,
Those of Rome are wise and sensible ;
Those of France tell us the truth every day."

The compositions borrowed either from classical
antiquity or from national traditions (*Chanson de
Roland, Doon de Mayence, Aliscans, Ogier le Danois*)
bore the common name of *chansons de geste*, because
they treated of the high deeds (L. *gesta*) of the heroes
of ancient time.   As we are not writing here a history
of French literature, we shall not enter into any
further details about these works ; we need only say
that in describing the lives and actions of men long
gone by, poets of the twelfth century could not help
ascribing to Charlemagne's contemporaries or even to
the companions of the King of Macedon, the manners
and customs amidst which they themselves lived ;
and so it is that the most complete and minute history of chivalry in all its details and particulars is to be
found in the works of the *Trouvères* (*Troubadours* in
Langued'oc) recited or sung by them and by their attending *jongleurs* in the palaces of the feudal lords, or
in the *cours d'amour* of Provence and Aquitaine.   We
may say in concluding this part of our subject, that
the literature of Southern France does not boast of
any *chanson de geste*, so far as we know, except the
Girartz de Rossilho, and an epic on Alexander the
Great by Auberi of Besançon, the first hundred lines
of which have alone been handed down to us.

The Crusades could not but infuse fresh vigour
into literature, either by stirring up the zeal of those

who had already been moved by the eloquence of
popular preachers, or by denouncing to universal contempt the cowards who refused to join the expeditions. Irony and faith on this occasion combined
their forces, and what sermons often failed to do was
accomplished by those short satirical pieces to which
the name of *sirvente* has been given (from *servir*,
says Dietz, because it is composed by a retainer in
the service of his master)—

> " Or s'en iront cil vaillant bacheler
> Ki aiment Dieu et l'onour de cest mont,
> Ki sagement voelent à Dieu aller,
> Et li morveus, li cendreus demourront."

> " Now the valiant bachelors will go
> Who love God and the honour of this world,
> Who wisely wish to go to God,
> And the cowards, the base, will remain."

Thus said the King of Navarre ; we can understand, however, that before leaving, a knight such as
Guillaume de Poitiers would turn many a time
towards the family castle, and exclaim, his eyes full
of tears—

> " Aissi lais tot quant amer suelh (*L. solebam*)
> Cavalairia et orguelh !
> Li départir de la doulce contrée
> Où la belle est, m'a mis en grant tristor.
> Laissier m'estuest (*me faut*) la riens (*chose*, L. *rem*) qu'ai plus amée
> Por Dom le Dieu servir, mon criator."

> " I leave here all that I used to love,
> Tournaments and magnificence.
> The fact of quitting the pleasant country,
> Where is my lady-love, has plunged me in great sorrow.
> I must leave what I have most loved,
> In order to serve the Lord God my creator."

Often a faint-hearted knight, having quieted his conscience by an insignificant expedition, tried to come back stealthily to his baronial halls; the *sirvente* immediately seized upon him, and denounced him to public contempt, adding in cutting invective to the curses of the Church—

> " Marques, li monges (*moines*) de Clunhic,
> Veuilh que fasson de vos capdel,
> O siatz abbas de Cystilh,
> Pus le cor avetz tan mendic (*pauvre*)
> Que mais (*mieux*) amatz dos buous et un araire,
> A Montferrat qu'alors estr' empernieur."

> " Marquis, the monks of Cluny,
> I wish that they may make of you their captain,
> Or that you may be abbot of Citeaux,
> Since you have a heart so base
> As to prefer two oxen and a plough
> At Montfernat, than to be emperor elsewhere."

One of the most formidable amongst these fighting troubadours was Bertram de Born, a Provençal nobleman, who spent his life in warring against his neighbours, destroying their castles, plundering their domains, and then slandering them in his *sirventes.* Dante has given him a place of honour in his "Inferno," where he represents him (canto xxviii.) carrying his head in his hands—

> " And so that thou may carry news of me,
> Know that Bertram de Born am I, the same
> Who gave to the young king (Richard of England) the evil comfort."

Bertram de Born called severely to task Philip Augustus and Richard Cœur-de-Lion, the latter of whom he ironically nick-named *yea and nay,* in order to taunt him for his irresolution. He urged them both

to go to the Holy Land ; then when the moment came
for starting, he, for his own part, remained at home,
and set his conscience at ease by composing a *sirvente*
against himself.   Thus it is that in the case of France
as well as of other countries, the popular literature of
the day throws almost as much light upon the political state of the country as professed chronicles and
histories ; but besides the *fabliaux*, the *sirventes*,
the *tensons*, and the *pastourelles* of the troubadours
and *trouvères*, there are several poetical compositions
which, under the name of *romans*, are nothing more
or less than historical compositions, possessing a certain amount of authenticity, and compiled from Latin
originals.   Thus we may name the " Roman de Rou "
and the " Roman de Brut," by Robert Wace (1162–
1182), of whom a distinguished modern historian,
Mr. Freeman, has said, " The name of Wace I can
never utter without thankfulness, as that of one who
has preserved to us the most minute and, as I fully
believe, next to the contemporary sketch-work, the
most trustworthy narrative of the central scene of my
history."   Respecting the word *roman* itself, we must
be careful to observe that it had by no means in the
Middle Ages the signification applied to it by modern
usage.   It denoted then a narrative containing a
greater or smaller proportion of real fact, and recording the deeds of historical characters.   We shall
say nothing about the " Roman de Brut," which refers
to the history of England ; but the " Roman de Rou "
is strictly and closely connected with France, and
deserves a mention here.   The following lines fix
the date of its composition—

" Mil et cent et soixante ans eut de temps et d'espace
  Puis que Diex en la Vierge descendi par sa grace :
  Quand un Clerc de Caën, qui et nom Maistre Wace,
  S'entremist de l'istoire de Rou et de sa race."

" One thousand one hundred and sixty years had elapsed,
  Since God, by His grace, came into the Virgin,
  When a Clerk of Caën, by name Wace,
  Wrote the history of Rollo, and of his race."

The poem we are now describing consists of seventeen thousand lines; the first part of it gives the
biography of the early Dukes of Normandy ; Rollo
(*Rou*, hence the title of the work), William Longue-
Epée, and Richard I. ; it is the least valuable portion,
from the historical point of view ; the second division,
on the contrary, based upon the chronicle of a certain William of Jumièges, is extremely precious for
the information it contains. The Benedictine scholars,
Montfaucon and Lancelot, used it as a kind of com-
mentary on the celebrated Bayeux Tapestry, which
gives, as all readers know, a pictorial view of the
Battle of Hastings, and the events which immediately
preceded it. The entire " Roman de Rou " takes
us as far as the reign of Henry I. (1106), and Robert
Wace was rewarded by the King of England with
a canonry in the church of Bayeux. The annalist
found a somewhat formidable rival in Benoit de
Sainte Maure, who, by the express command of
Henry II., wrote a history of the Dukes of Normandy, beginning with the invasions of the Northmen
under Hastings, and ending with the reign of William
the Conqueror. This chronicle, extending to twenty-
three thousand lines, is of second-rate historical merit.

The Crusades had their historians, as we may well

suppose,[1] the principal being Tudebod, Robert the
Monk, and especially William of Tyre. Out of the
materials supplied by these Latin chroniclers, a certain *trouvère* named Richard the Pilgrim, composed a
poem entitled "La Chanson d'Antioche," which was
revised and almost re-written during the thirteenth
century by Graindor, a native of Douai.

Richard the Pilgrim accompanied Godefroi de
Bouillon to Palestine ; he is supposed to have been
one of the retainers of the Count of Flanders, and he
appears to have died before the capture of Jerusalem.
The work which has immoralized his name is of equal
value if we consider it as a specimen of literary composition and a faithful record of the events which
marked the first Crusade. "Every page of his narrative bears evidence to the fact that he was an eye-wit-
ness of the incidents he relates, even in the most indifferent and casual circumstances. Talking, for instance,
of three knights who refused to do their duty, he says :
'I know well who they are, but I shall not name
them.' Thoroughly conscientious, Richard the Pilgrim
describes faithfully all the episodes of the Crusade,
and analyses with much impartiality the characters of
the various leaders, the motives of their actions, and
the feelings by which they were moved. Thus Bohemond is represented more than once as trembling, and
needing to be reminded of his duty. The Duke of
Normandy appears, exactly as the local historian
describes him, to have been, brave, but light-hearted,
impetuous, easily put out of temper, and allowing
himself too often to be prejudiced. A native of Northern France, our *trouvère* very naturally dwells more

especially upon the heroism of his *compatriotes.* The warriors of Flanders, Artois, and Picardy are those in whom he feels chiefly interested."[1] We shall have, later on, to dwell in greater detail upon the real *literary* historians of the Crusades ; but it would have been unfair to leave out in this chapter the early chroniclers of these important events.

France was gradually waking up from the kind of moral slumber which had weighed over it for upwards of four centuries ; the whole nation, bursting through its frontiers, had rushed off to Jerusalem, to Italy, to Germany, to England ; the spirit of adventure and of conquest had taken possession of every heart, and yet the indolent king, Philip I., seemed to share nothing of the enthusiasm and the energy so universal around him. Steeped in luxury and sensuality, he heeded little the progress of feudalism, the gradual destruction of the royal power, the sufferings of the lower classes, and the condition of the Church. Was that state of reckless self-indulgence and neglect of duty to last ? No ! Philip, indeed, satisfied himself with spending in tardy exercises of penance the last years of his reign ; he died in 1108 in Melun, after a reign of more than forty-seven years ; but his son, Louis VI., was destined to retrieve by his energy and his activity the faults of half a century, and to strike the first blow at the power of the aristocracy.

[1] Masson, " Mediæval Chronicles of France."

III.

LOUIS VI.—LOUIS VII.—THE COMMUNAL MOVE-
MENT.—SCHOLASTICISM.

(1108–1180.)

WHEN Louis VI. ascended the throne the royal
power was very much diminished, if we compare it to
what it had been in the time of Hugues Capet.   The

SEAL OF LOUIS VI.

countships of Paris, Sens, Orléans, and Melun constituted the whole of the royal domains ; but even within
these comparatively small limits the movements of

the king were by no means free. For instance, be
tween Paris and Etampes stood the fortress of the
lord of Montlhéry; between Paris and Melun the
Count of Corbeil exercised almost absolute authority,
and even at one time hoped to be at the head of a
fourth dynasty; between Paris and Orléans the frown-
ing walls of Puiset were a constant source of anxiety
to the Crown, and it required a three years' war to
reduce it to submission. In whatever direction the
eye might turn, it met the domains of feudal lords,
whose power and influence equalled, in every respect,
that of the king, and who, paying no attention to the
royal safe-conducts, plundered the pilgrims, levied
illegal and exorbitant fines upon travelling merchants, and acted in every respect as the most unscrupulous highwaymen. The king was thus, if we
may so say, hemmed in on all sides by that terrible
and compact organization of feudalism which, having
long since cast aside the ideal from which it originated,
now only represented the principle of brute force
against that of justice, order, and national unity.

The time had come for a revolution to take place ;
iniquity could not prevail for ever, and in the movement we are about to describe, the Crown and the
lower classes acted as allies to each other. The principle of association was at the bottom of the feudal
system; it formed likewise the starting-point of the revolution which ultimately destroyed that system. If
we trace back to its beginnings the history of industry, trade, and commerce, we find guilds and corporations rising everywhere, and imparting stability and
the elements of success to professions which could

have produced nothing if left to isolated action and individual effort. In like manner the old institution of serfdom having gradually disappeared, and the labourers and vilains having obtained the right of inheriting the land, or portion of the land, which they formerly tilled for their masters, associations of families were formed, hence the organization of parishes, and their grouping together for purposes of mutual protection. In the South of France, where traces of the old municipal institutions of the Romans were even then to be found, a still more decisive element of anti-feudalism existed, and speedily manifested itself.

The communal movement broke out almost simultaneously in various parts of the country ; Le Mans (1066), Cambrai (1076), were followed by Noyon, Beauvais, Saint Quentin, Laon, Amiens and Soissons. The following extracts from the charters of a Beauvais *commune*, will give a sufficient idea of all the others :

"All the men residing within the walls of the city and its suburbs, to whatever lord they may belong, the land which they occupy, shall swear the *commune*. Within the whole enclosure of the town, each one shall assist his neighbours loyally and according to his ability.

"The peers of the *commune* shall swear to favour no one for friendship's sake, to injure no one on the ground of private enmity ; they shall in every case give, according to their power, an equitable decision. All others shall swear to obey the decisions of the peers, and to assist in seeing that they are carried out.

"Whenever any man has done injury to a person who has sworn the *commune,* on a complaint of the

CATHEDRAL OF NOYON.

same being made, the peers of the *commune* shall punish the delinquent, either in his person or in his goods, deliberation having been held on the subject.

"If the culprit takes refuge in some castle, the peers of the *commune* shall refer to the lord of the castle or his representative, and if, according to their opinion, satisfaction is done to them against the enemy of the *commune*, it will be enough ; but if the lord refuses satisfaction, they shall do justice to themselves on the lord's property or on his retainers.

"If some foreign merchant comes to Beauvais for trading purposes, and if any one does wrong or injury to him within the municipal limits (*banlieue*), if a complaint is entered before the peers, and if the merchant can discover the malefactor in the town, the peers shall punish him, unless the merchant should be an enemy of the *commune*.

"No member of the *commune* shall give or lend his money to the enemies of the *commune* so long as war exists between them, for if he does so he has perjured himself ; and if any man stands convicted of having lent or trusted any thing to them, he shall be punished according to the decision of the peers.

"If it happens that the whole *commune* marches out of the town against its enemies, no one shall hold parley with the enemies, except by the leave of the peers.

"If any peer of the *commune*, having trusted his money to a resident of the town, that resident takes refuge in some castle, the lord of that castle, on complaint having been made to him, shall either return the money or drive the debtor out of his castle ; but

should he do neither of these things, justice shall be
taken against the men of that castle at the discretion
of the peers."

It is needless to observe that the *communal* movement was a source of great sorrow and irritation to
the nobles both clerical and secular. "*Commune*,"
says Guibert of Nogent (twelfth century), "is a new
and detestable name. This is what is meant by it—
Persons now only pay once a year to their lords what
they owe them. If they commit some crimes, they
have merely to submit to a fine legally fixed."

It is only fair to say that not a few amongst the
prelates, understanding the real nature and the
beneficial character of the communal movement, gave
to it the sanction of their name and their high
ecclesiastical position. Such was Baudri de Sarchain-
ville, Bishop of Noyon (1098), and it is interesting
to read the document by which he established (1108)
the *commune* in the chief town of his diocese.

"Baudri, by the grace of God Bishop of Noyon,
to all those who do persevere and go on in the faith.

"Most dear brethren, we learn by the example and
words of the holy Fathers that all good things ought
to be committed to writing, for fear lest hereafter they
come to be forgotten. Know then all Christians present
and to come, that I have formed at Noyon a *commune*, constituted by the counsel and in an assembly
of clergy, knights, and burghers ; that I have confirmed it by oath, by pontifical authority, and by
the bond of anathema, and that I have prevailed
upon our lord King Louis to grant this *commune* and
corroborate it with the king's seal. This establish-

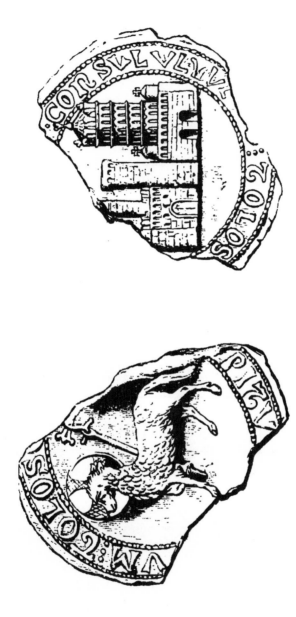

SEAL OF TOULOUSE COMMUNE (OBVERSE AND REVERSE).

ment formed by me, sworn to by a great number of persons, and granted by the king, let none be so bold as to destroy or alter. I give warning thereof, on behalf of God and myself, and I forbid it in the name of pontifical authority. Whoever shall transgress or violate the present law be subjected to excommunication; and whosoever, on the contrary, shall faithfully keep it, be preserved for ever amongst those who dwell in the house of the Lord."

The communal revolution, like most popular movements, was unfortunately stained in several places with deeds of violence, and the history of the *commune* of Laon is unquestionably one of the most dramatic episodes in the whole development of the Middle Ages. Gaudri, bishop of that town, had, on condition of a sum of money, allowed the inhabitants the permission of instituting an elective magistracy on the pattern of that of Noyon (1109). Three years later, repenting of the concessions he had made, he persuaded the king, whom he had invited to spend the Easter festivities at Laon (1112), to cancel the communal charter, promising him in return a sum of 700 silver *livres*. The news of this piece of treachery was soon spread abroad, and notwithstanding the protection given to Gaudri by a powerful body of knights, the episcopal palace was set on fire and the unfortunate bishop put to death.

It was the evident interest of the King of France to encourage and favour the communal movement; he thus secured for himself powerful allies against the barons who scorned his authority, and in his endeavours to restore order throughout his dominions he was assisted in the most efficient manner by the parish militias and the citizens of the various towns; whereas the knights and men-at-arms either forsook him entirely or gave him very little assistance in his efforts to restore peace and order throughout the kingdom, he found, on the contrary, the greatest assistance in the armed bands raised by the Church and the towns. We must add, to tell the whole truth, that Louis VI. so eager to favour the communal movement in the domains of the barons, did not tolerate a single one in his own; he wanted to be absolute master at home till the time when he might become master also over his turbulent vassals.

The relations between England and France were always those of two deadly enemies. With the view of checking the power of his rival, Louis VI. took up the cause of William Cliton, son of Robert, Duke of Normandy, who, defeated by his brother Henry at the battle of Tinchebrai (1106), had been kept as a prisoner in Cardiff Castle. This scheme would have materially strengthened the position of the King of France; unfortunately, the tide of war turned against Louis VI., who experienced a defeat at Brenneville (1119). We must remember at the same time that the English monarch was vassal of Louis as Duke of Normandy, and therefore he dare not push on the war to its last extremities. A series of events, however, contributed to favour the progress of the power of England in France. The terrible episode of the *Blanche-nef* left Henry with one child only, Mathilda; he married her to Geoffrey Plantagenet, eldest son of Foulques V., Count of Anjou, and thus the support

which Louis had hitherto found in the Angevin
princes against Normandy was henceforth lost. Later
on the marriage of Mathilda's son with Eleanora of
Guienne extended the power of England as far as
the Pyrenees.

The murder of Charles the Good, Count of Flanders, by the rebellious serfs and citizens of Ghent,
furnished Louis VI. with another occasion of exercising his rights as a suzerain lord, and of trying
to extend his authority. Accompanied by William
Cliton, to whom he promised the Countship of Flanders, he invaded the land, and obtained at first some
slight success; but the cities of Furnes, Lille, Ghent,
and Alost rose against the invaders and called to the
supreme power Thierry of Elsass. Cliton died in 1128
of a wound he had received before Alost.

The firm resolution entertained by the King of
France of re-establishing order in his dominions was
felt even south of the Loire, where the Count of
Auvergne and the Duke of Aquitaine learnt at
their own cost that deeds of violence would no
longer be tolerated. Amongst the king's last acts
was a signal and energetic measure in the same direction.. One of the most unprincipled and savage
banditti-lords of the day, Thomas de Marle, who had
played an important part in the rising at Laon, was
carrying on a system of brigandage on a thoroughly
extensive scale. He had locked up in the dungeon
of his castle a company of innocent traders, stripped
of their goods and their money by his men on the
high roads, notwithstanding the royal safe-conduct,
and he declined to let them depart unless they paid

him a considerable ransom.   He had as his motto the
proud couplet :

"Je ne suis roy ne comte aussy,
Je suis le Sire de Coucy,"

and he fancied himself in safety behind the walls of
his castle of Coucy, one of the strongest baronial residences north of the Seine.   The king, nevertheless,
marched against him at the head of his troops, and
Thomas de Marle, who had sallied forth with the
intention of laying an ambush, was wounded, made a
prisoner, and taken to Laon, where he died.

Louis VI. was incidentally led to perform a part in
the quarrel between the Papacy and the Empire, for
three popes, Gelasius II., Calixtus II., and Innocent
II., sought a refuge in France against the Imperial
forces.   In the year 1130 the king summoned at
Étampes a council which, on the proposition of the
celebrated Saint Bernard, declared Innocent II. to be
the rightful successor of Saint Peter.   Twelve months
afterwards another council assembled at Reims, was
attended by thirteen archbishops and two hundred
and sixty-three bishops.   Louis VI. appeared in person, and Innocent II. availed himself of the opportunity of crowning the monarch's son, Louis, ten
years old.   Louis VI. died of an attack of dysentery
on the 1st of August, 1137.   He had been nicknamed
le gros (the fat) on account of his corpulency.

The clever and enlightened course of policy
adopted by Louis VI. was carried on by his son, but
it led, in one of its applications, to an event which the
new king had scarcely anticipated.   The Pope had
named to the archbishopric of Bourges his own

nephew, regardless of the right of presentation which belonged to the Crown. Louis compelled the new prelate to vacate the see, whereupon the Count of Champagne offered a refuge to the disappointed ecclesiastic. The king had already some motives of complaint against the count. He resolved, therefore, upon punishing him, entered his domain, and burnt down the small town of Vitry; thirteen hundred persons who had taken refuge in the church perished. So wholesale a destruction weighed upon the king's existence; seized by remorse, he organized a Crusade, and found an apology and justification of his design in the state of affairs in the Holy Land. The Sultan of Aleppo had taken Edessa, and driven the Christians from one of their most important possessions. Would the kingdom of Jerusalem itself be safe? and was it not to be feared that the infidels, encouraged by their success, might in a very short time destroy a work which had cost so much blood and so much money? Pressing appeals were made to all the princes of Western Europe, and Saint Bernard became the apostle of the second Crusade (1144). We cannot dwell here upon the life and character of that truly remarkable man; sufficient to say that he was one of the most distinguished representatives of the mediæval clergy, and that, by his learning no less than by his earnest piety, he fully deserved the title of "The Last Father of the Church," which some historians have bestowed upon him. A monk, of the Order of Cîteaux, famed for the strictness of its discipline, he had himself founded in 1115 an establishment—an off-shoot of the original monastery at a

place called "The Valley of Wormwood," so designated either from the fact that the soil abounded with
that plant, or because the locality was infested with
robbers. Subsequently to the foundation of the new
monastery the valley assumed the more propitious
name of *Clairvaux* (Lat. *clara vallis*). Bernard was
abbot at the time of the preaching of the Crusade;
he placed himself at the head of the movement with
his wonted energy, but a great change had taken
place in public feeling, and instead of the spontaneous
élan which seized all classes of society in the days of
Peter the Hermit, it was necessary to levy a kind of
Crusade tax throughout the kingdom, independently
of rank and condition. Riots followed, and the king
started for his expedition, says a chronicler, in the
midst of curses and imprecations. The second
Crusade was nothing else but a series of failures; the
want of discipline of the soldiers and the stupidity of
the leaders brought about a first disaster. The only
anxiety which possessed the King of France was to
reach Jerusalem and to pray at the Holy Sepulchre.
This he contrived to do, and then the Crusaders,
deeming that it would be disgraceful for them to leave
Palestine without accomplishing at least one feat of
arms, determined upon attacking Damascus. Here,
again, their own imprudence led to a discomfiture.
Who should be prince of Damascus *if the town was
taken?* The Count of Flanders, said some; this
selection met with a great deal of opposition, but, as
the siege had to be raised, it did not so much signify,
and a very small number of the Crusaders returned to
Europe to tell the tale of the expedition.

Saint Bernard's reputation suffered considerably from this untoward episode. " He had confidently predicted its success, and was even said to have wrought miracles in attestation of his mission. The complaints against him were loud, bitter, and universal ; and he himself acknowledged his confusion at this inexplicable visitation of Divine Providence. He attributed it to the scandalous vices of the Crusaders, comparing them to the Jews of old, to whom God's

FIGURE OF SUGER IN CHURCH WINDOW.

prophet had solemnly promised the enjoyment of the Land of Canaan, but who were nevertheless ' overthrown in the wilderness' on account of their sins and unbelief." Saint Bernard died in 1153, and was canonized by Pope Alexander III. in 1174.

In contrast with the first Abbot of Clairvaux stands Suger, the great statesman, " the Father of his country," as his grateful contemporaries loved to call him. Born of poor parents in the neighbourhood of

Saint Omer, Suger was indebted for his early training
to the monks of the abbey of Saint Denis, who received him in their midst, and soon discovered his
ability and his high moral qualities. Louis VI., his
fellow-student at Saint Denis, conceived for him a
friendship which Louis VII. continued, and having
been elected abbot during his absence at Rome, he
rose to be invested with the highest powers in the
state. Named regent whilst the king was engaged in
the Crusade, he governed prudently and discreetly,
maintained order, and displayed the greatest talent as
a financier. He had always been opposed to the
Crusade, and urged upon the king the duty of " not
abandoning his flock to the rapacity of the wolves."

On his return to France, Louis VII. repudiated his
wife Eleanor for alleged misconduct. This step, justified, no doubt, from the point of view of morality,
was a political mistake, because the ex-queen, heiress,
as we have seen, of the duchy of Guienne, transferred
her vast domain to Henry Plantagenet, Count of
Anjou, Duke of Normandy, and heir-presumptive to
the crown of England (1152). The power of this
country, thus immensely increased, was still more so
when, two years later, Henry obtained for his sons
the hand of the Count of Brittany's only daughter.
Thus irritated by the rapid and constantly-increasing
power of his rival, Louis VII. avenged himself by encouraging the rebellious conduct of Henry's four sons.
The murder of Thomas à Becket (1170) is another
incident which helped him in his designs against
England. Having insisted with the Pope that the
blood of the archbishop should be avenged, he ob-

tained satisfaction. With the view of escaping from
a sentence of excommunication, Henry submitted to
all the humiliations which were imposed upon him,
and spent the last years of his reign in wars against
his own sons, his subjects, and the King of France.

The tragic death of Thomas à Becket belongs immediately and directly to the history of England ;
but it affected, more or less, the whole of Christendom, and therefore we are not astonished at finding it
described by a French writer :

" Since now and at so late a time (in the history of
the world) a new martyr is given to you, Garnier the
Clerk, a native of Pont Saint Maxence, thinks it right
to tell you the date of this event : it took place full
eleven hundred and seventy years after the incarnation." The chronicle we are now alluding to, written
in Alexandrine verses, is founded upon the well-known
" Historia Quadripartita," compiled under the direction of Pope Gregory XI. from materials supplied by
John of Salisbury, Herbert of Bosham, William of
Canterbury, and Alan, Abbot of Tewkesbury. The
poem is remarkably accurate in point of historical
detail : Garnier has spared neither time nor trouble in
collecting information from the most trustworthy
quarters :

" I have spent at least four years in making and
perfecting it (the poem), retrenching, adding, without
taking any account of my trouble." Further on, he
tells us "he went to Canterbury for the purpose of
getting the truth from the friends of Saint Thomas, and
those who had served him ever since he was a child."
. Impartiality is his chief object : " Truth and inte-

grity you may expect here, for I would not depart from the truth for any damages or death I might endure."

The views of Garnier respecting the murder of Thomas à Becket are those which might be anticipated from a Churchman and a *Frenchman ;* his opinion is that of the clergy during the twelfth century. "The prelates," he remarks, "are the servants of God ; and princes, therefore, ought to cherish them ; they are above kings, who should bend under them."

The communal movement continued during the reign of Louis VII. His father had granted or confirmed eight charters ; his own name appears on twenty-five such documents ; the population of the towns increased, barren tracts of land were cultivated, forests disappeared, and substantial encouragement was given to trade and industry. Louis VII. confirmed the privileges of the *Hanse* or guild of Paris merchants, which under the collective name of *marchands de l'eau de Paris,* had succeeded to the corporation of the *nautæ Parisienses.* This company or association, the most powerful of all those then existing, enjoyed the monopoly of carrying goods from the bridge of Le Pecq, near Saint Germain on Laye, to the higher part of the river. They levied a toll on all provisions brought into Paris ; their armorial device was a ship, which subsequently became that of the metropolis, with the motto *Fluctuat nec mergitur.* The foundation stone of the Cathedral of Notre Dame was laid in 1168 by Pope Alexander III. We have already said that Louis VII. caused his son and heir to be consecrated during his own lifetime ; he further directed that the ceremony should always take place at Paris.

We cannot close our account of the reign of Louis VII. without giving a sketch, if ever so slight, of the intellectual movement which was going on in France, during the administration of the first Capetian monarchs.

Under the name of *Schola Palatii* Charlemagne had established in connection with every cathedral church (circular of 789), schools for the elementary teaching of children, and, besides, seminaries where the higher branches of the sciences were studied, under the supervision of competent teachers. Tours, Metz, Fontenelle in Normandy, Ferrières near Montargis, and Aniane in Languedoc, thus became centres of intellectual progress : the curriculum of learning was called the *trivium* and the *quadrivium*, and embraced the seven liberal sciences, as enumerated in the following distich :

" *Gramm(atica)* loquitur ; *Dia(lectica)* vera docet ; *Rhet(orica)* verba colorat ;
Mus(ica) canit ; *Ar(ithmetica)* numerat ; *Geo(metria)* ponderat ; *As(tronomia)* colit astra."

There was of course a school attached to the metropolitan church of Paris, and thus it happened that the foundation of the University of Paris came to be ascribed to Charlemagne, although the real founder of it, as a matter of fact, was Philip Augustus. A vestige of the old tradition is still preserved in the circumstance that the annual festival of the University of France takes place on the day of Saint Charlemagne. The University of Paris was really an association of guilds of schools, on the pattern of the other corpora·

tions, and its headquarters were on the south bank of the Seine, at and near the Montagne Sainte Geneviève, still regarded as the centre of what is called *le quartier Latin.* The importance of the various schools belonging to the University of Paris may be gathered from merely naming a few of the distinguished men who there taught and were there educated. Thus Ulger, Bishop of Angers, Albéric de Reims, Archbishop of Bourges, Gauthier de Mortagne, Bishop of Laon, Michel de Corbeil, Dean of Saint Denis, who, after having refused the Patriarchate of Jerusalem, was consecrated Archbishop of Sens. Some of the most distinguished members of the University of Paris were foreigners, and to mention only a few Englishmen out of a list which might easily be extended, we shall quote almost at random, Adam de *Parvo Ponte*, Bishop of Saint Asaph, Robert de Béthune, Bishop of Hereford, Cardinal Robert Pulleyn, and finally Nicolas Breakspeare, who was elected to the Papacy under the name of Adrian IV.

Of all the schools comprising the University of Paris during the Middle Ages, that of Saint Victor has remained the most illustrious; it was founded by Guillaume de Champeaux, in 1108. "Whilst it endeavoured," says Canon Robertson, "to reconcile the scholastic method of inquiry with practical piety, it was especially opposed to the dialectical subtleties which were now in fashion, and was itself inclined to mysticism. The most famous teachers of this school were Hugues—a Saxon, according to some writers, while others suppose him a native of Ypres—who died in 1141; Richard, a Scotchman, who died in

1170; and Gauthier, who, in 1174, wrote against 'the four Labyrinths of Gaul,' under which names he denounced Abélard, Gilbert de la Porrée, Peter Lombard, and his disciple, Peter de Poitiers." [1]

Hincmar, Alcuin, Eginhard, and Scot Erigena, to name only these, had given to the Carlovingian dynasty a kind of intellectual character, and the great theological disputes of the mediæval epoch were anticipated by the sharp controversy, in which were engaged, on the one side, the Monk Gotteschalck, and, on the other, Rabanus Maurus, Bishop of Mentz. Theology and philosophy at that time were identical expressions, and arguments on points of doctrine often meant nothing less than efforts to assert the right of intellectual freedom against the claims of authority. Condemned by two councils for having stated that the doctrine of predestination is to be found in the writings of Saint Augustine, Gotteschalck had refused to retract, and had been shut up for life by Hincmar in a cloister; Scot Erigena, Bérenger, and Roscelin suffered persecution in various forms for the boldness of their ideas, and when the dispute between the *Realists* and the *Nominalists* broke out, the tide of theological bitterness was at its height.

When we talk of *universal* ideas, we may suppose either that they are mere ideas, or real existences, just as real as, for instance, an individual horse, tree, or man. The latter view had been the one acknowledged as orthodox, and it had on its side the authority of Plato and of Saint Augustine; the former was sanctioned by Aristotle. Roscelin,

---

[1] "History of the Christian Church."

Canon of Compiègne, stood up on the side of Nominalism, and having boldly applied his tenets to an explanation of the doctrine of the Trinity he was accused of Tritheism, and compelled to retract. He had to leave France, and fled to England, where he further excited great dissatisfaction by maintaining that the sons of clergymen could not legally receive ordination. He then returned to France, found a kind and sympathetic friend in Yves de Chartres, was through his mediation reconciled to the Church, and appointed a canon of the church of Saint Martin at Tours.

The philosopher, however, whose name has become the most illustrious in the history of the times, was Abélard, a pupil of Roscelin, and subsequently of Guillaume de Champeaux. The romantic story of his love with Héloïse, has chiefly made his name known to the public, but he was equally distinguished as a theologian and a teacher. Born in 1079, at a village near Nantes, he became extremely popular as soon as he began lecturing, and his excessive vanity led him into difficulties from which he never extricated himself. Saint Bernard, always on the watch against heretical doctrines, had not much trouble in discovering the dangerous propositions maintained by Abélard in his "Introduction to Theology," and he brought forth against him the charge of sharing the errors of Nestorius, Pelagius, and Arius. The councils of Soissons (1121), Sens (1140), condemned him, and the doctors assembled on the former of these occasions obliged him to burn with his own hands the dangerous treatise. Prohibited from teaching, and ordered to be confined for life, Abélard repaired to the Abbey of Cluny, where he was most kindly received by Peter the Venerable. He there spent two years in study and devotional exercises, and having been removed to the priory of Saint Marcel, near Châlon-sur-Saone, he died there in the sixty-third year of his age, April 21, 1142.

We must not suppose that the endless discussions carried on by the schoolmen of the Middle Ages derive their importance from the fact that they cleared a few theological difficulties, about which no one really cared. The great, the ever-momentous question at issue then was *liberty of thought*, and the right of examining, and dissenting from, the tenets propounded by the Church of Rome. In this long quarrel, the *Realists* represented the principle of freedom, and the *Nominalists* that of submission.

IV.

LOUIS VII., whose reign we have just been describing, was the eldest of six sons : three had taken
orders ; Robert was the head of the house of Dreux,
and Pierre founded that of Courtenay, which still
exists in England. Philip II., surnamed *Augustus*
because he was born in the month of *August* (1165),
ascended the throne at the early age of fifteen. His
reign marks an important epoch in the history of
France ; it coincides with the beginning of a revolution
which destroyed the feudal system and placed in the
hands of the king all the powers of the country. The
vigilance and energy of the new king baffled the
activity of the barons who still attempted to rule
independently of their liege lord. As a result of the
wars he had to undertake, we must name the acqui-
sition of the countships of Amiens, Valois, and Vermandois (1183); in 1191 he obtained by right of
inheritance the important province of Artois, and
thus the immediate domains of the Crown were
extended as far as Flanders. He reduced to obedience

the Duke of Burgundy, the Lord of Beaujeu, and the Count of Châlons ; he persecuted the Jews (1182) ; with the help of the communal militia he stamped out an insurrection attempted by the *Cottereaux*—a band of robbers who infested the central provinces of France.

The rivalry between France and England found fresh fuel in the events which marked the third Crusade (1190-1191). Jerusalem had fallen into the power of the infidels (1187). Since the accession of Godefroi de Bouillon, eight European kings, all French, had reigned in the Holy City, and the last, Guy de Lusignan, defeated at the battle of Tiberias, had now become the prisoner of Saladin. A vigorous effort was made throughout Christendom to improve a situation which had grown very serious ; the emperor, Frederick Barbarossa, took the initiative ; Richard Cœur de Lion followed, accompanied by Philip Augustus. The expedition arrived at Saint Jean d'Acre, which was retaken by the Crusaders. The "lion-hearted" soon made his personality felt in the most decided manner, and earned by his reckless courage, his determination, and his perseverance, a reputation which extended even to the Mohammedan population of the country. If we may believe an Eastern historian, his fellow countrymen used to rebuke their startled horses by uttering his dreadful name. "Do you think," said they, "that King Richard is on the track, that you stray so wildly from it ?" He directed from the first the chief operations of the siege, and acquired over his fellow Crusaders, over Philip especially, an ascendency which could not be but very galling to a man so impatient of control as the King of France.

" We laud and honour the courage and high achieve-
ments of the King of England, but we feel aggrieved
that he should, on all occasions, seize and maintain a
precedence and superiority over us, which it becomes
not independent princes to submit to. Much we might
yield of our free-will to his bravery, his wealth, his
zeal, and his power ; but he who snatches all as a
matter of right, and leaves nothing to grant as a
matter of courtesy and favour, degrades us from allies
into retainers and vassals, and sullies, in the eyes of
our soldiers and subjects, the lustre of our authority,
which is no longer independently exercised."

This speech of the Grand Master of the Templars,
in Sir Walter Scott's " Talisman," exactly represents
the feelings of Philip Augustus in his relations towards
the King of England. Acre having once surrendered,
he resolved upon leaving the Holy Land immediately,
for the express purpose of destroying the power of
Richard. Before starting, he renewed, indeed, the
engagements which bound him to respect the territories, the interests, and the rights of the English
monarch ; but he tried during his stay at Rome to obtain from Pope Celestine III. a deed releasing him
from this engagement. This being useless, he determined upon releasing himself by force, and sought the
alliance of Prince John, who had long been plotting
to supplant his brother, and who consented to do
homage to the King of France, not only for Normandy
and the other English possessions on the Continent,
but for England itself. In the meanwhile Richard
contrived to escape from a captivity in which the
Emperor of Germany had unjustly kept him (1194) ;

he arrived in Normandy at the head of a powerful
army, and defeated the French at Frettival. As for
John, whose baseness was only equalled by his cruelty,
he sought to propitiate his brother by putting to the
sword three hundred French soldiers whom he had
invited to a banquet at Évreux. Pope Innocent, then
interfering, obliged the rival monarchs to sign a five
years' truce (January, 1199. Two months afterwards
Richard was killed before the castle of Chalus, in
Limousin.

John Lackland, now having become king, had as an
enemy the prince whose alliance he had so recently
sought, and who was only anxious for a pretext to
renew hostilities. The murder of young Arthur, which
occurred then (1204), seemed to justify the ambitious
projects of Philip Augustus. He had made up his
mind to vindicate the rights of John's nephew to the
throne of England, on consideration of homage for the
possessions of the English Crown in France ; he now
summoned the murderer to appear in person before
the court of the twelve peers (chief vassals of the
Crown), and, having received a refusal, he marched
into Normandy, took possession of the chief towns in
the duchy, including Rouen, and, following his career
of success, re-annexed Poitou, Anjou, and Touraine
to the royal domains. Vainly did Pope Innocent III.
endeavour to bind down the two monarchs by a peace.

Not even so cowardly a man as John could submit
to such humiliations, and he formed a league with the
Emperor of Germany, Otho IV., the Counts of Flanders and Boulogne, and all the princes of the Netherlands. They were to invade France by the northern

frontier, whilst he, with an English army, attacked it
by the south-west. Louis, the eldest son of the king,
marched into Poitou against John, whilst Philip, with
a large body of knights and the communal militia,
took the road to the north. He met the enemy at
the bridge of Bouvines, between Lille and Tournai
(July 27, 1214). The Flemings felt so confident of
victory that they had already divided the country between themselves. Philip Augustus ordered a mass
to be celebrated ; he then commanded bread and
wine to be brought, and having had some slices
(*soupes, sups, sops*) cut, he ate one, and addressing the
men who were near him, he said, " I request all my
good friends to eat together with me in remembrance
of the twelve apostles who ate and drank together
with our Lord ; and if there shall be any one of you
who entertains thoughts of evil or of treachery, let
him not draw near." Then came forward my Lord
Enguerrand de Coucy and took the first sop ; Count
Gauthier de Saint Pol took the second, and said to the
king, " Sire, it will be seen to-day whether I am a
traitor ! " This he said because the king suspected
him on account of certain bad reports. The Count
of Sancerre took the third sop, and then the other ·
barons, and the crowd was so great that all could not
reach the table (*buffet*) on which the sops were placed.
This seeing, the king was very joyous, and he exclaimed to the barons : " My lords, you are all my
men, and I am your king, whatever I may be, and I
have loved you all very much. . . . Therefore, I beseech you, maintain on this day my honour and yours,
and if you see that the crown is better on the head of

one of you than on mine, I shall willingly part with it." When the barons heard him thus speak, they began to shed tears, saying : " Sire, thanks, for God's sake ! We will have no other king but you ! Now ride boldly against your enemies, and we are prepared to die with you ! "

The two armies remained for some time at a short distance from each other without daring to begin the action, and the French were retiring by the bridge of Bouvines to march in the direction of Hainault, when the enemy, by attacking the rear, obliged them to turn round.

" Philip," says his chaplain, Guillaume le Breton, who was present during the action, " was resting then under a tree, near a chapel, with his armour unfastened. At the first noise of the fight, he entered the chapel to make a short prayer, armed himself quickly, and jumped upon his charger with as much joy as if he was going to a wedding or a festival. Then shouting out, ' To arms ! warriors, to arms !' he rushed forwards, without waiting for his banner. A valiant man, Gallon de Montigni, carried on that day the oriflamme of Saint Denis, a standard of bright red silk. The bishop-elect of Senlis, Guérin, arranged the *batailles* in such a manner that the French had the sun at their back, whilst the enemy had it in their eyes. Three hundred burghers of Soissons, vassals of the Abbot of Saint Médard, and who fought on horseback, began the action at the right wing by charging audaciously the knights of Flanders. These hesitated for some time to try their courage against commoners. However, the cry of ' Death to the French !' raised by one

of them, animated them, and the Bourguignons, led
by their duke, having reinforced the people of Soissons,
the *mêlée* became furious. Count Ferrand was fighting
on that side of the army."

" When the action began the communal militias were
already beyond Bouvines ; they recrossed the bridge
in all haste, ran in the direction of the royal standard,
and came to place themselves in the centre, in front
of the king and of his *bataille.* The German knights,
in the midst of whom was the Emperor Otho, charged
these brave men, and riding through them endeavoured
to reach the King of France ; but the most renowned
amongst Philip's men-at-arms threw themselves in
front of them and stopped them. During this *mêlée*
the German infantry passed behind the cavalry, and
arrived at the place where stood Philip. They dragged
him from his horse, and, when he was on the ground,
they endeavoured to kill him. Montigni waved the
oriflamme as if to ask for assistance. A few knights
and the men of the *communes* ran up, delivered the
king, and replaced him upon his horse ; he immediately rushed back into the thick of the fight. It
was the emperor's turn to feel in danger of being
taken. Guillaume des Barres, the bravest and the
strongest man in the whole army, the happy adversary
of Richard Cœur de Lion, whom he had twice overcome, already held Otho, and was striking him violently, when a crowd of Germans rushed upon him.
They killed his horse, but though dismounted, he extricated himself, and with sword and dagger cleared
the ground around him. Otho thus managed to
escape."

"On the right wing Ferrand, Count of Flanders, had
fallen into the hands of the French ; at the centre, the
emperor and the Germans were in full flight ; but, on
the left, Renaud de Bourgogne and the English held
their ground.   They had driven before them the
militias of Dreux, Perche, Ponthieu, and Vimeu.   'At
this sight,' writes a chronicler, ' Philippe de Dreux,
Bishop of Beauvais, was distressed, and, as *he happened
to hold a club in his hand*, forgetting his episcopal
dignity, he struck the leader of the English, knocked
him down and many others with him, breaking limbs
but shedding no blood.   He recommended those who
surrounded him to declare that this great slaughter
was their work, for he feared lest he should be accused
of having violated the canons and committed a deed
unlawful for a bishop.'   The English were soon in
full rout except Renaud, who had arranged a company
of sergeants on foot in the shape of a double circle
bristling with long spears.   From the centre of this
circle he rushed forth as from a fortress, taking refuge
within it at times to take rest.   At last, his horse
being wounded, he fell and was made prisoner.   Five
other counts and twenty-five knights-bannerets had
already been captured."

The above description of the battle of Bouvines,
translated from M. Duruy's " History of France," is
given here in detail on account of the extreme importance belonging to the event.   The immediate
results, indeed, if we consider territorial aggrandise-
ment, were null for the French king, but he had re-
pelled a formidable invasion, defeated an emperor and
a king, and proved to some of his ambitious vassals

that any sinister intention they might have against the crown would be both promptly and signally defeated. To quote M. Guizot, " The battle of Bouvines was not the victory of Philip Augustus alone over a coalition of foreign princes ; the victory was the work of king and people, barons, knights, burghers, and peasants of Ile-de-France, of Orléanais, of Picardy, of Normandy, of Champagne, and of Burgundy. And this union of different classes and of different populations in a sentiment, a contest, and a triumph shared in common, was a decisive step in the organization and unity of France. The victory of Bouvines marked the commencement of the time at which men might speak, and indeed did speak, by one single name, of *the French.* The nation in France and the kingship in France on that day rose out and above the feudal system." We do not wonder, therefore, to find that the return of Philip Augustus to Paris had all the features of a triumphal march ; rejoicings were universal, and the enthusiasm of the people displayed itself in every possible manner. Crowds collected to see the Count of Flanders, so powerful lately, but now wounded and disabled, borne about in a litter where he was manacled and loaded with fetters. "There you are, Ferrand," they exclaimed, "bound and fettered ; you can no longer kick and lift your stick against your master!" He remained for the space of thirteen years a prisoner at the Louvre (1227), a commemorative church called *l'abbaye de la victoire,* was built near Senlis to celebrate the event.

Foulques, priest of Neuilly-sur-Marne, undertook at that time the missions which had previously been per-

formed with such success by Peter the Hermit and
with comparative failure by Saint Bernard. At the
suggestion of Pope Innocent III. he preached a
Crusade. Jerusalem was beginning to excite very little
interest, and the princes of Western Europe were too
much engrossed by their feuds at home to think of
the Holy Land, the Saracens, and the empire founded
by Godefroi de Bouillon. It is quite true that the eloquence of the Abbot of Clairvaux had kindled the
utmost enthusiasm at first in the breast of his hearers,

SEAL OF ST. BERNARD.

and the shouts of "Diex el volt! Diex el volt!" had
re-echoed in answer to his appeals ; but, as we have
seen above, the excitement proved very short-lived,
and artificial means were absolutely necessary to
render the Crusade possible. It was very much the
same in the present case. However, the expedition
having been resolved upon, the question of itinerary
remained to be settled. The general opinion decided
against an over-land journey, and a deputation was
sent to hire ships from the Venetians. The sum asked

THE VOWING OF A CHURCH.

by the Republic was 85,000 silver merks, besides half the conquests made by the Crusaders. So large a sum could not be paid down at once, so the Venetians granted a delay provided the invaders would help them to take possession of Zara in Dalmatia. Consent was given. Further, by the advice of their Italian friends, they determined to make Constantinople the basis of their operations, and having thus settled the preliminary difficulties, they started.

It is interesting that the first French prose writer worthy of that name should have been the historian of the fourth Crusade; we mean Geoffroi de Villehardouin, who took a part in it himself and related, so to say, his own experiences. Born about the year 1167, Villehardouin was a member of one of the most distinguished families in Champagne, and had filled with distinction the important post of *marshal* of that province, when, in 1199, he was prevailed upon by Count Thibault to join the Crusade. One of his companions, Geoffroi de Joinville, had for his nephew the celebrated friend and biographer of Saint Louis. Villehardouin was one of those who went to negotiate with the Venetians about the conveyance of the troops to the Holy Land. After the taking of Constantinople he received as a reward for his services the Marquisate de Montferrat with the gift of a fief in Thessaly, and he died there about the year 1213. The work in which Villehardouin gives us the account of the Crusade is entitled " La Conqueste de Constantinoble," and with all its shortcomings in the way of accuracy and historical fidelity, it is a most interesting work. The events it describes are those comprised between 1198 and 1207.

The Crusading Princes having resolved upon going to Constantinople, the young Prince Alexios offered to be their guide on condition that they should restore to the throne his father, Isaac Angelos, whose power had been usurped (1203). Villehardouin describes in a very picturesque manner the effect produced upon the Crusaders by the first view of Constantinople. "Those who had never seen it did not believe that there could be so rich a city in the whole world. When they beheld those lofty walls and rich towers by which it was surrounded, and those rich palaces and lofty churches of which there were so many that no one could believe it who had not seen them with his own eyes; and when they saw the length and the breadth of the city, which was the sovereign of all other cities, know ye that there was not a man whose flesh did not tremble, nor was it great wonder if they were moved, for never since the creation of the world was so high a deed undertaken by any nation."

Constantinople was defended by an army of 60,000 men, but they gave way most ignominiously, the city was taken by storm (July 18, 1203), and the old emperor, released from captivity, was reinstated upon his throne. This unfortunate monarch had made to the Crusaders promises which he could fulfil only by grinding down his subjects with taxes. A fresh revolution was the result. Alexios was strangled, and Murtzulph, who usurped the power, ordered the gates of the city to be closed against the Christians. Another siege was the result (March, 1204), disgraced on the part of the Crusaders by the most horrible excesses. The establishment of a Frankish empire at Constanti-

7

nople prevented the expedition to the Holy Land.
Baldwin IV., Count of Flanders, was elected Emperor ;
the Marquis de Montferrat received the title of King of
Macedon ; there were Dukes of Athens and of Naxos,
Counts of Cephalonia, Lords of Thebes and of
Corinth. The Venetians retained for themselves a
whole district of Constantinople, together with all the
seaports and islands belonging to the empire. But
this new organization had no elements of stability ; it
would have required a greater amount of military force
than was available, and the collapse took place in 1261,
when the Greeks recovered Constantinople. " For
thirteen years the Emperor Baldwin bore about with
him an empty title which won for him the commisera-
tion or the contempt of thousands who could not be
brought to stir hand or foot in his service. His pretensions were maintained by his son Philip, and
through his grand-daughter Catherine passed to her
husband, Charles de Valois, brother of Philip the
Fair of France." [1]

The next event we have to describe in connection
with the reign of Philip Augustus is the one which
illustrates in the saddest manner the spirit of intoler-
ance which characterized the Middle Ages. We allude
to the crusade against the Albigenses. We have said
elsewhere that the river Loire separated as a broad
line of demarcation, two forms of civilization essentially different from each other. In the north (*pays
de Langue d'oil*) the Teutonic element prevailed ;
manners were rough, commerce in a most rudimentary
state, literature imperfect, luxury, comparatively un-

[1] Cox, "The Crusades."

known, and peace a very rare exception. In the south
(*pays de Langue d'oc*), on the other hand, literature
had reached a high state of perfection, commerce had
introduced ease and luxury, and the administration of
the towns gave all the conditions of peace and
material prosperity. But an over-refined state of
civilization often leads to a loose state of morality, and
later on libertinism is almost as a rule associated
with free thinking. Such was the case south of the
Loire. Heresies and sects rapidly multiplied, the best
known being that of the *Albigenses*, thus named
because their headquarters were in the town of Albi.
They held the philosophical doctrines of the Mani-
chæans, that is to say, they admitted two Gods,
identified respectively with the principles of good and
evil, some of them believing further that the creator
of evil had himself been created by the good deity,
and had fallen from his first estate by rebellion. Be
it as it may, Raymond V., Count of Toulouse, sent in
1177 a formal complaint against the heretics to the
abbot and community of Citeaux ; and it is further
supposed that he urged the Kings of France and
England to agree upon certain strong measures for
the suppression of the heterodox doctrines. Innocent
III., on his part, was fully alive to the danger which
threatened the Church, but his first efforts met with
no success. In 1203, however, he appointed two
legates, of whom Pierre de Castelnau is the best
known, for the exclusive purpose of putting down
heresy in the province of Languedoc; and these
monks proceeded at once to the discharge of their
task, powerfully assisted by a Spanish priest, Dominic

de Guzman, belonging to the diocese of Osma.   In
the meanwhile the Count of Toulouse had died, and
his successor Raymond VI. was suspected of favouring
the Albigenses.   Everything was done to frighten
him into orthodoxy ; but even a sentence of excommunication had no effect ; and finally a gentleman of
his household murdered the legate, Pierre de Castelnau,

SEAL OF SIMON DE MONTFORT.

near Saint Gilles (January 15, 1208).   This tragedy
led to the preaching of a crusade, in which the Pope
offered to those who would join it the advantages
enjoyed by the faithful who went to defend the Holy
Land.   The war soon assumed the character of an
international rather than a religious contest.   Under
the leadership of Simon de Montfort, the whole of

Langued'oil invaded Languedoc, and the result was the destruction of southern civilization and of the *gai savoir*. The greatest ferocity marked all the incidents of the war: thus fifteen thousand persons were slaughtered at the siege of Béziers; the powerful Counts of Toulouse, the Viscounts of Narbonne and Béziers were dispossessed, and the King of Arragon, who had come to their assistance, fell at the battle of Muret (1213).

Simon de Montfort profited by the disaster which had thus visited the south, for the Papal legate gave over to him the domains of the Languedoc barons; but he was killed under the walls of Toulouse; and his son Amaury, unable to face the universal reprobation of the conquered populations, offered his domains to the King of France. This proposition, declined at first, was finally accepted.

It is interesting to find how the barbarity exercised against heretics and infidels is reflected in the popular literature of the time, and recognized as a matter of course, and as the distinctive mark of all really Christian governments. Thus in the romance entitled "Floire et Blanceflor" we find a curious example of religious zeal carried on to painful extremities. Floire, the hero, son of a heathen prince, becomes a convert to Christianity, and no sooner is he received within the fold of the Church than he compells all his subjects to follow his example:

> "Qui le baptesme refusoit,
> Ne en Diu croire ne voloit,
> Floire les faisoit escorchier,
> Ardoir en fu ou destrenchier."

> " Those who refused baptism,
>   And who would not believe in God,
>   Floire caused them to be flayed alive,
>   Burnt in the fire, or beheaded."

The compulsory baptism of the Saxons by Charlemagne was a case which the *trouvère* might adduce,
but the question still remains whether the stake and
the sword have ever made real converts, and the
history of the Albigenses is there to supply a negative
answer. The only good result of the crusade was the
unity of France, and the fusing, the welding together
of two races into one nationality, capable henceforth
of holding its own against all foreign enemies, whether
German, Italian, or English.

We must now say a few words about the relations
of Philip Augustus with the Papacy. They were not
of a very amicable character. On one occasion the
king was decidedly wrong, on the other he was right.
His first wife, Isabella of Hainault, having died, he
married Ingelburge, daughter of the King of Denmark ; but, strange to say, he at once conceived a
strong aversion towards her, repudiated her almost
immediately after the marriage, and obtained a
sentence of nullity from a council summoned at Compiègne. This step was followed by his espousing
Agnès de Méranie, the beautiful daughter of the
Count of Istria. So gross a violation of all the laws
of morality and of decency could not remain un-
punished, and after vain efforts to bring Philip Augustus
to reason, Innocent III. placed the kingdom under a
sentence of interdict, which meant the entire cessation
of all religious services, except the administration of

baptism to new-born infants and of extreme unction to the dying. This melancholy state of things lasted eight months. In vain did the king deprive of their sees the prelates who observed the interdict ; in vain did he imprison Ingelburge. He was at last, compelled to yield, and taking back the Danish princess, he separated from Agnès, who died broken-hearted in 1213.

The second occasion on which Philip Augustus

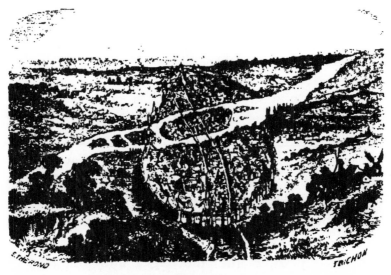

PARIS UNDER PHILIPPE AUGUSTE.

resisted the Pope was when, despite the threats of Innocent III., he took possession of the fiefs which John Lackland had lost by his felony. Here he was perfectly right, and he brought his undertaking to a prosperous issue.

Philip Augustus did much for the administration and police of the kingdom, the beautifying of the city of Paris, and the extension of commerce and

industry. We have already said that the earliest
statutes of the Paris University were his work. He
took the greatest pains with the administration of
justice, established an improved fiscal system, and
was the author of a most valuable institution, named
La Quarantaine-le-roi. By virtue of this enactment,
whenever any crime or injury had been committed, all
private wars which would have resulted from it were
strictly prohibited for a period of forty days, in the
meanwhile the King had the offender arrested and
punished.

Philip Augustus died in 1223, and was succeeded
by his son Louis, of whom all that can be said is that
he was the son and the father of two great monarchs.
On his mother's side (Isabella of Hainault) he descended from Charlemagne, so that by a fortunate
coincidence he united in his own person the rights both
of the Carlovingians and of the Capetians. He
conquered over the English part of Poitou, Aunis,
La Rochelle, Limoges, and Périgueux. Continuing
the war against the Albigenses, he took possession of
Avignon, obtained the submission of the entire south-
west of the Rhone, with the exception of Toulouse
and Guienne, thus carrying on the work of territorial
unity. Royal *seneschals* and bailiffs were appointed,
at Béziers, Beaucaire, and Carcassonne. Louis VIII.
was only 39 years old when he died, on the 8th
of November, 1226.

WALLS OF CARCÁSSONNE.

V.

SAINT LOUIS, TO HIS RETURN FROM HIS FIRST CRUSADE.
(1226—1254.)

LOUIS VIII. had married Blanche of Castile, a princess remarkable both for her personal attractions and for her moral and intellectual qualities. She combined with deep religious views and earnest piety the greatest firmness of character and political skill of no mean order. She had four sons—Louis, who succeeded to the throne, Robert, Count of Artois, Alphonse, Count of Poitou, and Charles, Count of Anjou and of Maine. The crown was on the head of a mere child, only eleven years old, and the regent was both a woman and a foreigner. The barons thought the occasion an excellent one to recover their lost authority, and accordingly they made an alliance against Queen Blanche. She proved, however, too clever for them, and the confederacy utterly failed. Amongst the rebellious barons the most powerful was Thibaut, Count of Champagne, who, not satisfied with the accomplishments of a knight and a soldier, aimed also at being considered a lover of literature, and even wrote poetry. Whether the beauty of Blanche captivated him, or her remonstrances put him to shame, it would be difficult to decide now, although the probability is that both causes had a share in influencing him on the side of loyalty; at any rate, he separated himself from his former confederates, and became the staunchest champion of the regency. The queen, in her turn, defended Thibaut from the attacks of the rebellious nobles, and he having, through an inheritance, become King of Navarre, made over to the Crown the countships of Blois, Chartres, and Sancerre. Two other barons held out obstinately for a long time, namely, Philip Hurepel, the late king's half-brother, who was irritated at having his supposed claims to the regency set aside in favour of a foreign woman, and Mauclerc, Count of Brittany. The death of the former of these noblemen and the submission of the latter came opportunely to strengthen the power of the Crown. A treaty signed in 1229 secured to one of the king's brothers the domains of the Count of Toulouse, and a marriage between another prince of the royal family and the heiress of Provence, further enlarged the kingdom of France. Thus the reign began most auspiciously, and even when the majority of the king was proclaimed (1230), Blanche of Castile retained all her influence and her share in the management of affairs.

The treaty of 1229 just alluded to put an end to the Albigensian difficulties and brought about the pacification of Southern France; but in order to prevent the recurrence of heretical opinions, an ecclesiastical court was established at Toulouse by virtue of a council held that same year. It was styled *the In-*

quisition, and its members were selected from the order of Dominicans. The baneful influence exercised by the tribunal of the inquisition over Christendom has often been described, and need not be more than alluded to again. Suffice it to say, that it was the

SAINT LOUIS.

most formidable engine of ecclesiastical despotism the world ever saw.

Under the careful and judicious training of his mother, Louis IX. became a model king, a pattern of all the virtues which most befit the ruler of a great nation, especially if we consider the troublous times during which he had to live. Let us quote on that subject a few extracts from the *naïve* and beautiful memoir for which we are indebted to his friend and confidential adviser, Jean, Sire de Joinville.

"The holy king loved truth so much that even to the Saracens and infidels, although they were his enemies, he would never lie, nor break his word in anything he had promised them.

"In his conversation he was remarkably chaste; for I never heard him, at any time, utter an indecent word, nor make use of the devil's name, which, however, is now very commonly uttered by every one, but which, I firmly believe, is so far from being agreeable to God that it is highly displeasing to Him.

"My good lord the king asked me if I should wish to be honoured in this world, and afterwards to gain paradise; to which I answered that I wished it were so. 'Then,' replied he, 'be careful never knowingly to do or say anything disgraceful, that, should it become public, you may not have to blush and be ashamed to say, "I have done this," or "I have said that."' In like manner he told me never to give the lie, or contradict rudely whatever might be said in my presence, unless it should be sinful or disgraceful to suffer it, for oftentimes contradiction causes coarse replies and harsh words, that bring on quarrels, which create bloodshed and are the means of the deaths of thousands."

It is very amusing to see, every now and then, honest Joinville scandalizing the pious king by the frankness of his answers, which were not strictly orthodox.

"The good king, once calling me to him, said he wanted to talk with me on account of the quickness of understanding he knew I possessed. In the presence of several persons he added : ' I have called these two monks, and before them ask you this question respecting God. Seneschal, what is God ?' 'Sire,' replied I, 'He is so supremely good nothing can exceed Him.' 'In truth,' answered the king, 'that is well said, for your answer is written in the little book I have in my hand. I will put another question to you, whether you had rather be a leper, or have committed, or be about to commit, a mortal sin ?' But I, who would not tell a lie, replied that I would rather have committed thirty deadly sins than be a leper."

"When the two friars were gone away he called me to him alone, making me sit at his feet, and said : 'How could you dare to make the answer you did to my last question ?' When I replied, 'Were I to answer it again I should repeat the same thing,' he instantly said : 'Ah! foolish idiot, you are deceived ; for you must know that there can be no leprosy so filthy as mortal sin, and the soul that is guilty of such is like the devil in hell. . . . . I therefore entreat of you, first for the love of God, and next for the affection you bear me, that you retain in your heart what I have said, and that you would much rather prefer having your body covered with the most filthy leprosy than suffer your soul to commit a single deadly sin, which is of all things the most infamous."

Passages such as those we have just quoted, and many others which might be adduced, give us a true insight into the character of Louis IX., scrupulously honest, high-minded, influenced throughout his life by the principles of Christianity, the incarnation of justice, adherence to duty, and patience in long-suffering. His defects were a certain deficiency of clear ideas in carrying out his designs, a want of firmness in his resolves, and a certain inability to exercise stern authority. This appeared most in the Crusades, to which we shall have occasion to refer by and by at greater length.

The English were still endeavouring to secure a footing in France by exciting the barons to revolt. Defeated at Taillebourg and at Saintes, they would probably have been entirely driven out of the kingdom, had it not been for the scruples of the king. Here again his innate honesty appeared in all its force, in what others would have called unnecessary strictness. The royal domains had been extended to three times their original dimensions by the acquisitions made during the last fifty years. Louis objected to what was the result of two confiscations. By virtue, therefore, of a treaty which was signed only in 1259, he left to the King of England the duchies of Guienne and Gascogne, on condition that he should do homage for them to the French Crown ; he also obliged those lords who held fiefs from both crowns to choose between the two suzerains.

Driven out of Italy by the emperor, Frederick II., Pope Innocent IV. took refuge in France, and held (1245) at Lyons a council, in the course of which he preached another Crusade. The popularity of these expeditions had waned to a considerable extent, and thoughtful people, instead of being led to take the

cross in a moment of enthusiasm, now coolly discussed
the results to be obtained from a war against the
infidels.[1]

> " Hom puet bien en cest payx
>   Gaaingnier Dieu sens grant damage ;
>   Je di que cil est foux nayx
>   Qui se mest en autrui servages,
>   Quant Dieu peut gaaingnier sayx
>   Et vivre de son héritage. . . .
>   Je ne faz nul tort à nul home
>   N'uns hom de moi ne fait clamour,
>   Je cuiche tost et tien grand soume
>   Et tieng mes voisins à amour. . .
>   Je vueil entre mes voisins estre
>   Et moi déduire et solacier. . . .
>   Distes le Soudant vostre maistre
>   Que je pris pou son menacier :
>   S'il vient deça, mal me vit naistre
>   Mais lui ne l'irrai pas chacier. . . .
>   Sermoneiz ces hauz coroneiz,
>   Ces gran doiens et ces prélaz. . . .
>   Clerc et prélat doivent vengier
>   La honte Dieu, qu'il ont ces rentes. . . .
>   Ils ont à boire et à mengier. . ..
>   C'il vont à Dieu par telle sente,
>   Fol sont s'il la vuelent changier,
>   Car c'est de toutes la plus gente. . .
>   Hom dit : ce que tu tiens, si tiens,
>   Ci at bien mot de bone escole. . . .
>   Si crois par S. Pierre de Rome
>   Qu'il me vaut miex que je demour."

> " A man can very well in this country
>   Obtain God without running much risk ;
>   I maintain that he is a born fool
>   Who places himself under the dependence of others,
>   When he can secure God,
>   And, withal, live in his inheritance. . . .
>   I do wrong o no man,
>   And no man complains of me.

---

[1] See Lenient's " Satire en France au moyenâge."

I go to bed early and sleep soundly,
And I love my neighbours. . . .
I wish to live amongst my neighbours,
And enjoy and solace myself. . . .
Tell the Sultan, your master,
That I don't care for his threats.
If he should come here so much the worse for me ;
But I shall not go in pursuit of him. . . .
Preach to those high-crowned princes,
Those great deans and prelates. . . .
Clerks and prelates should avenge
The shame cast upon God, for He bestows upon them
    their incomes. . . .
They have plenty to eat and to drink. . . .
If they can go to God by such a path
It would be foolish in them to change it ;
For of all it is the pleasantest. . . .
Some one says : ' Lord, part what thou hast.'
This is certainly a sound thought.
I believe, by the name of S. Peter of Rome,
That is better for me to stay here."

Thus said the *trouvère* Rutebeuf in his " Desputizon du Croisé et du Décroisé," and he was only expressing the opinion of all sensible men ; but Saint Louis who, struck down by a severe illness (1244), had made a vow to go to the Holy Land, thought that the time had come for him to carry out his intention. After making the necessary preparations, he took ship at the harbour of Aigues-Mortes (1248), at the head of a considerable army, leaving his mother, Blanche, for this time also, regent of the kingdom. Some of the Crusaders embarked at Marseilles, and, amongst others (somewhat reluctantly), the brave Seneschal of Champagne, Jean, Sire de Joinville.

"It was the month of August in this same year (we quote the honest chronicler's own story) that we

SAINT LOUIS STARTS FOR THE CRUSADE.

embarked at the rock of Marseilles, and the ports of the vessel were opened to allow the horses we intended carrying with us to enter. When we were all on board, the port was caulked and stopped up as close as a large tun of wine, because, when the vessel was at sea, the port was under water. Shortly after, the captain of the ship called out to its people on the prow, 'Is your work done? are we ready?' They replied, 'Yes, in truth, we are.'"

"When the priests and clerks embarked, the captain made them mount to the castle of the ship, and chant psalms in praise of God, that He might be pleased to grant us a prosperous voyage. They all, with a loud voice, sang the beautiful hymn of 'Veni Creator,' from the beginning to the end; and while they were singing, the mariners set their sails in the name of God. Instantly after, a breeze of wind filled our sails, and soon made us lose sight of the land, so that we only saw sea and sky, and each day we were at a farther distance from the place from which we had set out."

"I must say here, that he is a great fool who shall put himself in such danger, having wronged any one or having any mortal sins on his conscience; for when he goes to sleep in the evening, he knows not if in the morning he may not find himself under the sea."

This extract, taken from Joinville's "Life of Saint Louis," is a good specimen of one of the best models of French mediæval literature. The friend of Saint Louis possesses all the picturesque qualities of Ville-hardouin, together with a tenderness, a pathos which we do not find in the "Conqueste de Constantinoble.'

The flotilla forming the expedition arrived safely to the Egyptian shores, and the city of Damietta was taken on the 7th of July, 1249. Unfortunately, the Crusaders wasted much valuable time before continuing their journey towards Cairo, and the Mamelukes, cheered by the hesitations of their enemies, defeated them at Mansurah (February, 1250). One passage from Joinville's account of the battle may appropriately be given here :

"After some little time, the Count Peter of Brittany came to us who were guarding the small bridge from Mansurah, having had a most furious skirmish. He was so badly wounded in the face that the blood came out of his mouth as if it had been full of water, and he vomited it forth. The Count was mounted on a short, thick, but strong horse, and the reins and the pommel of his saddle were cut and destroyed, so that he was forced to hold himself by his two hands round the horse's neck, for fear the Turks, who were close behind him, should make him fall off. He did not, however, seem much afraid of them, for he frequently turned round, and gave them many abusive words, by way of mockery."

The battle of Mansurah cost the life of many a noble and stalwart knight, amongst others one of the king's brothers, the Count d'Artois.

"Thus," says Joinville, "as we were riding together, Father Henry, prior of the hospital of Ronnay, who had crossed the river, came to him (Saint Louis) and kissed his hand, fully armed, and asked if he had heard any news of his brother, the Count d'Artois. 'Yes,' replied the king, 'I have heard all:' that is to say, that he knew well he was now in Paradise. The prior, thinking to comfort him for the death of his brother, continued : 'Sire, no King of France has ever reaped such honour as you have done ; for with great intrepidity have you and your army crossed a dangerous river to combat your enemies ; and have been so very successful that you have put them to flight and gained the field, together with their warlike engines, with which they had wonderfully annoyed you ; and concluded the affair by taking possession this day of their camp and quarters.' "

" The good king replied that God should be adored for all the good He had granted him ; and then heavy tears began to fall down his cheeks, which many great persons noticing were oppressed with anguish and compassion on seeing him thus weep, praising the name of God, who had enabled him to gain the victory."

Not only was the Crusading army surrounded by the enemies, it had also to suffer from the plague, which did sad havoc amongst the troops, striking down Joinville himself and his chaplain.

" My poor friend," we continue our quotations, "was as ill as myself ; and one day when he was singing mass before me as I lay in my bed, at the moment of the elevation of the host, I saw him so exceedingly weak that he was near fainting ; but when I perceived that he was on the point of falling to the ground, I flung myself out of bed, sick as I was, and taking my coat, embraced him, and bade him be at his ease, and take courage from Him whom he held in his hands. He recovered some little ; but I never quitted him till he had finished the mass, which he completed, and this was the last, for he never after celebrated another, but died. God receive his soul !"

Louis IX. had married, in 1234, Marguerite, daughter of Raymond Bérenger IV., Count of Provence. She insisted upon accompanying her husband on the expedition, and shared with the greatest fortitude and devotedness all the dangers to which the king was exposed. Whilst in France, she had had much to suffer from Blanche of Castile, who, notwithstanding all her brilliant qualities, was imperious, jealous, and exacting. Removed from her influence, Marguerite gave herself up exclusively to the duty of cheering her husband, encouraging him amidst all his difficulties, and bearing her full share of the dangers attending the unfortunate expedition.

"You must know, also, that the good queen was not without her share [of miseries], and very bitter to her heart, as you shall soon hear. Three days before she was brought to bed, she was informed that the good king, her husband, had been made prisoner, which so troubled her mind, that she seemed continually to see her chamber filled with Saracens ready to slay her ; and she kept incessantly crying out, ' Help! help !' when there was not a soul near her. For fear her child should perish, she made a knight watch at the foot of her bed without sleeping. This knight was very old, not less than eighty years, or perhaps more ; and every time she screamed he held her hands and said, ' Madam, do not be thus alarmed ; I am with you, quit these fears.'"

SAINT LOUIS IN PRISON.

" Before the good lady was brought to bed, she ordered every person to leave her chamber except the ancient knight ; she then cast herself out of bed on her knees before him, and requested that he would grant her a boon. The knight, with an oath, promised compliance. The Queen then said, ' Sir Knight, I request on the oath you have sworn, that should the Saracens storm this town and take it, you will cut off my head before they seize my person.' The knight replied that he would cheerfully so do, and that he had before thought of it, in case such an event should happen."

The European knights were finally compelled to yield themselves prisoners, together with the king, whose spirit and lofty bearing inspired the Saracens with respect. The price required previous to the conclusion of a treaty and the release of Louis IX. was a very heavy one, viz., the surrender of Damietta and of several fortresses which the Christians still held in Palestine, besides a sum of 500,000 livres (£408,280 of modern English money). The King of France flatly refused to comply with the second clause of the proposition, declaring that he had no power to give-up what was not his own, but the property of the other Christian princes and religious orders. Finally, the Sultan agreed to the terms named by Louis, the giving up of Damietta and the sum we have just mentioned : he was even astonished that the king had not objected to the payment of so great a ransom. " By my faith," said he, " the Frank is liberal not to have haggled about the money. Go tell him that I will give him 100,000 livres towards it."

On the 7th of May, 1250, the Crusaders left the shores of Egypt, and on the 14th they reached Palestine, and landed at St. Jean d'Acre.

Louis IX. remained in the Holy Land for the space of four more years, visiting all the towns still held by the Christians, repairing the fortifications wherever necessary, and endeavouring to put down the private feuds which had broken out in several quarters between certain barons. Of all the men who had embarked with him at Aigues-Mortes the great majority returned to France; his two brothers were of the number, and when a discussion took place on the advisability of a prolonged stay of the army in the East, an overwhelming majority voted against it. The very few Crusaders who chose to remain with Saint Louis would have been utterly unable to attempt the conquest of Jerusalem, and the king, to whom the Sultan of Damascus offered every facility if he wanted to make *a pilgrimage* to the Holy City, refused the courteous proposition. He would not go there except as a victor and by force of arms. He was at Sidon at the beginning of 1253, when the news reached him that Queen Blanche of Castile, his mother, had died in Paris on the 27th of November, 1252.

"This information," says Joinville, "caused him such grief that he was two days in his chamber without suffering any one to see him. On the third, he sent one of his valets to seek me; and on my presenting myself he extended his arms, and said, 'Ah! Seneschal, I have lost my mother!'"

"'Sir,' replied I, 'I am not surprised at it, for you know there must come a time for her death; but I am indeed greatly so, that you, who are considered se great a prince, should so outrageously grieve ; for you know,' continued I, ' that the wise man says, whatever grief the valiant man suffers in his mind, he ought not to show it in his countenance, nor let it be publicly known, for he that does so gives pleasure to his enemies and sorrow to his friends.' "

The death of the Queen Dowager created, as may be supposed, great sensation throughout France ; numerous letters reached Saint Louis begging for his speedy return. Therefore, leaving Geoffroi de Sargines at the head of one hundred knights to protect the Christians in Syria, he started on the 24th of April, 1254, from St. Jean d'Acre, arrived at Hyères on the 8th of July, and reached Paris on the 7th of September.

During the absence of the king several scandalous instances of abuse of authority had taken place on the part of the clergy, which led to seditions of a serious character. The most important was the revolt of the *Pastoureaux* (L. *pastores*=shepherds), caused, in the first instance, by the cruelty of the Chapter of Notre Dame of Paris. The peasants of the village of Chastenai, having refused to pay the taxes, a great many of them were shut up in prison, and, notwithstanding the entreaties of the Queen Regent, their wives and children shared the same fate. Other abuses of the like description led to a general outbreak, and in 1254 the revolt of the *Pastoureaux* took place. The chronicler, Guillaume de Nangis, tells us that "some chiefs of banditti, in order to deceive simple folk and excite the people to a Crusade, announced by inventions full of deceit, that they had had visions of angels; the holy Virgin Mary, they added, had appeared unto them, commanding them to take the cross and to assemble an army of shepherds and the most common people, chosen by the Lord, for the purpose of delivering the Holy Land and the King of France, who was a prisoner in that country. They represented the circumstances of their visions painted on banners, which they caused to be raised aloft before them."

The rebellion broke out, first, in Flanders and Picardy, the leader being an unknown man called the *Master of Hungary*—eloquent, of a commanding appearance, and speaking fluently several languages. He assumed the priestly rights, administered the sacraments, celebrated marriages, and the populace, excited by his appeals to rebellion, put to death the clergymen, whether regular or secular, who were imprudent enough to wander through the rural districts. Queen Blanche began by taking the *Pastoureaux* under her protection, and even held a conference with the *Master of Hungary*; but this mistaken kindness did not last long, and the terrible scenes which occurred at Orléans opened her eyes to the necessity of dealing severely with the rebels. The master had been holding forth to a large assembly, when a student of the university interrupted him, saying that he was a heretic and a deceiver; a tumult immediately arose, the student was killed, and a general *mêlée* took place; the bishop interdicted the city. The *Pastoureaux* then continued their march southwards; at Bourges they met with the first severe check they had encountered, and were driven out of the city by the infuriated inhabitants. The *Master of Hungary* was pursued and put to death. The extraordinary enthusiasm which they had excited in the first instance subsided almost as suddenly. The fact is that the clergy spread abroad a report to the effect that the *Pastoureaux* were paid by the Sultan of Babylon to slaughter as many Christians as they could ; on the other hand, it was asserted, with perhaps more truth, that the revolutionists were Albigenses, and that a fresh effort was being made to revive a damnable heresy. At any rate, the collapse was complete ; a number who had made their way as far as Bordeaux had to retire under the threats of Simon de Montfort, Earl of Leicester, who governed there in the name of the King of England ; others went to Marseilles, and then dispersed, not without leaving some of their adherents in the power of the common hangman, who made them pay for the rest.

The rebellion of the *Pastoureaux* helped to hasten the return of Saint Louis from Palestine. On arriving in Paris he promised to devote the remainder of his reign to the better administration of justice, and to the reforms which the state of the kingdom rendered absolutely necessary.

VI.

SAINT LOUIS ; END OF THE REIGN—LITERATURE,
ARTS, AND SCIENCES DURING THE THIRTEENTH
CENTURY.

(1254–1270.)

THE reforms made by Louis IX. were of so important a character and led to such weighty consequences
that they require to be examined a little in detail.
Let us notice, in the first place, the suppression of
judicial duels—a strange institution which placed
right at the mercy of skill and physical strength ;
this was merely an extension of *La Quarantaine-le-roi*,
and it was universally welcome. Another most noteworthy change must be mentioned. According to
the rules of feudal society, every lord and baron administered justice within the limits of his own domains,
appeal being allowable to the suzerain : (1) If the
baron refused to render justice (*défaut de droit*) ; (2)
when the condemned person thought the sentence
unfair (*pour faux jugement*). Louis IX. encouraged
appeals made *directly* to the Crown, and then gradually
the baronial courts became subordinate to that of the
king. The *cour du roi*, or parliament, under various
names existed in France from the earliest days of the

monarchy. It was presided over by the king, and consisted of the *peers* or feudatories of the Crown. Gradually the chief officers of the Crown (*ministeriales domini regis*), such as the chancellor, the bread-bearer (*panetier*), the butler (*bouteiller*), the chamberlain, were required to sit with the peers, notwithstanding the complaints made by these. The substitution of written evidence instead of trial by combat was a further reform, and lawyers had to take an important part in the work done by the *cour du roi ;* the chief amongst these were Pierre des Fontaines and Philippe de Beaumanoir. It is natural to suppose that the importance thus given to written texts led to a revival of the study of law ; already in the eleventh and twelfth centuries some Italian cities, Bologna in particular, had become celebrated by the teaching of certain lecturers deeply versed in the mysteries of Roman jurisprudence, and Irnerius saw crowds of pupils attend his lessons. Justinian was translated into French during the reign of Philip Augustus, and law schools were opened at Montpellier, Orléans, and Angers. Thus science joined effectually in the war against feudalism, and Saint Louis authorized in Languedoc and in other places the use of the Roman law by preference to the old customs and traditions of the Franks, the Visigoths, and the Burgundians.

In order to make quite sure that his commands and enactments were duly carried out, Louis IX. was in the habit of sending through the various provinces visitors who, like Charlemagne's *missi dominici*, had to report on the cases of injustice, infringement of the laws, &c. High social position, rank, and dignity were ineffectual to shield an offender from deserved punishment. M. Chéruel (" Dictionnaire des Institutions ") mentions two remarkable cases which illustrate this fact. Charles d'Anjou, the king's own brother, had taken possession of a piece of land against the will of the original owner, promising to pay the full value. He was obliged to restore it. The Sire de Coucy had caused three young men to be hanged for poaching. Notwithstanding the intervention of the whole baronage of France, he was condemned to a very heavy fine. It was only in the case of Jews and heretics that Louis IX. was unrelentingly severe. " No one," said he, " should discuss with Jews unless he is a great clerk and a perfect theologian ; but when a layman hears the Christian faith evil spoken of, he should defend it not only with words, but with a sharp-cutting sword, which he should thrust through the miscreant's body as far as it will go."

The work of Joinville contains two passages which have become classical, and which we shall quote here as illustrating most admirably the personal part which the king took in the administration of justice :

" The king had his task arranged in such manner that My Lord de Nesle and the good Count of Soissons, together with us all who were around him, after attending mass, used to go and hear cases tried at the court of requests. And on returning from church, His Majesty would sit at the foot of his bed, then made us all sit around him, and asked us whether there was any case to be settled which could not be settled without him ; we accordingly named them to him, whereupon he sent for the contending parties

SAINT LOUIS RENDERS JUSTICE.

and said to them : 'Why do you not take what our men offer to you ?' Then they answered : 'Sire, it is because they offer too little.' Then he said : 'You ought to take that from him who would make it over to you.' And the holy man thus worked with all his might to keep them in a proper and peaceful way."

And further on :

"Many a time it happened that in summer he would go and sit in the forest of Vincennes after mass, lean against an oak, and bid us sit around him. Then those who had business to transact came to speak to him, without being hindered by ushers or any other people. He then asked with his own lips : 'Is there any one here who has a suit ?' Then those who had, rose, and he said : 'Be silent, all of you, and you shall be heard one after another.' Then he called my Lord Pierre de Fontaine and my Lord Geoffroi de Villette, and said to one of them : 'Despatch me that case.' And when he saw aught to amend in the words of those who spoke for him, or in the words of those who spoke on behalf of others, he himself corrected it with his own lips. In order to despatch the cases, I have often seen him come into the Paris gardens dressed in a camlet coat with an overcoat of woollen stuff without sleeves, a cloak of black taffetas fastened round his neck, neatly combed, having no cap, but merely a hat with white peacock's feathers on his head. He had carpets spread out for us to sit upon, and all those who had business for him to settle stood around him, and he heard the various cases according to the fashion I have mentioned above in the wood of Vincennes."

9

It will seem astonishing, perhaps, that in this long
account of French jurisprudence during the reign of
Louis IX., we have said nothing of the code of laws
known by the name of "Établissements de Saint
Louis." The fact is that this document, important
as it may be from a certain point of view, has no
character of authenticity, and the anonymous person
or persons who compiled it gave it the designation by
which it is known, merely to secure for it as much
popularity as possible. Many reasons might be
adduced to prove that it does not belong to the reign
of Louis IX., and the date assigned to it (1269) is
amply sufficient to show the mistake of historians who
still consider it as a monument of the holy king's
legislative talents. It is not likely that, on the eve of
starting for the Crusade, he could have found leisure
enough to discuss matters of jurisprudence which are
both complicated and difficult to settle.

The high roads had become much safer in consequence of the abolition of private warfare, and also
because every person was made responsible for the
police of the highways within the limits of his domains.
In Paris the king instituted a special body of armed
police (1254), called the *guet royal*, and consisting of
twenty foot and twenty horse sergeants. It was commanded by an officer styled the *chevalier du guet*
(Lat. *miles gueti*).

The first general rule on the French coinage was
established in 1265. The king asserted his right of
allowing the royal currency to circulate throughout the
realm, and he prohibited the barons from coining gold
pieces. This decree favoured in a notable way the

development of commerce and industry, for the reason
that the king's money being of the right weight and
value, it soon superseded the baronial coinage. The
nomination of Estienne Boisleve (or Boileau) as Provost of Paris, turned out to be also an excellent
measure. He drew up under the title of "Livre des
métiers" the statutes and laws which had at various
times been fixed by the guilds or corporations of
tradesmen and artificers, and he did so in order that
in case of lawsuits and discussions there might be a
text-book to which the contending parties could
appeal. From that curious document we know what
the professions and trades were which during the
thirteenth century gave employment to the greatest
number of hands. Armourers, of course, held the
foremost rank ; some workmen exclusively forged the
spurs ; others devoted themselves to adorn with
heraldic devices the various parts of the dress, trappings, &c. The *heaumiers, fléchiers*, and *arbalestriers*
dealt respectively in helmets, arrows, and cross-bows ;
then there was the more peaceful but highly fashion-
able guild of merchant-furriers, whose wares excited
an admiration bordering upon madness : " Pelles
castorum (*beavers*) et marturum (*martins*) quæ nos
admiratione sui dementes faciunt." Each corporation
had its appointed shops or stalls in the market-places,
and the general aspect produced a picturesque and
varied sight. A contemporary poet describes to us
in the following lively manner his walk through one
of these gatherings of tradesmen and artisans :

> " Au bout par deça regratiers
> Trouvé barbiers et cervoisiers,

> Taverniers et puis tapissiers ;
> Assez près d'eux sont les merciers.
> À la côte du grand chemin
> Est la foire du parchemin ;
> Et après trouvai les pourpoints. . . .
> Puis la grande pelleterie. . . .
> Puis m'en revins en une plaine,
> Là où l'on vend cuirs crus et luine ;
> M'en vins par la féronerie ;
> Après trouvai la baterie,
> Cordouaniers et boureliers,
> Selliers et fremiers et cordiers."

> " At the end, beyond the (stalls of) the retail grocers
> I found the barbers and dealer in beer,
> The eating-houses and upholsterers' shops ;
> Near them are the mercers.
> By the highway side
> Is the parchment fair ;
> Then I found the jackets (jacket-makers, tailors),
> Then the dealers in furs. . . .
> Then I returned by a plain,
> Where is sold raw leather and wool ;
> I came next the quarters of the ironmongers ;
> Then I found the coppersmiths,
> Shoemakers, and dealers in horse-hair,
> Saddle-makers, farmers, and rope-makers."

It would take us too long to go through the whole list. Fairs played, of course, a great part in the history of mediæval commerce. The principal French ones were those held at Falaisse (*foire de Guibray*) in Champagne, and at Saint Denis, near Paris (*foire du Landit*, or *Lendit*). The origin of this last name is as follows: in 1109 a supposed fragment of the true cross having been brought to Paris, the bishop of the diocese ordered a meeting (*indictum*, hence *L'indit*, and by corruption *Landit*) to be held in the plain of Saint Denis, so that the people might come to look

at the relic. In course of time the *indictum* became
an annual fair, which lasted several days, and led to so
much disorder, owing to the presence of the scholars
belonging to the Paris University, that in Jean de
Meung's continuation of the " Roman de la Rose," we

SEAL OF LOUIS IX.

find the substantive *Landit* used in the sense of a
drunken bout.

To conclude these remarks on the administration
of Louis IX., and the general character of his government, we would say that the accession of the third

estate to power dates from his reign.   He granted, it
is true, a few communal charters, but municipal independence pleased him as little as feudalism, and he
encouraged as much as he could the transformation of
the communes into "royal cities," which depended
upon the Crown, whilst they were governed by mayors,
councillors, and other magistrates elected by the
burghers.   Thanks to this interference of the king,
France escaped the danger of falling into the anarchy
which was for so many centuries the curse of Italy,
leaving it a prey to the ambition and intrigues of the
Emperors of Germany.

Saint Louis endowed Paris with several foundations,
some of which still subsist, and have rendered much
service ; we shall name only two here, viz., the Hospital of the *Quinze-vingts* and the *Sorbonne.*   The
former of these establishments was created in 1254,
for the reception of three hundred gentlemen (15 × 20)
who had lost their eyes during the Crusade through
the cruelty of the Saracens ; it is now one of the best
known hospitals in Paris.

With reference to the Sorbonne, it was one of the
earliest colleges connected with the University of
Paris, having been founded in 1202 by the king's
confessor, Robert Sorbon or de Sorbonne, thus called
from the village of Sorbonne, his native place.   It
became in course of time an exclusively theological
school, and obtained such reputation that the historian
Mézeray, who flourished during the seventeenth
century, styles it *Le concile permanent des Gaules.*

The firm attitude which Saint Louis preserved towards the Papacy has caused him to be regarded as

the author of a deed called the *Pragmatiquesanction*, which asserts the liberties of the Gallican Church, and guarantees the free election within the limits of the realm of France of all bishops, archdeacons, prebendaries, canons, and other dignitaries of the Church. The authenticity, however, of this document is now generally discarded, and only ignorance or prejudice can ascribe the slightest weight to it.

The good king, in the midst of all his administrative reforms, had never forgotten the claims of the Christians in the East on the sympathy of their Frankish brethren, and in 1270 he determined to start for another Crusade. On this occasion the Seneschal of Champagne flatly refused to follow him. "Those who advised him to start," says Joinville, "committed a great sin, considering the extreme weakness of his body, for he could bear neither the motion of a vehicle nor that of a horse. His weakness was so great that he allowed me to carry him in my arms from the hotel of the Count of Auxerre, where I took leave of him, to the convent of the Franciscan friars (*Cordeliers*), and, weak as he was, if he had only remained in France, he might have lived long enough and done many good works. About his voyage to Tunis I shall neither say nor relate anything, for, thank God, I was not there, and I will not say or write in my book anything of which I am not certain." Saint Louis died under the walls of Tunis on the 25th of August, 1270, and after an interval of twenty years the Crusaders had to retire from the Holy Land.

Whilst these things were going on in Egypt and in

Palestine, Charles of Anjou, brother to the King of France, had accepted from Pope Urban IV., as a fief, the kingdom of Sicily (Naples and Sicily), which Manfred had usurped, to the prejudice of his nephew Conradin still young. He marched into Italy at the head of an army of French and Provençal knights, was crowned king at Rome on the 6th of January, 1266, and gained, on the 26th of February following, the Battle of Beneventum. To this expedition can be traced the pretentions raised from time to time by the French Crown to the kingdom of two Sicilies.

The progress of literature and the fine arts during the thirteenth century must now engage our attention, and we find there, as well as in questions of politics, results which deserve to be described somewhat in detail. If we turn, first, to literature properly called, the two names of Villehardouin and Joinville stand pre-eminent amongst prose writers, and the merits of him who wrote "Conqueste de Constantinoble" appear the more conspicuous if we compare him with his dull continuator Henri de Valenciennes. In the walks of poetry we have to notice a period of decay so far as the romances of chivalry (*chansons de geste*) are concerned; the age of enthusiasm is gone, and the *trouvères* have lost their originality. In a previous chapter we have attempted a classification of the principal subjects treated by the poets who aimed at describing the high deeds of ancient heroes; we shall now consider separately the *cycle of Charlemagne* which is the most decidedly French of the three. For the sake of clearness it may be subdivided into three minor *gestes*. 1. *Geste du Roi*, where the glory of

Roland casts into the shade even that of Charlemagne.
2. *Geste de Garin de Montglane*, the hero of which is
Guillaume au Cort-nez, who won the Battle of Alis-
camps. 3. The *geste de Doon de Mayence*, taken up by
the exploits of Renaud de Montauban and Ogier le
Danois. Besides these three great branches or series
of poems, we must not forget several smaller *gestes*,
such as the *cycle de la Croisade (Chanson d'Antioche)*,
the *geste des Lorrains (Garin le Lohérain)*, the *geste de
Blaives (Amis et Amile)*, &c., &c. The peculiarity of
the *trouvères* of the thirteenth century was that, instead
of composing original poems, they were satisfied for
the most part with remodelling old compositions and
clothing them with new dresses. Thus Graindor of
Douai, taking Richard the Pilgrim as his pattern,
recast the "Chanson d'Antioche ;" thus, again, Jean
Bodel wrote "Chanson des Saisnes" (Saxons) or
"Guitéclin (Witikind) de Sassoigne" (Saxony) from
an old poem ; Adenès le roi, so called because he was
"King of the Minstrels," modernized also "Berthe aus
grands piés," "Beuves de Comarchis," and "Les en-
fances Ogier." Amongst what may be called the *original* romances of the thirteenth century we may
name Jacques Forest's "Roman de Jules César," the
"Roman du bel écu," or "Frégus et Galienne" by
Guillaume de Normandie, Pyram's "Parthénopex de
Blois, Gilbert de Montreuil's "Roman de la Violette"
imitated by Boccaccio and from which Shakespeare
borrowed the story of Cymbeline; Adenès le roi wrote
the romaunt of "Cléomadès," and, to complete this long
list, we may mention "Floire et Blanceflor," the work
of an author whose name is not exactly known.

The poem, however, with which the thirteenth century in its decline must ever be chiefly associated is the famous "Roman de la Rose," begun by Guillaume de Lorris about 1262, and finished by Jean de Meung about 1305. The former part of the work is an extraordinary association of mystic tenderness and of coarse sensuality, of chivalrous gallantry and of scholastic subtlety ; the latter half breathes the spirit of keen satire together with longings after a reformation which, if Jean Meung had had his way, would have been of the most sweeping character.

TROUBADOURS.

The voice of the *troubadour* no longer resounded ; *Tensons, Sirventes, planhs, aubades* were gone for ever, and at the time immediately preceding the reign of Louis IX. the principal monument of Languedoc literature was a long-rhymed chronicle which has lately been published, and which was the work of two distinct poets ; the first part, composed between 1210 and 1213, is directed against the Albigenses ; the second, to which the date of 1218 or 1219 can be assigned, is inspired, on the contrary, by intense hatred of the Crusaders, and is fairly entitled to be called a poem.

If we were to enumerate all the *trouvères* who flourished during the reign of Saint Louis we should be drawn far beyond the limits of this chapter. Rutebeuf, the genuine precursor of Villon, must be named, however, amongst the most distinguished ; his style is elegant and natural, full of imagination, pathos, and genuine sentiment. The *lays* and *fabliaux*, whether anonymous or assignable to well-known authors, may be defined as miniature romaunts or tales characterized chiefly by the spirit of satire, and not unfrequently by a *vis comica* bordering upon coarseness ; the name of Marie de France must ever be associated with these compositions, and if she had written nothing but the " Lay du Frêne "(containing the germ of the touching story of *Griselidis*) and the " Ysopet " (a collection of fables imitated from classical antiquity), she would still deserve not to be forgotten. The pretty story of " Aucassin and Nicolette" is one of the gems of thirteenth-century literature, but the best known of all the compositions belonging to that time is undoubtedly the " Roman de Renart," which is claimed by Germany and the Netherlands as well as by France, and which with its numerous branches and subdivisions is the embodiment of the satirical tendency of the Middle Ages. The days of chivalry are gone, and instead of Charlemagne, Turpin, Oliver and Roland, Ogier, Naime, and Huon, we find ourselves summoned before an assembly of animals, where the chief parts are taken by the lion (*Noble*), the fox (*Renard*), the wolf (*Ysengrin*), the bear (*Brun*), the wild boar (*Beaucent*), &c. The triumph

of cunning over brute force and of hypocrisy over
violence forms the subject-matter of the " Roman de
Renart ; " it runs through the works of Gauthier de
Coinsy and the innumerable *Bibles, castoiements*, and
dits which the erudite authorities of the " Histoire
Littéraire de la France " have so carefully analysed.

Suppose now we take one of the poems just enumerated, suppose, instead of a consecutive narrative,
we introduce each of the *dramatis personæ*, telling his
story and expressing his own opinions, we have immediately the drama under its twofold manifestations
of sacred (*mystères* and *moralités*) and secular (*farces*).
The mysteries were dramatized episodes of the Bible
and of the legends of the saints, the principal, besides
the "Mystère de la Passion," being that of Saint Nicolas
by Jean Bodel, a native of Arras, whom we have already
mentioned ; the earliest comedy or *farce* deserving to
be named is the " Jeu de la feuillie," and the earliest
comic opera, if we may use such a name, is the " Jeu
de Robin et de Marion," both works being by another
native of Arras, Adam de la Halle, surnamed the
hunchback no one knows why, and who distinctly
repudiated a sobriquet for which, as it seems, his
personal appearance did not give the slightest pretext : " On m'apele *bochu*," said he, " mès je ne le sui
mie."

Between the essentially lyric poetry of the *troubadours* and the decidedly satirical strain of the *trouvères*,
we find, as a transition, Thibaut, Count of Champagne.
Himself a pupil of the *troubadours*, and like them an
Epicurean by taste, notorious for the laxity of his
morals and the scandal of his life ; he shared also

their freedom of thinking, and their spirit of opposition to the Church. Bound by his oath, he was compelled to take a part in the crusade against the Albigenses, and to fight Raymond, Count of Toulouse ; but the following lines prove that his sympapathies were really on the side of the southern knights, and it would be difficult to find, even in Jean de Meung's bold poetry, a more bitter denunciation of the Holy See than in Thibaut de Champagne's sixty-fifth song.

> " Ce est des clers qui ont laisser sermons
> Pour guerroier et pour tuer les gens,
> Jamais en Dieu ne fuit tels homs créans.
> Nostre chief fait tous les membres doloir.
>
> .   .   .   .
>
> Papelars font li siècle chanceler
>
> .   .   .   .
>
> Ils ont tolu joie, et solas et pais,
> Sen porteront en enfer le grant fais."

" There are clerks who have forsaken sermons
In order to fight and to kill people.
Such men never did believe in God.
Our head (Innocent III.) makes all the limbs suffer.
The followers of the Pope cause the world to totter,
They have carried away joy, and solace, and peace.
Therefore they shall carry to hell the great burden (of their misdeeds)."

We cannot believe that so strict a king as St. Louis approved all the sentiments of the poets who were his contemporaries ; at the same time he granted valuable privileges to the minstrels, jugglers, and other members of the brotherhood, and particularly exempted them from paying toll at the bridges. The minstrels in lieu thereof might treat the collector to a tune or a song, and the juggler might make his monkey cut a caper or two. The well-known French proverb, " Payer en monnaie de singe " ($=$ to deceive a person by false promises), has arisen from that ancient custom.

The various branches of literature we have thus been considering are French exclusively—French by the form in which they are expressed, and by the inspiration under which they were written. If we now come to a more serious topic, to pulpit eloquence, we still find the vernacular language used, although monuments are very scarce and very imperfect. It was natural that preachers should retain in their sermons what may be called the ecclesiastical idiom, and that they should bestow upon *Latin* discourses most of their care and attention ; but they remem- bered that if often they had to preach *ad cleros*, their audiences consisted more frequently still of common and illiterate people, who could not have understood them if they had used the language of the Church ; we are therefore led to adopt the opinion arrived at by several learned historians, to wit (1) that all the sermons addressed to the faithful, even those written in Latin, were preached entirely in French ; (2) that the sermons intended for the clergy were, generally, preached in Latin. Maurice de Sully, Bishop of Paris, who died in 1196, composed a set of sermons intended to be a manual or guide for the priests of his diocese ; it is written in Latin, being in the first instance meant as a kind of authorized book, to be employed by those who had no talent or leisure for original composition ; but, at the same time, the pre- late expressly directed that these sermons should be addressed to the whole congregation of faithful, and accordingly, as the final clauses of two MSS. expressly state, they were to be read in French. We have the authority of the chronicler, Humbert de Romans, to state that the early Dominican friars, even those of German origin, preached in that language, and one of them, Jourdain of Saxony, holding forth to a congregation of knights in Palestine, after having apologized for his imperfect knowledge of French, made frequent use of German words and phrases. The custom of thus intermixing the vernacular idioms with Latin gradually gained ground, and led in course of time to the macaronic style which characterizes the sermons of Michel Menot and Olivier Maillard.

The transition from pulpit eloquence to church architecture is a natural one, and we are thus led to consider the state of the fine arts during the reign of Louis IX. It may be said that the renovation of church architecture took place shortly after the year 1000. Up to that time, in the construction of sacred buildings, nothing more was aimed at but the imitation of the ancient *basilica*. No sooner was the Christian world delivered from the terrors of the day of judgment, which so many had proclaimed as about to be ushered in with the eleventh century, than, as if it had been through a desire of expressing substantial gratitude to the Deity, the whole population set about erecting cathedrals, parish churches, abbeys, and monasteries. From the school of Cluny, and other similar establishments, came forth architects of the greatest merit, and the Gothic style of construction made its first appearance. The principal cathedrals

SAINT WULFRAN, À ABBEVILLE

NOTRE DAME OF PARIS.

10

belonging to that epoch are those of Chartres, Bourges,
Amiens, Paris, and Rouen; nor must we forget the
Sainte Chapelle, one of the most elegant specimens
of Gothic architecture which the metropolis of France
can boast of.

It has often been noticed that what may be called
lay or secular architecture followed closely the same
type as the one adopted for the erection of churches;
the reason for this is twofold.   In the first place,
religious establishments held the foremost rank in the
social order; and, secondly, the monks alone being
architects, painters, sculptors, and decorators, they
could scarcely help introducing in the economy of
secular buildings the usual way they had of drawing
a plan, and carrying out its execution.   The art of
sculpture and that of painting made considerable
progress in France during the thirteenth century.
M. Viollet le Duc tells us that so far as drawing is
concerned, together with the correct observation of
movement, composition, and even expression, the
French artists cast off the trammels of conven-
tionalism long before the Italian ones. " The paintings and vignettes which the thirteenth century has
bequeathed to us are the proof of that fact, and fifty
years previous to Giotto, we had amongst us painters
who had already realized the progress ascribed to the
pupil of Cimabue.   From the twelfth century to the
fifteenth drawing becomes modified ; fettered at first
by the traditions of Byzantine art, it begins by shaking
off these rules of a particular school; without abandoning style, it looks for principles derived from the
observation of nature.   The study of gesture soon

attains to a rare delicacy, then comes a search after
what is called expression. . . . As early as the second
half of the thirteenth century we recognize striking
efforts of composition ; the dramatic idea finds its
place, and some of the scenes betray powerful energy."
Mural and decorative painting had more difficulties
to contend with, but they also showed decided progress.

The influence of the Church could not but be much
felt in music, and when we speak of that art, as it
flourished during the Middle Ages, we must be understood to refer to plain chant, motets, hymns, and in
general to psalmody. Modern music may be said to
have sprung into existence when Gothic architecture
had attained its perfection ; and it would have been
strange if Saint Louis, so anxious to have Divine service celebrated with all possible perfection, had not
given his attention to music. The names of several
organists have been handed down to us, and the
cathedral church of Notre Dame in Paris claims the
most celebrated amongst them ; Léonin, for instance,
and Pérotin. The king did not care for secular
music, and whilst most of the high barons had
minstrels as part of their household, Louis IX. had
none. When Marguerite de Provence came to
Sens on her coronation, her father brought with
him a minstrel and six troubadours ; these did
not remain 'at Court, but at the same time they
were handsomely remunerated, and on the statement of expenses made for the occasion, we find
112 livres, 20 sols, and 12 deniers for the minstrels,
together with 10 livres paid to the minstrel of the

Count de Provence.   The list of musical instruments in use during the Middle Ages was a long one ; besides the organ, the lyre, and the harp, we find the violin (*vielle*, *rote*, *rebec*), the guitar or guiterne, the doulcemer (*dulcimer*), the trumpet, the sackbut, the drum, &c.   The *nacaire* or *naquaire*, mentioned by Joinville, seems to have been a kind of cymbal, and the dulcimer very like our piano.

The industrial arts claim also a mention here, and as a matter of course the improvements of every kind introduced into church architecture and decoration, told upon carpentering, carving, the " craft and mystery " of joiners, goldsmiths, silversmiths, and blacksmiths.   Tombs, relic-cases, stalls, lecterns, fonts, incense-boxes, candelabra, crucifixes—in fact, all the articles used for ecclesiastical purposes, all the monuments belonging to the church were executed with a degree of perfection and of taste which has never been surpassed.

In conclusion, the thirteenth century marks the most brilliant epoch of the Middle Ages, and in that epoch the reign of Saint Louis forms, so to say, the central point.   After the death of that glorious monarch, decay sets in, the old order of things falls gradually to pieces, and to the prevalence of honour, courage, loyalty, and self-sacrifice succeeds the triumph of insolence, cowardice, treachery, avarice, and selfishness.

VII.

PHILIP III.—PHILIP IV.
(1270-1314.)

WHY Philip III. should have been surnamed "the Bold" (*le hardi*) it would be difficult to say. He had inherited the meekness and the piety of his father, but none of his other virtues, and the contemporary chronicles have very little to say about him. Charles de Valois was the French prince who occupies the stage of history during the last few years of the thirteenth century, and around him is gathered all the interest which belongs to the country of the *fleurs-de-lys*. It is even still a matter of doubt whether Philip knew how to write; at any rate, his mind absolutely lacked culture. During his reign, however, the royal power went on acquiring strength, and fresh provinces were added to the kingdom; in fact, he inherited from almost every member of his family. The death of his brother, Jean Tristan, brought to him the province of Valois; his uncle Alphonso left to him nearly the whole of Southern France : Poitou, Auvergne, Toulouse, Rouergue, Albigeois, Quercy, Agénois, Comtat Venaissin ; finally he got possession of Navarre by marrying his son Philip to the daughter of the Count of Champagne, who was also king of that fertile province. It is true that Agénois was restored to England, and the Comtat to the Pope, but still the authority of the new monarch extended over nearly all the country comprised between the Loire and the Pyrenees, and a few attempts of resistance having taken place, they were speedily put down.

Charles d'Anjou, as we have already said, was at that time the real French king. Count of Florence, King of Naples and Sicily, a Roman senator, imperial vicar in Tuscany, lord of most of the cities in Northern Italy, he might have been satisfied with the immense power then concentrated in his hands. The political state of Europe had singularly favoured his ambitious plans. Germany was without an emperor ; Italy was rent asunder by the feuds between the Guelphs and Ghibelines ; a dispute on points of doctrine had separated the Eastern from the Western Church ; and the empire of Constantinople was threatened as the focus of a dangerous schism. Charles d'Anjou took advantage of this state of things ; he aimed, not only at being Emperor of the East, but at taking possession of Jerusalem and of Egypt. Such exorbitant pretensions could not be tolerated, and even Pope Gregory X. saw the necessity of stemming the torrent. He contrived to bring about a reconciliation between the conflicting factions in Italy, secured the election of Rodolph of Hapsburg to the throne of Germany, and put an end to the schism at the council of Lyons. When he died Nicolas III., his successor, adopted the same policy. The danger thus minimized was entirely removed in consequence of the event which is known as the *Sicilian Vespers*. A Calabrian physician, lord of the island of Procida, had been for some time travel·ling about for the purpose of stirring up enemies against Charles d'Anjou. Having secured the active co-operation of Don Pedro, King of Arragon, he organized a conspiracy, and selected Sicily as the spot where the rising was to take place. That island, ground down by the tyranny of Charles, drained of its financial resources, subjected to the most iniquitous system of taxation, was treated with insolence by the French, who took every opportunity of asserting their superiority over the wretched inhabitants. " On Easter Monday (March 30, 1282) the population of Palermo, according to custom, had gathered together for the purpose of attending vespers on the hill of Monreale. A young lady of noble birth was in the crowd, accompanied by her betrothed lover ; a Frenchman approaches her, charges her with having weapons concealed under her clothes, and attempts to search her in the most indecent manner. He is immediately killed, and his death becomes the signal of a universal massacre. Measures to that effect had been taken beforehand, the houses inhabited by the French, for instance, were all marked with a peculiar sign during the previous night. No one escaped who could not pronounce the letter c in the Italian fashion. The whole of Sicily followed the example of Palermo." [1] In the meanwhile Don Pedro, accompanied by Procida, started for Sicily, at the head of a powerful fleet, which took possession of the Straits of Messina

[1] Bordier and Charton, " Histoire de France."

Charles d'Anjou did not repose much confidence in his own sailors ; he raised the siege of Messina which he had been blockading, and crossed over to Italy, having to suffer the humiliation of seeing his ships destroyed. It is said that he kept biting his sceptre out of sheer rage. Finding that fortune was abandoning him, he exclaimed, "Grant, O my God, that the descent may take place by slow steps and gently." After several prolonged and unhappy efforts to continue the struggle Charles d'Anjou died on the 7th of January, 1285, declaring that "he had undertaken the enterprise of the kingdom of Sicily rather for the benefit of the Holy Church than for his own private advantage."

His uncle now dead, Philip III. had to bear the brunt of the war against Spain, and to avenge the honour of the Valois family. A crusade was preached against Spain, and the King of France crossed the Pyrenees at the head of a splendid army, which some historians estimate at twenty thousand cavalry and eighty thousand infantry ; a powerful fleet coasting along the shore was to keep this large force amply supplied, as well as to assist it in case of need. The town of Elne taken after a desperate resistance, seemed to be the prelude of great things ; but the French lost two months in besieging Gerona, and when that place had capitulated, the invaders were so reduced by the climate, the heat and pestilential diseases, that they were obliged to retrace their steps and to return home. Philip had just time to reach Perpignan before he died (October 5, 1285). His fleet had been defeated, and a week after the death of the King of France, Don Pedro occupied Gerona.

Amongst the monuments of French dramatic literature during the Middle Ages there is one which we shall mention here, not on account of any merit it possesses, but because it refers to an extraordinary incident in the reign of Philip III. It is entitled " Le Jeu de Pierre de la Broce," and is preceded by a *complainte* or dirge on the same person. Now, Pierre de la Brosse, belonging to a very humble family, had been originally barber to Philip III. Being extremely clever, ready-witted, and sharp, he contrived to gain the confidence of his master, and to become Prime Minister. Philip was married twice ; his first wife, Isabella of Arragon, died shortly before her husband ascended the throne. In 1274 he took as his consort Mary of Brabant, and the following year, Louis, the eldest of his sons by Isabella, having died of poison, as it was supposed, Pierre de la Brosse managed to persuade the king, that Mary of Brabant was guilty of the crime, and that she had formed the plan of despatching in like manner the other children, in order to secure the throne for her own offspring. Philip, of course, was extremely angry, and determined upon having his wife burnt alive ; but the princes of the blood and the chief lords, to whom he communicated his suspicions, persuaded him not to act too rashly. Before he followed out his intentions he should make all necessary inquiries, and consult some person learned in sorcery and witchcraft. They selected a nun of Nivelle, in Brabant, the dominions of the queen's father, and sent to her for the purpose of consultation the Bishop of Dol and a Knight-Templar. " Tell from me to the king," answered the

oracle, "that he must not believe the slanderous
reports circulated about his wife ; for she is good
and loyal both towards him and towards all his
family, and her heart is sincere." Some historians
add that the nun went on to say that the young
prince had been poisoned by a man who enjoyed
the king's confidence. No other but Pierre de la
Brosse was evidently meant by this designation.

Whether the last part of the story is true or not,
the Prime Minister became suspected in his turn, and
soon paid the penalty of his misdeeds. Mary of
Brabant was still treated as if she was guilty, and
confined to her apartments. The Count d'Artois,
who was a relation both of the king and of the
queen, having offered to maintain her innocence in
single combat, and no one accepting the challenge,
she re-appeared in public. About that time a packet
of letters was delivered to the king, coming from
Spain and addressed to Pierre de la Brosse ; on
opening it, proof was found that the Prime Minister
had been carrying on a treasonable correspondence,
and he was immediately arrested on that charge,
tried in Paris, and condemned to be hanged. Thus
it was that Mary of Brabant was avenged of the
vilest and boldest accusation ever put forth ; from
that time she lived in perfect harmony with her
husband ; she had three children, one son who, prior
to his ascending the throne, was Count d'Evreux, and
two daughters.

Before taking leave of Philip the Bold, we must not
forget to mention two facts which are of importance
as illustrating the decay of feudal institutions. In the

first place, by granting (1272) a patent of nobility to
his treasurer Raoul, the king gave the earliest
instance on record in French history of a commoner
being admitted into the aristocracy ; secondly, leave
was granted for commoners to enjoy the possessions
of fiefs. Thus nobility ceased to be a natural quality
which could neither be lost nor purchased ; it was
reduced to a privilege conferred to this or that man
by the accident of his birth or the good pleasure of
the king, to the prejudice of his equals. Any one
was qualified to exercise the rights it implies, and to
discharge the duties resulting from it.

Philip IV. was seventeen years old when he
ascended the throne, and from the very beginning
of his reign it was quite evident that the power was
in the hand of the legists. The days of feudalism
had passed away for ever, and a period of transition
was commencing. Under the old system, as there
was no administration properly so called, government
agents did not exist ; as the vassals of the Crown
were compelled to do military service, there was no
mercenary troops, no need to provide for the pay
of a permanent army. Things now were totally
different ; the royal domain included two-thirds of
France instead of half a dozen towns as heretofore ;
hence the necessity of a host of judges, notaries,
provosts, seneschals, counsellors, &c. It was the same
in matters of war ; whereas formerly, as a general
rule, warlike expeditions were confined within rela-
tively small limits, now troops had to be moved
towards the Pyrenees, the Rhine, the Garonne, the
shores of the Mediterranean. Fleets were indispens-

able, and the feudal militia could not suffice. Now
law-agents must be paid; seneschals appointed by the
king will not explain the law *gratis*, counsellors insist
on being remunerated for giving advice. In like
manner, if the feudal militia is not equal to the
exigencies of a campaign, mercenary troops must be
called in; they are subjected to strict discipline, and
their services can always be depended upon; but
they very naturally require to be paid; and if the
Genoese galleys (as in the case of the war with
Flanders) are retained in addition to the ships from
Poitou and Normandy, money must be forthcoming.
We thus see that Philip the Fair (*le bel*, such was
his surname) was very short of money, and as the
expenses kept increasing whilst the national income
remained the same, France seemed on the eve of a
bankruptcy. Philip tried several means of replenish-
ing the exchequer, but he was very unwise in the
schemes he adopted, and whilst grinding down the
people, he did no good to the State. One of his
first plans was to extort money arbitrarily out of the
Jews and Lombards—the bankers of those days.
Driven from France the Jews carried their riches
into foreign lands, the Lombards concealed theirs, and
commerce came to a standstill. Now, Philip turned
coiner and this, of course, did not mend matters;
he ordered all the old coinage to be melted, with the
view of altering its value; further, under the pretence
of enforcing the sumptuary laws, he confiscated the
gold and silver plate of those persons who had not
a large fortune, and caused it to be cast into the
smelting furnace out of which it came in the shape

of *livres* and *sous parisis*, nominally equal in value to what they used to be, but really worth much less ; the consequence was the ruin of industry. His endeavour to raise taxes in Flanders led to a rebellion ; his bold endeavour to get money out of the Church ended in a quarrel with Pope Boniface VIII. ; we shall see presently the mysterious history of the Templars and the destruction of the order.

Philip the Fair was not naturally of a fighting disposition ; as soon as he could, he got rid of useless warfares by treaties and peaceful arrangements, and set about extending his domains by marriages and other quiet contrivances. His union with the heiress of Navarre and Champagne procured to him two important provinces ; a sentence of parliament deprived the heirs of Hugh de Lusignan to the profit of the French Crown, which was thus put in possession of Marche and Angoumois ; finally, Philip's .second son took to wife the heiress of Franche Comté. Remained the countship of Flanders and the duchies of Guienne and Brittany. Here fighting was a matter of absolute necessity, and Philip tried first what he. could do in Southern France. Edward I., King of England, was at the same time Duke of Guienne, and might have proved a dangerous adversary for Philip had he not been entirely absorbed by the affairs of Wales and of Scotland. Philip's army marched into Guienne, whilst his fleet plundered Dover. The Count of Flanders had sided with Edward ; Philip invaded his domains and defeated the Flemings at Furnes (1295). Thanks to the intervention of the Pope, peace was concluded between

France and England, the treaty being confirmed
by the marriage of the daughter of Philip the Fair
with the son of the King of England. Thus it
happened that prospective claims to the crown of
France were enjoyed by England—claims which later
on Edward III. knew how to put forth, and to support by the power of his arms. Hitherto Philip had
sided with the Scotch; he abandoned them to his
new ally, who in his turn forsook the Count of
Flanders. Thus deserted, this prince was struck
with terror; he came in person to surrender to
Philip, and Flanders was annexed to the kingdom
of France.

Common sense should have suggested to Philip
the advisability of treating the Flemings with kindness, or, at any rate, with a certain amount of courtesy.
Unfortunately he adopted a totally different course,
and sent amongst them as a governor, Jacques de
Châtillon, who thought that he had nothing to do
but to get as much money as he could out of a rich
and thriving population, and to convince them that
their riches would avail them nothing against the
power of the *fleurs-de-lys*. He began by depriving
the citizens of their municipal elections, and of the
right of managing their own affairs. This ill-judged
measure alienated the upper classes. His next act
was to oblige the workmen to pay to the Crown one
fourth of their daily salary. This irritated the poor.
An amount of agitation took place which Châtillon
did not anticipate, although the ill-will of the
Flemings had manifested itself on the very first day
of the French occupation. The centre of the move-

ment was at Bruges, which Châtillon had visited
with his wrath ; he had confiscated the privileges
of the town, dismantled it, and was constructing
a citadel with the view of keeping the citizens in
order. A massacre of the French took place on
May 17, 1302, and precautions were taken by the
inhabitants to prevent the foreign knights from
retaliating. Chains were drawn across the streets,
and all the available bridles and saddles seized by
the magistrates for the purposes of furnishing an
improvised body of cavalry. The report that the
King of France was advancing at the head of an
army of sixty thousand men only served to exasperate the people of Bruges, who were nearly the only
part of the population which seemed determined to
fight. "Attacked before Courtrai, they coolly awaited
the French, having taken up their position at the
back of a semi-circular ditch, concealed both by
branches of trees and by the bulrushes which filled the
marshes. A priest celebrated mass, and at the moment
of the devotion, each man taking up a little earth
raised it to his lips, thus showing that he joined in
the communion with his fellow-citizens. The French
were full of confidence ; in order to have the whole
honour of the victory, they pushed aside the Italian
archers who formed a kind of auxiliary force. They
had the advantage at first ; but the Count d'Artois
having crossed the ditch was killed close to the
banner of Flanders, and the horsemen who followed
him stumbled upon one another in utter confusion.
Thus disabled and helpless, they became the easy
victims of their enemies, who made of them a terrible

slaughter. Twelve thousand sergeants-at-arms were then killed in a marsh, which subsequently received the name of the *Blood Marsh*. We are told that on the field of battle the gold spurs of the knights were measured by the bushel "[1]

We may imagine how joyfully the news of Philip's defeat was received at Rome, Florence, Toulouse, and Bordeaux. It is true that the French avenged their honour at Mons-en-Puelle (1304), but the king having besieged Lille, a general rising of the whole of Flanders took place, and Philip drew back ; he obtained Douai, Lille, Béthune, Orchies, and the whole of French Flanders situated between the Lys and the Scheldt, and as a kind of compensation he gave back to the Flemings their count, who did him feudal homage for his domains. Thoroughly ruined by the war, he returned to his kingdom, and found there great irritation caused by the famine, the alteration of the coinage, and the other financial measures which he had so injudiciously forced upon the people. He now turned his attention towards the Pope, and thought he would replenish his exchequer at the expense of the Church.

As early as 1296 differences had arisen between Boniface VIII. and Philip the Fair, on account of certain taxes which the king wished to levy on ecclesiastical property. " Between the famished king," says M. Michelet, "and the hungry starved to death, there was some one rich, and that *some one* was the Church, archbishops and bishops, canons and monks —monks ancient, belonging to the order of Saint

---

[1] Bordier and Charton.

Benedict ; monks modern, styled mendicant friars—
they were all rich, and vied with each other in point
of opulence. All that tonsured society throve on
the blessings of heaven and the fat of the land.
It was a small and happy community, obese and
shining, in the midst of the great famished people,
which was beginning to look at them with an
unfavourable eye."

Concord seemed however to be re-established for a
short time, and Boniface VIII., as an earnest of good
will, pronounced the canonization of Louis IX. This
was only a brief respite, and the proud interference
of the Pope in the home policy of France made
things worse than ever. One of the Papal legates,
Bernard Saisset, an ambitious and violent man,
Bishop of Pamiers, used on a certain occasion offen-
sive and even treasonable language towards the King
of France, and what was more, in the king's own
presence. Philip could not brook such insolence ; he
caused Bernard Saisset to be arrested, and requested
the Archbishop of Narbonne, his metropolitan, to
pronounce his canonical degradation. The archbishop having referred to the Pope, Boniface VIII.
by way of answer, fulminated the famous Bull
Ausculta, fili, which resulted in his being shamefully
treated, and in his meeting finally with a pitiable
death. The whole of this affair was characterized
on both sides by acts of violence which would have
narred the best cause, and which did equal injury to
the King of France and to the Pope. The drift of
the Bull will be seen from the following quotation :

"God has set me, though unworthy, above kings

II

and kingdoms, having imposed upon me the yoke of apostolic servitude, to root out and to pull down, to destroy and to throw down, to build and to plant, in His name. Wherefore let no man persuade you that you have no superior, or that you are not subject to the supreme head of the ecclesiastical hierarchy. He who thinks so is a madman, and if he persists in his error, is convicted as an infidel. . . .

"Although it is certain that the nomination to all benefices belongs to the Pope, and that you have no right to any such patronage without the consent of the Holy See, you oppose our collations, and claim to act as judge in your own cause. You drag before your tribunals the bishops and other clergy of your kingdom, both regular and secular, even for matters concerning property which they do not hold from you in fief. You exact from them tenths and other imposts, although laymen have no authority whatever over the clergy. You hinder the bishops from employing the spiritual sword against offenders, and from exercising their jurisdiction over conventual houses. You observe no moderation in disposing of the revenues of vacant episcopal sees which you call by an abuse, '*Droit de régale*.' You squander these revenues, and turn into plunder what was a means of preserving them intact."

The Bull *Ausculta, fili*, accompanied by the one known as *Salvator mundi*, and by three others, was issued on the 3rd of December, 1301 : it had been preceded by the Bulls *Ineffabilis amoris* (February 7, 1297) and *Clericis laïcos* (February 24, 1296). Whilst denouncing the bad administration of Philip the Fair, and the iniquitous taxes which he imposed upon his subjects, Boniface VIII. was perfectly right, and he was well aware that the tax called *maltôte* (L. *malè tolta*=unfairly raised), exacted from certain large towns had caused rebellions, at Rouen, for instance (1292); but, on the other hand, he formed on the power of the Papacy ideas which were no longer admissible. The days of Gregory VII. had gone never to return, and the lawyers who really governed the kingdom under the name of Philip, endeavoured to establish the rule of Roman law which gives to the king absolute power, including that of interfering in the administration of the diocese. Hence a deplorable quarrel. Supported by the unanimous vote of the States-General (1302), Philip threatened Boniface with a council, before which he meant to summons him; the Pope in his turn prepared a Bull for the deposition of the king. This was too much; one of the agents of Philip the Fair, Guillaume de Nogaret, was in Italy, at Anagni, the birthplace of Boniface VIII., who had himself repaired there from Rome. Nogaret had contrived to gain the support of the inhabitants, and was accompanied by Sciarra Colonna, a nobleman of Roman origin, and a mortal enemy of the Pope. We should remark that Nogaret's grandfather had been formerly burnt alive as belonging to the sect of Albigenses; he could not, therefore, feel very favourably disposed towards the Holy See. He entered Anagni at the head of four hundred men, and marched towards the palace amidst the cries of "Death to the Pope! Long live the King of France!" Boniface was

sitting· on his throne, arrayed in his pontifical vestments, with the tiara on his head, holding a cross
in one hand, and the keys of St. Peter in the other.
Being ordered to abdicate, he said, "Here is my neck,
here is my head; betrayed like Jesus Christ, if I must
die as He did, at any rate, I shall die a Pope."
Thereupon Sciarra Colonna tore him from his throne,
struck him in the face with his iron gauntlet, and
would have killed him on the spot, had not Guillaume
de Nogaret interfered. Addressing Boniface, the
Frenchman said : "O thou wretched Pope, consider
and behold the kindness of my lord the King of
France who, for ever so distant as his realms are
from thine, by me protects and defends thee."

The people of Anagni, however, recovered at last
from the stupor in which they had been plunged by
the arrival of the French; they rose, drove away the
invaders, set the Pope at liberty, and conducted him
back to Rome. He died shortly after of shame and
anger at the affronts to which he had been submitted.
Benedict XI., who succeeded Boniface on the siege of
St. Peter, wanted to avenge him by excommunicating
Nogaret, Colonna, and all those who had assisted
them. The sentence virtually reached the king ; one
month after the Bull was fulminated the new Pope
died, most probably of poison.

Philip the Fair now contrived to secure the tiara
for an ecclesiastic of his own choice, and who would
not hesitate to accept any terms the French monarch
might think fit to make. This was Bertrand de Got,
Archbishop of Bordeaux ; he assumed the name of
Clement V., was consecrated at Lyons, and abandon-

ing Rome, came to settle at Avignon (1308), where he was at the disposal and under the thumb, so to say, of the king. Then commenced what has been called the second Babylonish captivity; the successors of Clement V. remained in Avignon till the year 1376.

The scandalous bargain thus made between the Pope and Philip has been characterized in three doggrel lines, which we find quoted by Walsingham :

> ' Ecclesiæ navis titubat, regni quia clavis
> Errat.   Rex, Papa, facti sunt unica cappa.
> Hoc faciunt *dodes*, Pilatus hec, alter Herodes."

One of the conditions imposed by the king upon the Pope was the destruction of the Order of the Temple. Why should those warrior-monks be so rich?   In the time of the Crusades they might have given as an excuse that they spent their money in levying troops for the delivery of the Holy Land ; but now that these expeditions were abandoned, there seemed no need for the knights to have in their treasure-house 150,000 gold florins, besides silver and precious cups, vases, and other specimens of goldsmith's work.   Then was not the order a standing menace against the power of the king?   They numbered 15,000 knights, in addition to an immense number of retainers ; they possessed throughout the whole extent of Christendom upwards of 10,000 manorial residences, to say nothing of fortresses which could set at defiance the united forces of Europe.   Finally, their orthodoxy was more than doubtful, and they constituted a standing scandal to the Church.   They worshipped the devil under the shape of a cat, they were Mahometans in

disguise, they held mysteries which no profane eye
was allowed to see, and to which no outsider was
admitted, &c., &c. It would be perhaps rash to deny
that the Templars were not uniformly blameless from
the point of view of morality, and that their religious
opinions were not strictly orthodox ; but confessions
obtained under the influence of torture are unworthy
of belief, and it is only too clear now that the suppression of the Order of the Temple was the result of
Philip the Fair's covetousness and love of money.
By a clever stroke of policy he thought of associating
the nation with him in his design, and summoned
the States-General at Tours. In the meanwhile
popular opinion instigated by Philip the Fair had
been excited against the Papacy, and satirical literature was brought in to take the king's part and to
further his designs. The most signal instance of this
rather unscrupulous attack is to be found in the
" Roman de Fauvel," composed by François de Rues.
Fauvel, an imaginary being, half-man and half-horse,
is represented as a kind of idol before which popes,
cardinals, princes, bishops, monks, are prostrated.
Every one claims the privilege of *torcher Fauvel*
(caressing Fauvel), and the expression *torcher Fauvel*,
coined at that epoch, has remained as the synonym
of *to cabal, to intrigue, to act unscrupulously.* Fauvel is
the embodiment of falsehood, pride, and sensuality.

> " De Fauvel descent Flaterie,
> Qui du monde a la seigneurie,
> Et puis en descent avarice,
> Qui de torcher Fauvel n'est nice,
>   Vilenie et vanité,
> Et puis envi et fauseté."

" From Fauvel proceeds flattery,
   Which exercises the lordship in this world ;
   Thence proceeds also avarice
   Which has no scruple in caressing Fauvel,
      Vileness and vanity,
   And then envy and falsehood."

Of the condemned Templars the poet says :

" Hélas ! Hélas ! c'est bien raison ;
   Car ils ont, trop longue saison,
   Cette orde vie demenée ;
   Si régnassent plus longuement,
   Crestienté certenement
   S'en fust partout envenimée."

" Alas ! alas ! it is quite right (that they should be
      condemned) ;
   For they have too long
   Led this disgraceful life ;
   If they had reigned for a longer period,
   Christendom certainly
   Would have been thoroughly poisoned."

Thus excited, the deputies to the States-General
pronounced unanimously the condemnation of the
unfortunate Templars, and gave to the unscrupulous
despot the full sanction to seize upon the rich prey
which he had so long been coveting (May, 1307).
All the towns of any importance were represented at
Tours as well as all the prelates and the great
majority of the nobility. Thus it might be said with
a certain amount of plausibility that the entire nation
believed in the guilt of the knights, though at the
same time the accusation brought against them was
utterly false and calumnious. But Philip the Fair
was accustomed to such procedure, and already, five
years before, when the States-General of 1302 pro-

nounced the deposition of Boniface VIII., they had falsified the Papal bull in the most scandalous manner with the view of finding a ground for their accusations.

Fifty-four Templars were burnt alive in one day at Paris alone, and similar executions took place in all the principal provincial towns. The Pope, at the council of Vienne (1312), pronounced the suppression of the order throughout Christendom; their riches were to be handed over to the Knights Hospitallers, but we need scarcely say that Philip the Fair managed to secure a large portion of the spoil. He obtained all the coin found in the chief house of the order, besides two-thirds of the furniture and of the money owing to them, and a considerable amount of landed property.

VIII.

PHILIP THE FAIR—LOUIS X.—PHILIP V.—CHARLES
IV.—PHILIP VI.
(1314–1328.)

THE reign of Philip the Fair was marked, as we have
already seen, by events of the most extraordinary, and,
we may almost say, the most revolutionary character.
The administration of France furnished the king
with an opportunity of carrying out his scheme of
reforms, and we are bound to say that although his
laws were stamped with the mark of despotism,
some of them, many of them, we should say, manifested a true idea of the principles of government.

The Paris parliament existed in an elementary
form under the reign of Philip Augustus and Saint
Louis, but it was reserved for Philip the Fair to give
to it a regular constitution, and make of it a real
court of justice. By his decree of 1302, he separated
the functions of the parliament into three classes,
according as they were of a political, judicial, or
financial nature. The first belonged to the Council of
State (*Grand Conseil* or *Conseil Étroit*); the second fell
under the cognizance of the Parliament properly
so called ; the third pertained to the Court of Ac-

counts (*Cour des comptes*).   With reference to the
parliament, it was definitely constituted by virtue
of the ordinances of 1291 and 1302, and comprised
three distinct courts (*chambres*) :—1. The *Chambre des
requêtes* judged the cases immediately brought before
the parliament.   2. The *Chambre des enquêtes* decided
upon the cases about which an appeal had been
made to the parliament.   3. The *Grand' Chambre*, or
Chambre des plaidoiries judged the cases which had
been previously examined in the *Chambre des enquêtes.*

In addition to the Paris parliament, Philip the
Fair had also thought of establishing a special one
at Toulouse for the trial of cases amenable to Roman
law ; but the resistance which he encountered from
the local authorities obliged him to give up his plan,
and to be satisfied with annexing to the Paris
parliament an additional *Chambre des enquêtes* reserved for the examination of cases which could not
be judged according to the principles of feudal
legislation.   The parliament was to meet twice a
year for sessions of two months each, in the building
called *Palais de la cité*, and subsequently known as
Palais de justice. The Normandy *Exchequer* was
retained by Philip the Fair ; founded at the time of
the Norman invasion, it had been, up to the fourteenth century, a feudal court peculiar to the
province, meeting twice a year, at Easter and
Michaelmas, and holding its sessions alternately at
Rouen, and Caën.   King Philip directed that the
sittings of the Exchequer should take place for the
future at Rouen exclusively, under the presidency of
magistrates appointed by the Crown.   Finally, Philip

IV. regularized the *grands jours* of Champagne held at Troyes, and which used to meet for the trial of cases which the ordinary tribunals were unable to deal with.

We have now come to the last years of an eventful reign, and it remains for us to notice two episodes of a tragic character which marked its conclusion.

In his poem entitled "Le grand Testament," the celebrated Villon says:

> "Semblablement où est la royne
> Qui commanda que Buridan
> Fut jetté en ung sac en Seine."

This queen was Marguerite de Bourgogne, wife of Louis le Hutin, who, being found guilty of adultery, was strangled in her prison in 1314, by order of the king. As for Buridan, whether he was tied into a sack or not and cast into the Seine, is still a matter of doubt, the probability being that the whole episode is nothing but an absurd tale. At any rate, he lived to be one of the most distinguished professors in the University of Paris. It is certain, however, that the three daughters-in-law of Philip the Fair led a most scandalous life, and that the Tower of Nesle in Paris was the scene of their crimes. Having been found out, they were arrested and sent to prison. One of them, as we have just said, was strangled, another committed suicide, and the third was ultimately taken back by her husband. Their accomplices, Gautier and Philip d'Aunay, were flayed alive on the Place de Grève.

The unfortunate Knights-Templar supply us with

materials for the last act of the tragedy   The principal dignitaries of the order had been lingering in prison for the space of six years, and seemed to be forgotten.   In 1313, having been summoned before a pontifical court, they were condemned to seclusion for life.   The Grand Master, and another visitor or master, then suddenly recanted all their previous confessions and avowals, says Guillaume de Nangis, to the astonishment of every one.   The cardinals who sat on the commission delivered them over to the custody of the Provost of Paris, till a more serious and thorough deliberation had taken place the next day ; but as soon as the noise of that incident had reached the ears of the king, who happened to be in his royal palace, having communicated with his friends and *without summoning the clerks*, by a prudent advice, in the evening of the same day, he had both Jacques de Molay, the Grand Master, and the other visitor, burnt to death on the same pile in a small island of the Seine, between the royal garden and the church of the Hermit friars of Saint Augustine.   (This island is now the place on the Pont-neuf where stands the statue of Henry IV.) M. Michelet, who quotes the narrative of Guillaume de Nangis, adds : " This execution, done without the knowledge of the judges, was evidently a murder." The expression is not too strong.

Philip the Fair was only forty-six when he died, November 29, 1314, leaving three sons who reigned successively.

Louis X., *le Hutin* (the quarrelsome), occupied the throne only for the space of eighteen months (1314–

1316), and his tenure of office was marked, in the first place, by an abortive expedition against Flanders, and in the second by a feudal reaction which very nearly destroyed the work of Philip the Fair. The barons were particularly anxious to ruin the *alter ego* of the late king, Enguerrand de Marigny; he was accused on the most futile charges, by Charles de Valois, brother of the late king, a violent and meddlesome prince, who put himself forward as the champion of the barons and the avenger of tottering feudalism. It would not have been difficult for Marigny to defend himself, had he been allowed to do so ; but his death was a matter determined upon beforehand, so they brought forward against him a charge from which there was no escape—that of sorcery, and he was hanged in Paris at Monfaucon. His only crime was that of having been Philip the Fair's confidential adviser. Pierre de Latilly, Chancellor of France, and Raoul de Presle, Advocate-General, were put to the torture ; Nogaret was ruined. This was the last effort of the feudal system ; it died hard, it died fighting, but its days were over.

Louis X. left only one daughter : five months after his death, his widow, Clémence of Hungary, had a son, John, who only lived eight days. Was the Princess Jeanne to succeed to the throne ? No, said the Salic law, and accordingly the States-General proclaimed as king Philip, brother of "the quarrelsome" monarch, who thus became Philip V., surnamed *le Long*. He was called to the throne in 1316, after a regency of five or six months. It is curious that whereas the right of inheriting fiefs was recognized

by feudal law for women, it was distinctly forbidden
in the case of Salic domains, and the question has
arisen whether this measure was a wise one or not.
M. Duruy remarks (" Histoire de France," vol. i. p.
382), that several royal houses, that of Austria, for
instance, owed their greatness to the opposite principle.
The Salic law, excellent as it was to insure the independence of a small state, was less necessary for
a powerful monarchy.   France was too important
to be absorbed by any power, and if we suppose a
foreign prince acquiring it by virtue of a marriage,
he would have, on the contrary, extended it, by the
addition of his own domains.   What would have
happened, for instance, if Edward III. of England
had come to the throne of France, instead of Philip
V.—Edward, essentially French by his mother, his
habits, his language, and part of his possessions, since
he was Duke of Guienne, and Count of Ponthieu?
The consequence would have been that, instead of
the mere countship of Valois, Guienne, Ponthieu,
and, for a time, England, would have become part
of the royal domains.   A few French barons might
have had to yield to English ones, but France would
have been spared the hundred years' war.   England
has never had but foreign kings—Saxons, Danes,
Normans, Angevines. Welsh, Scotch, Dutch, Germans; she is none the worse for that.

The reigns of Philip V. (1316-1322), and of Charles
IV. (1322-1328), were not remarkable for military
exploits, but for administrative measures of the
greatest importance.   Laws for the organization
of the Court of Accounts, for the improvement of

trade and commerce, &c., were enacted. Philip V. even planned a scheme for the reform of the monetary system, and the unity of weights and measures. By granting to commoners patents of nobility, Philip V., following the example of Philip the Bold, renewed the aristocratic element of the nation, ensured its duration, but, at the same time, destroyed its spirit. Under the feudal *régime*, nobility was one of the attributes of military fiefs; when it sunk, as we have already said, to the humiliating condition of a commodity which might be obtained for ready money, its original and distinctive quality completely disappeared.

At an epoch like the one of which we are treating, when the whole of society seems in a state of transformation, it is natural that a great amount of anxiety should manifest itself, and that deeds of violence should frequently occur. The Jews and the lepers fell under suspicion, and crimes were ascribed to them which, utterly groundless as they were, became a reality in the minds of ignorant and prejudiced people. It is easy to understand why the disorder of the finances, the debased character of the coinage, and the various fiscal measures introduced by Philip the Fair should have irritated the nation against the Jews. Nor is it more astonishing that the terrible mortality resulting from misery and imperfect sanitary rules should have made the unfortunate lepers suspected of contemplating the destruction of the population. A plot formed between the Jews and the lepers was seriously supposed to exist; the Jews were the instigators and the lepers their agents. The Lord of Parthenay, says a chronicler, wrote to the king that a certain tall leper, seized on his estates, had confessed having received from a rich Jew some money and some drugs. These were composed of human blood, urine, and consecrated wafers. The whole, thoroughly mixed up, dried and pounded, was placed in small bags, fastened to weights, and thrown into wells and fountains. The same chronicler reports having seen one of these bags; a leper woman who was passing by, fearing to be caught, threw behind her a bag tied with a string, which was immediately brought before a judge. Being opened, it was found to contain the head of a snake, the feet of a toad, and some woman's hair saturated with a black and stinking liquor. The whole, cast into the fire, did not burn—a sure proof that it was some deadly poison. Excited by such terrible stories, the people rose against the Jews and the lepers, and a great many of them were put to death.

Nor must we forget a fresh rising of the *Pastoureaux* (1320). As in the days of Saint Louis a number of poor people, shepherds, peasants, assembled themselves together with the intention, they asserted, of going to the Holy Land, and recovering it from the infidels. Led by an unfrocked priest and a monk they marched into Paris, committing on their way all kinds of violence. At the Châtelet the provost wanted to prevent them from entering; they threw him headlong from the top of the stairs; they went off then to the Pré-aux-clercs, where they drew themselves in battle array. Marching, finally, out of Paris.

they proceeded southwards till they came to Toulouse. There they were put to flight ; batches of twenty or thirty were sent to the gallows at a time ; the others dispersed and gave up their vain attempt.

Philip the Fair was carried off by death at the early age of forty-six ; Louis le Hutin at twenty-seven ; Philip the Long at twenty-eight ; Charles the Fair at thirty-four—all in the prime of life. Was this a visitation from heaven on the family of the remorseless king who had insulted Boniface VIII., perhaps poisoned Benedict XI., and burnt the Templars alive ? The common people thought so, and saw with a kind of satisfaction the end of a line of kings whose latest representatives had brought such scandal upon the Crown of France.

About Charles IV. himself (Charles le Bel, 1322– 1328) there is little to be said. The great object of his life was to get money, and with this aim in view he had recourse to all sorts of tricks and contrivances ; the coinage was debased, the Jews were plundered, and on the faith of his promise to organize a Crusade, he obtained from the clergy the equivalent of four years' tithes. Export duties were levied on all goods, public offices were put up for sale, and those who had received *gratuitously* their appointment to certain posts, that, for instance, of keeper of the seals, were obliged either to give them up or to pay a specified sum fixed by the king. Philip V. had issued a decree strictly forbidding the alienation of Crown lands. Charles IV. compelled the owners of such lands to restore not only the value of these lands, but the interest dating from the time of purchase. A poem, composed about that time, and called "Baudouin de Sebourc," shows what the general feeling was about money and the lust of riches. "What is money" (*argent*), says the author, "and why was it thus named?" The answer does not show a deep acquaintance with etymology, but it is an amusing proof of the irritation then existing against misers and the precursors of Shylock.

> " Un déable d'enfer le fist argent nomme ;
>   Car il *art* tout le monde, si lons qu'en set aller,
>   N'est si petit enfès, c'est légier à prouver,
>   S'on li donne un denier, qui n'en laist le plourer."

> " A clerk from hell caused it to be named money,
>   For it consumes (**L.** *ardere*) the whole world, so far as you can go ;
>   And there is not so small a child (this is easily proved)
>   Who does not leave off crying, provided you give him a penny."

Strange to say, the Paris Parliament was no respecter of persons, but sent to the gallows barons as if they were mere commoners. This was the case with Jourdain de Lille, lord of Casaubon, who, although guilty of eighteen capital crimes, had been forgiven by the king. Persisting in his career of wickedness, he was summoned to appear before the court of Parliament. He began by killing the official who delivered the message to him, and then entered Paris with an escort of nobles and lords from Aquitaine. Notwithstanding this piece of impertinence, meant to strike the government with awe, Jourdain de Lille was seized, dragged to the gallows at a horse's tail, and despatched without further ceremony ; and yet he was nephew of the Pope, and strenuous efforts had been made by the whole French nobility to obtain once more his pardon.

Charles IV. favoured the revolution which in England ended in the dethronement of Edward II., and he received the homage of young Edward III. for the provinces of Guienne and Ponthieu ; he did not live long enough, however, to profit by that revolution. He died nearly at the same time as the English monarch, leaving as regent of the kingdom Philip de Valois, grandson of Philip the Bold. The question of succession to the throne of France was a difficult one to solve. Supposing that the widow of Charles IV. should be confined of a daughter, to whom would that succession belong—to Philip de Valois, or to Edward III. of England, who was grandson of Philip the Fair by his mother Isabeau ? The English put forth their claims in favour of Edward on the ground that if, by virtue of the Salic law, Isabeau was precluded from reigning over France, no law whatever extended that prohibition to her son. The argument on the French side was this : Isabeau could not transmit a right which she did not herself possess ; and, besides, even if the principle laid down by the English were admitted, the throne would belong, not to Edward, but to the son of the Duchess of Burgundy, daughter of Philip V. The Hundred Years' War, as it is generally called, had its origin in the difficulty of solving this problem.

Philip de Valois made himself popular during his regency by certain measures designed for the public benefit, so that when the queen dowager had been confined of a daughter, he ascended the throne and was anointed king at Reims without much opposition (May 29, 1328). On the 25th of May following he arrested and sent to the gallows Remy, the treasurer of Charles IV.

Louis, Count of Flanders, was at that time engaged in putting down a rebellion which had broken out amongst the inhabitants of the western part of his domains, chiefly at Bruges and in the neighbourhood. He was present at the consecration of Philip de Valois, and begged for his assistance against the rebels. The King of France readily complied with the wishes of his vassal, and the *rendezvous* of the army was fixed at Arras on the festival of St. Magdalen. Out of rivalry against Bruges, Ghent sided with the count ; but sixteen thousand Flemings marched upon Cassel and pitched their tents on the summit of the hill where that town is situated ; they had hoisted a huge banner, on which was painted a cock with the motto :

> " Quand ce coq ici chantera,
>   *Le roi trouvé* (the *found*, *i.e.*, pretended king) ci entrera.'

They occupied an unassailable position. In order to compel them to leave it, Philip sent some forces, which laid waste the territory of Bruges. The leader of the rebels, named Zanekin (Johnny-kin, little John), not being able to restrain the ardour of his men, determined upon offering battle to the French ;. but he made use, in the first place, of a stratagem which would enable him to judge how far they were prepared, and whether the victory which the Flemings were confident of gaining would be an easy one. Disguising himself as a fishmonger, he penetrated into the French camp, and found the leaders and barons enjoying themselves as if no danger was near at hand. The Flemings took advantage of this, and rushed upon the French camp. It was three o'clock in the afternoon ; the knights were engaged in playing at dice, and the soldiers were resting around the heaps of forage, laughing and telling humorous anecdotes. The king, who had just dined and was enjoying his siesta, fortunately received from his confessor news that the camp was being attacked. He got on horseback half armed, and the knights rallied around him. The *marshals of the army* were in readiness ; they bore the first brunt, and gave time for the main body to come up. The incidents which had formerly taken place at Mons-en-Puelle were now repeated. The Flemish showed exactly the same hurry, and the French the same want of fore-thought.

" And on a day they of the garrison of Cassel departed out to the intent to have discomfited the king and all his host. And they came privily, without any noise, in three batayles well ordered ; whereof the first batayle took the way to the king's tents, and it was a fair grace that the king had not been taken, for he was at supper, and all his company, and thought nothing of them ; and the other batayle took the strait way to the tents of the King of Behaygne (Bohemia), and in manner they found him in like case ; and the third batayle went to the tents of the Earl of Hainault, and in likewise had near taken him. These hosts came so peaceably to the tents, that with much pain they of the host could awe them, whereby all the lords and their people had been slain, and the more grace of God had not been ; but in manner by miracle of God these lords discomfited all three batayles, each batayle all by itself, all in one hour. In such wise, that out of sixteen thousand Flemings there escaped never a person, captains and all were slain. And the king and lords of France knew not one of another, nor what they had done, till all was finished and atchieved ; for they, in three sundry parties, one from another ; but as for the Flemings, there was not one left alive, but all lay dead on heaps, one upon another, in the said three sundry places." [1]

The fact is, that either from prudence or pride of displaying their accoutrements, the Flemings, though all infantry, had taken into their heads to wear the heavy armour usually worn by cavalry troops. They were well protected no doubt, but could not move. The Ccunt of Flanders, on his return home, put to death ten thousand more of the rebels in three days. Philip de Valois came back to France followed by fifteen hundred hostages. " I have worked for you," said he, proudly to the Count, " I have worked at my own expense, and at that of my barons ; I restore to you your estates conquered back and in peace ; look to it that justice be kept there, and that I be not obliged to return on account of any failure on your part ; for if I am obliged to return, it will be your loss and my profit."

These words commended themselves so thoroughly to

[1] Froissart.

the attention of the Count of Flanders that he established in his dominions the reign of terror—inquests,
confiscations, tortures of every kind were the order of
the day ; the rebellious cities lost their privileges and
were dismantled. The military exploits of Philip VI.
seemed, even in the eyes of the English, to confirm his
pretensions as the lawful King of France. Edward
III. came over to Paris, did homage for the Duchy of
Guienne, and returned home marvelling at the high
state of the Court of France. Surrounded by an
array of kings, princes, and barons, Philip gave a series
of splendid entertainments, which, if they ruined the
country, secured for the monarch the reputation of
being the greatest sovereign in Christendom.

Wars and tournaments, festivities and deeds of high
emprise, treaties and marriages ;—what writer would be
found to celebrate worthily the *fasti* of the decaying
Middle Ages? Villehardouin and Joinville had sung
of the Crusades, the chronicles of Saint Denis originated, as some suppose, by Suger, were a kind of
official record of events ; but it needed some poetical
imagination to delineate the life and civilization of the
fourteenth century. Froissart presented himself, and
has won immortality, thanks to one of the most remarkable chronicles on record. Gifted with a real
passion for observing, knowing and relating all that
was worth attention, we fancy we can see him travelling from spot to spot, making friends everywhere by
his agreeable manners, his lively temperament, his
talent as a poet, and availing himself of the *otium
cum dignitate* which he enjoyed for the purpose of
taking notes of all the deeds of valour and chivalry

which were performed throughout the battlefields of
Europe. His own declaration to that effect is quite
characteristic :

"Now consider you who have read my book, or
who read it now, or purpose reading it, or who will
hear it read, consider, I say, how I can have known or
collected so many facts of which I treat, and which I
propose in so many parts ; and, to inform you of the
truth, I began early, at the age of twenty ; I likewise
came into the world with high deeds and adventures ;
in these, also, I took more delight than in any other
things. . . . I travelled throughout the greater part of
Christendom, and wherever I went I enquired of
ancient knights and squires who had taken part in
deeds of arms, and knew how to speak properly of
them, and also of certain trustworthy heralds, with
the view of verifying and justifying all these matters.
Thus it is that I have collected this high and noble
history . . . and, by the grace of God, I shall continue
it as long as I live ; for the more I am in it, and the
more I work at it, the more it pleases me ; for just as
the gentle knight or squire who loves arms becomes
perfect by persevering and continuing in the same, so
I become apt and I enjoy the more I work and toil
on this matter."

The reader must not seek in the pages of Froissart
for that spirit of patriotism which imparts to history
its highest value, and makes it so instructive. Although
using the French tongue as the medium through which
to address the public, Froissart cannot be called a
French chronicler ; nay, it is almost a subject of astonishment that he did not show greater partiality for

the English. The fact is, he was the historian of chivalry, not of one single nation, and provided he could record the catastrophes of tournaments, battles, or other such daring exploits, his motto was:

"Tros Rutulusve fuat, nullo discrimine habebo."

It may further be remarked, in connection with Frois-

FROISSART.

sart, that if all the splendours of feudal society revive in his pages, yet they are the splendours of an order of things on the verge of decay. Villehardouin and Joinville described the power of chivalry; Froissart gives us its mere brilliancy, its romance, if we may say so.

We shall have many an extract to quote from him whom M. Michelet designates as the Walter Scott of the Middle Ages. By way of conclusion to the present chapter we cannot do better than transcribe a paragraph from his English translator, Sir John Bourchier, Lord Berners :

"The most profitable thing in the world for the institution of the human life is history. The continual reading thereof maketh young men equal in prudence to old men, and to old fathers stricken in age it ministereth experience of things. More, it yieldeth private persons worthy of dignity, rule, and governance ; it compelleth the emperors, high rulers, and governors to do noble deeds, to the end they may obtain immortal glory ; it exciteth, moveth, and stirreth the strong hardy warriors for the great laud they have after they be dead, promptly to go in hand with great and hard perils, in defence of their country; and it prohibiteth reprovable persons to do mischievous deeds, for fear of infamy and shame."

If such be the uses of history, what a fund of moral instruction can be obtained from the events of that tragic period which, beginning with the reign of Philip VI. and ending with that of Charles VII., brought France and England as bitter enemies on the battle-field, and known by the name of *the Hundred Years' War !*

IX.

PHILIP VI. (CONCLUDED) — THE HUNDRED YEARS' WAR.
(1328–1350.)

THE Hundred Years' War began, it may be said, in Flanders. Philip VI., who was constantly endeavouring to bring Edward III. into trouble, and to check the power of England, had for a long time systematically stirred up the Scotch against the English, and, so far as it was possible for him, helped them in their attempt to assert their independence. After a protracted contest, Edward was successful, and having defeated the Scotch, he immediately set to work to find an opportunity of attacking France. That opportunity soon presented itself.

Robert, prince of the royal blood by his marriage with one of the daughters of Charles IV., claimed the countship of Artois, which was retained by his aunt, and after her decease, by her daughters. In order to justify his pretensions, he forged certain documents, and bribed false witnesses to give evidence in his favour. The lawsuit resulting from this affair showed that Robert had in all probability poisoned his aunt and one of his cousins. Condemned by the court of

peers to lose his domains and to banishment for
life (1332), Robert sought refuge in Brabant, and
with the view of avenging himself, he practised certain incantations which were to end in the death of
John, the son of the King of France. This new
misdeed was discovered, and would have resulted in
a fresh trial on the ground of sorcery. Now in those
days a person convicted of that supposed crime was
invariably put to death. Thoroughly frightened,
Robert disguised himself, went over to England,
presented himself at the court of Edward III., and
urged him to go to war against France.

The Count of Flanders, Louis de Nevers, vassal,
as such, of Philip VI., had about this time managed,
unfortunately, to excite the animosity of his subjects
by extorting money out of them, depriving them
of their privileges, and punishing severely all those
who offered any resistance. Commercial interests
bound England and Flanders closely together, so
that the policy of both countries was identical. Led
by a popular chief, the Brewer Arteveldt, the Flemings
drove away the Count Louis, and invoked the help
of. Edward III. (1336). They would have felt some
scruple in revolting against their suzerain, the King of
France ; accordingly Arteveldt persuaded Edward to
assume the title which he had often himself claimed
as his own ; and thus in attacking Philip VI., they
might say they were taking up arms against a pre-
tender and usurper.

The war in Flanders was fruitless ; if the French
were ignominiously defeated in a naval engagement
at the Sluys, they proved more fortunate at Saint

Omer, and Edward met with a check before Tournay
(1340). A truce was concluded, and when hostilities
recommenced, it was Brittany and no longer Flanders
which supplied the pretext. As for Arteveldt, he came
to a tragic end. Seeing himself on the point of being
discomfited, he attempted to give the sovereignty of
Flanders to the young Prince of Wales, thus de-
frauding the Count of Flanders of his rights; but
his scheme failed, and he was massacred at Ghent by
the populace in 1345.

The succession to the Duchy of Brittany must now
be described, as it led to a renewal of hostilities between
France and England. The Duke, John III., had died
childless, leaving a niece and a brother. The niece,
daughter of an elder brother, had married Charles of
Blois, a prince of the royal family of France; she
claimed the Duchy as her lawful inheritance, and had
on her side Philip VI., and the *French* portion of the
province. The competitor, John IV. de Montfort,
brother of the late duke, was supported by the
Breton Bretonnants and the King of England. M.
Michelet has given us in his history of France a
curious portrait of Charles of Blois, the *nominee* of
Philip; it is worth quoting here :

" He went to confession morning and evening, and
heard four or five masses daily. He never travelled
except accompanied by a chaplain, who carried about
with him some bread, wine, and water, in order to
celebrate mass on the way. If he saw a priest pass by,
he jumped from his horse into the mud. He several
times went barefooted in the snow on a pilgrimage to
the shrine of Saint Yves, the great saint of Brittany. He

used to put pebbles in his shoes, would not allow the
vermin to be removed from his hair-cloth, fastened
round his waist three ropes with knots which entered
into his flesh so that it was piteous to behold. When
he said his prayers, he struck his breast so furiously
that he became pale and then *as green*. One day he
stopped within two yards of the enemy and ran a
great danger, because he wanted to hear mass. At the
siege of Quimper, his soldiers were on the point of
being overtaken by the tide 'If it is the will of God,'
said he, 'the tide can do us no harm.' The town was
taken by storm, and a good number of the inhabitants put to the sword. Charles de Blois went first to
the cathedral to thank God. He then stopped the
massacre."

The city of Nantes had been besieged by the
French ; the Count de Montfort, made prisoner, was
taken to Paris, and shut up in the tower of the
Louvre. His wife then gave proof of an energy and
determination which cannot be praised too much, and
Froissart seems to take delight in relating her deeds
of courage and of daring. The episodes of the siege
of Rennes and of Hennebon may be appropriately
quoted as instances both of Jeanne de Montfort's
intrepidity and of the chronicler's picturesque talent.

" When the sweet season of summer approached,
the lords of France, and divers others, drew towards
Bretayne with a great host, to aid Sir Charles de
Blois to recover the residue of the Duchy of Bretayne.
They found Sir Charles de Blois in Nantes ; then
they determined to lay siege to Rennes ; the Countess
of Mountfort had well prevented the matter, and had

set there for captain Sir William of Cadudall Breton. The lords of France came thither, and did much trouble with assaults; howbeit they within defended themselves so valiantly, that their enemies lost more than they won. . . . When the city of Rennes was given up, the burgesses made their homage and fealty to the lord, Charles of Blois; then he was counselled to go and lay siege to Hennebon. . . . When the countess and her company understood that the Frenchmen were coming to lay siege to the town of Hennebon, then it was commanded to sound the watch-bell alarm, and every man to be armed and draw to their defence. . . . The countess herself wore harness on her body, and rode on a good courser from street to street, desiring her people to make good defence; and she caused damosels and other women to cut short their kyrtels, and to carry stones and pots full of chalk to the walls to be cast down to their enemies.

"This lady did then a hardy enterprise; she mounted up to the height of a tower, to see how the Frenchmen were ordered without; she saw that all the lords, and all other people of the host, were all gone out of their field to the assault; then she took again her courser, armed as she was, and caused 300 men on horseback to be ready, and she went with them to another gate where there was no assault; she issued out and her company, and dashed into the French lodgings, and cut down tents, and set fire to their lodgings; she found no defence there, but a certain of varlets and boys, who ran away. When the lords of France looked behind them, and saw their lodgings a-fire, and heard the cry and noise there, they returned to the field crying, 'Treason! treason!' so that all the assault was left. When the countess saw that, she drew together her company, and when she saw she could not enter again into the town without great damage, she took another way, and went to the castle of Brest, which was not far thence. . . . They of the town (of Hennebon) wist not where the countess was become, whereof they were in great trouble, for it was five days or they heard any tidings. The countess did so much at Brest, that she got together a five hundred spears, and then about midnight she separated from Brest, and by the sun rising, she came along by the one side of the host, and came to one of the gates of Hennebon, the which was opened for her, and therein she entered, and all her company, with great noise of trumpets. . . ." [1] At last a succour from the English caused the siege to be raised.

The Kings of France and of England were gradually led to take an active personal share in the war; Edward III. came to Brittany in 1342, and was present at the sieges of Vannes, Rennes, and Nantes. In the meanwhile John of Normandy gathered together an army of upwards of forty thousand men, besides a large number of knights and barons. The forces met at Malestroit, but the deficiency of provisions and the inclemency of the weather had caused such an amount of sickness on both sides, that the Papal legates obtained (January 19, 1343) a truce which was to last till Michaelmas, 1346.

[1] Book i. caps. 79, 80.

The treachery of which the French king was guilty towards Clisson and fourteen other Breton lords contributed much to strengthen Edward's cause in France. Clisson had been a prisoner in England and had been handsomely treated—too handsomely, perhaps. It is said that the Earl of Salisbury, in order to avenge himself on Edward for seducing his wife, informed Philip of a secret agreement concluded between his master and Clisson. The King of France immediately invited the fifteen Bretons to a tournament, had them arrested and put to death without a trial. The brother of one of them, who happened to be a priest, was exposed on a scaffold and stoned to death by the mob. A short time after the King of France despatched in the same summary way three barons of Normandy ; he tried in vain to seize upon the Count d'Harcourt who contrived, however, to escape, and proved as useful to the English as Robert d'Artois had been.

Edward resolved upon avenging the death of Clisson, and the war recommenced more determinately than before. The Earl of Derby landed in Guienne, took possession of La Réole and Port Sainte Marie, and advanced as far as Angoulême. The King of England had collected a powerful fleet and wished to penetrate into Southern France, but a storm drove him back to the British Channel, and acting on the advice of the Count d'Harcourt, he disembarked with an army of upwards of thirty thousand men at La Hougue Saint Vast on July 22, 1346, and after having made himself master of a few small towns, he arrived under the walls of Caën on the 26th of the same month.

"When they of the town who were ready in the field saw these three batayles coming in good order, with their banners and standards waving in the wind, and the archers, the which they had not been accustomed to see, they were sore afraid, and fled away toward the town without any order or good array, for all that the constable could do ; then the Englishmen pursued them eagerly. When the constable and the Earl Tankerville saw that, they took a gate at the entry and saved themselves and certain with them, for the Englishmen were entered into the town ; some of the knights and squires of France, such as knew the way to the castle went thither, and the captain there received them all, for the castle was large. The Englishmen in the chase slew many, for they took none to mercy." [1]

At last the citizens took courage, defended themselves in their houses, and upwards of five hundred Englishmen had been killed or wounded, when Edward ordered the massacre to cease, promising quarter to every one. Louviers, Pont de l'Arche, Poissy, Vernon, and Saint Germain fell into the power of the English who came within sight of Paris having burnt Bourg la Reine and Saint Cloud.

In the meanwhile Philip had got together a large army, and was marching against the enemy. Edward re-crossed the Seine at Poissy, and retreated towards the district of Ponthieu, wishing to put himself in safety behind the Somme. All the fords of this river were in the hands of the French, and the one at. Blanquetaque, more especially, was defended by one

[1] Froissart, chapter 124.

thousand men-at-arms and five thousand Genoese archers. Edward forced his way through it, but seeing that he could not retreat any further, he halted, prepared for a battle and drew up his forces on the slope of a hillock near Cressy (August 27, 1346).

"The Englishmen, who were in three batayles, lying on the ground to rest them, as soon as they saw the Frenchmen approach, they rose upon their feet, fair and easily, without any haste, and arranged their batayles. . . The lords and knights of France came not to the assembly together, in good order, for some came before, and some came after, in such haste and evil order, that one of them did trouble another. When the French king saw the Englishmen, his blood changed, and he said to his marshals : 'Make the Genoese go before, and begin the battle in the name of God and Saint Denis.' There were of the Genoese cross-bows about a fifteen thousand, but they were so weary of going a-foot that day, a six leagues, armed with their cross-bows, that they said to their constables : 'We be not well ordered to fight this day, for we be not in the case to do any great deed of arms; we have more need of rest.' Their words came to the Earl of Alençon, who said : 'A man is well at ease to be charged with such a sort of rascals, to be faint and fail now at most need.' Also the same season there fell a great rain and an eclipse, with a terrible thunder, and before the rain there came flying over both batayles a great number of crows, for fear of the tempest coming. Then anon the air began to wax clear, and the sun to shine fair and bright, the which was right in the Frenchmen's eyes, and on the Englishmen's backs. . . . The English archers stepped forward one pace, and let fly their arrows so wholly and so thick, that it seemed snow ; when the Genoese felt the arrows piercing through heads, arms, and breasts, many of them cast down their cross-bows, and did cut their strings, and returned discomfited. When the French king saw them fly away, he said : ' Slay these rascals, for they shall let and trouble us without reason.'   Then ye should have seen the men-at-arms dash in among them, and killed a great number of them ; and ever still the Englishmen shot where as they saw thicker press.   The sharp arrows ran into the men-at-arms, and into their horses, and many fell, horse and men, amongst the Genoese, and when they were down, they could not rise again ; the press was so thick that one overthrew another " (book i. chap. 130).

The Genoese fought with considerable determination ; but besides the fact that they were tired out by a long march, the heavy rain had utterly spoilt the strings of their cross-bows, and unfitted them for service.   The English archers, more prudent, had unfastened theirs, and concealed them in their head-dresses (*chaperons*).   The order given by King Philip to slay the Genoese mercenaries created, as may well be imagined, the greatest confusion, and the English took advantage of this first incident in the day's adventures.   One of the most exciting episodes connected with the battle of Cressy is the one of which the old King of Bohemia was the hero: we give it here as we find it in Froissart :

" The valiant King of Bohemia, called John of

Luxemburgh, son to the noble emperor Henry of
Luxemburgh, for all that he was nigh blind, when he
understood the order of the batayle, he said to them
about him : 'Where is the Lord Charles, my son ?'
His men said : 'Sir, we cannot tell, we think he be
fighting ;' then he said : 'Sirs, ye are my men, my
companions and friends in this journey (*journée*) ;
I require you bring me so far forward, that I may
strike one stroke with my sword.' They said they
would do his commandment, and to the intent that
they should not lose him in the press, they tied all
the reins of their bridles each to other, and set the
king before to accomplish his desire, and so they went
on their enemies. The Lord Charles of Bohemia, his
son, who wrote himself King of Bohemia, and bore
the arms, he came in good order to the batayle ; but
when he saw that the matter went awry on their
party, he departed, I cannot tell you which way. The
king, his father, was so far forward, that he strake a
stroke with his sword, yea, and more than four, and
fought valiantly, and so did his company ; and they
adventured themselves so forward that they were
there all slain, and the next day they were found in
the place about the king, and all their horses tied each
to other " (*ibid.*).

Philip VI. was hurried off the field of battle after
having experienced a defeat such as had never been
heard of before. Eleven princes, eighty knights-
bannerets, twelve hundred knights, and thirty thousand
soldiers were killed. Accompanied by five gentlemen,
the King of France arrived during the night before
the castle of Broye, and knocking at the gates, ex-

claimed : " Open ! open ! It is the unfortunate King of
France!" The next day the *communes* of Rouen and of
Beauvais, the retainers of the Archbishop of Rouen, and
the troops of the Grand Prior of France, knowing what
had happened, came to take part in the battle ; they
had lost their way. The English fell upon them and
put them to the sword.

Edward had resolved to carry on to a successful
issue the work so triumphantly begun ; he led his
army to Calais and besieged the town (September 3,
1346). The only way to take it was by famine, for the
walls were strong beyond the possibility of making a
breach in them. With the prospect of spending several
months, perhaps the whole winter under the fortifications of Calais, the English set to work to build a
regular town where they settled themselves most
comfortably, thoroughly provided with, not only the
necessaries, but the luxuries of life. " There was," says
Froissart, " every thing to sell, and a market place to
be kept every Tuesday and Saturday for flesh and fish,
mercery ware, houses for cloth, for bread, wine, and all
other things necessary, such as came out of England
or out of Flanders, and they might buy what they
list " (cap. 133).

Philip VI. of course resolved to do what he could
for the relief of Calais, and he set to work to collect
an army. Unfortunately, from different causes, the
mustering of the troops took a very long time, and it
was only in July, 1347, that they were ready ; then all
the approaches to the town were either impracticable
from the state of the ground, or occupied by the
English ; so that the French army had to disperse

after having vainly displayed their banners and standards before the unfortunate citizens who, reduced to the last extremity, saw themselves obliged to surrender at discretion. Edward required that six of the leading citizens should come to his camp in their shirts, with halters round their necks, bringing him the keys of the castle and of the town, and imploring his mercy. Eustache de Saint Pierre, and five friends and relatives of his volunteered to plead on behalf of their fellow citizens, and went off to the camp under the conduct of Walter de Manny.

"When Sir Walter presented these burgesses to the king, they knelt down and held up their hands and said: 'Gentle king, behold here we six, who were burgesses of Calais, and great merchants: we have brought to you the keys of the town and of the castle, and we submit ourselves clearly into your will and pleasure, to save the residue of the people of Calais, who have suffered great pain. Sir, we beseech your grace to have mercy and pity on us, through your high nobleness.' Then all the earls and barons, and other that were there, wept for pity. The king looked felly on them, for greatly he hated the people of Calais for the great damages and displeasures they had done him on the sea before. Then he commanded their heads to be stricken off; then every man required the king for mercy, but he would hear no more in that behalf. Then Sir Walter de Manny said: 'Noble king, for God's sake refrain your courage; you have the name of sovereign nobleness, therefore now do not a thing that should blemish your renown, nor to give cause to some to speak of

you villanously. Every man will say it is a great
cruelty to put to death such honest persons, who
by their own will put themselves into your grace to
save their company.' Then the king uryed (*turned*)
away from him, and commanded to send for the
hangman; and said: 'They of Calais have caused
many of my men to be slain, therefore these shall die
in like wise.' Then the queen, being great with
child, knelt down, and sore weeping, said: 'Gentle
sir, since I passed the sea in great peril, I have desired
nothing of you; therefore now I humbly require you,
in the honour of the Son of the Virgin Mary, and for
the love of me, that ye will take mercy of these six
burgesses.' The king beheld the queen, and stood
still in a study a space, and then said: 'Dame, I
would you had been as now in some other place; you
make such request to me that I cannot deny you;
therefore I give them to you, to do your pleasure
with them.' Then the queen caused them to be
brought into her chamber, and made the halters to be
taken from their necks, and caused them to be new
clothed, and gave them their dinner at their leisure;
and then she gave each of them six nobles, and made
them to be brought out of the host in safe-guard, and
set at their liberty" (cap. 146).

The Calaisians were turned out of their city except
a few who renounced their nationality, and preferred
acknowledging Edward as their king; Calais became
an English colony. Edward seemed to be triumphant
everywhere; the Scotch had been defeated, and
Charles de Blois, the ally of the King of France, had
been made prisoner at the siege of La Roche de

Rien. In the meanwhile the two adversaries were equally weary of the war ; Pope Clement VI. offered his mediation, and on the 28th of September, 1347, a truce was signed which was to last ten months, each of the two kings retaining possession of what he actually got.

The plague soon came to add its horrors to those entailed by war. The *black death*, as it was called, after having visited the greater part of Europe, invaded France. In a great many places, the chronicler tells us, out of twenty persons, as many as eighteen were carried off. The mortality was such in the Paris hospital (*Hôtel-Dieu*) that for a long time they transported daily five hundred corpses in carts to the cemetery of the Innocents. Again on this occasion the Jews were accused of poisoning the public fountains, they were in many places attacked, murdered, or burnt alive. One-third of the whole population of Europe died of the plague, and in Paris alone eighty thousand persons were fatally struck.

These dreadful calamities, according to all appearances endless, had the natural effect of rousing the people to a state of religious enthusiasm bordering upon frenzy. Hence the *Flagellants*, who endeavoured to appease the wrath of heaven by the most terrible. acts of self-inflicted mortifications. They bore red crosses aloft ; half naked, they scourged themselves with whips in which were fastened iron nails, and went about singing hymns, of which the following is a specimen—

"Or avant, entre nous tous frères,
Battons nos charognes bien fort

En remembrant la grant misère
De Dieu, et sa piteuse mort,
Qui fut pris en la gent amère
Et vendus et trais à tort
Et bastu sa char (*chair*) vierge et dère (*dear*)
Au nom de ce battons plus fort."

The Flagellants started from Germany, went to the Netherlands, and entered France by Picardy and Flanders. They numbered nearly eight hundred thousand persons at Christmas (1349). They originally recruited their numbers from the peasants and the common people ; later on they were joined by gentlemen, noblemen, and even ladies. When the danger was over, or thought to be so, the sense of gloom and despair gave way to a frantic desire of enjoying life, and a thirst for merriment of every description. Nothing was seen but festivals, marriages, and christenings. The royal family set the example of such dissipation, and the old king married his son's betrothed, Princess Blanche, his cousin, only eighteen years of age. The young prince took to wife, instead, the heiress of Auvergne and Burgundy, whilst the grandson married the daughter of the Duke de Bourbon. Philip de Valois died soon after (1350).

If we now turn our attention to the home administration of Philip VI., we find several points which deserve to be mentioned here. In the first place, let us notice the establishment of the salt tax (*gabelle*, from the German *gabe*). By virtue of a decree dated March 20, 1343, the king created for the benefit of the Crown a monopoly of the sale of salt throughout the kingdom. Commissioners were appointed whose business it was to establish stores where every family was obliged to supply itself with salt ; a tax was fixed at the discretion of the government, and no one was allowed to sell the quantity left unused after the wants of the family had been fairly and honestly met. The salt tax levied temporarily at first, and suppressed for a time in 1356, was definitely reinstated by Charles V., and only done away with in 1790. The utter incapacity of Philip de Valois was apparent from the reckless deeds to which his foolish prodigality compelled him to have recourse. He kept altering the coinage, creating fresh taxes, and he even confiscated the property of the Italian merchants settled in France.

Important territorial acquisitions must likewise be noticed. Humbert II., Count of Vienne, and known by the title of *Dauphin* of Viennois, because the family bore a *dolphin* on their coat of arms, sold his domains to Philip for 120,000 florins (1349). One of the conditions of the transaction was that the eldest son of the King of France should ever henceforth be styled *Dauphin*. The town of Montpellier was likewise purchased from the King of Majorca.

X.

JOHN II. — THE HUNDRED YEARS' WAR (CONTINUED)—ETIENNE MARCEL.—THE JACQUERIE. (1350-1364.)

THE reign of King John (*Jean le Bon*) is one of the most tragic and eventful in the whole history of Mediæval France. He was in point of character very much like his father—brave but violent, lavish in his expenditure, impetuous, and reckless. "*Le Bon*," says M. Michelet, " means here. the *trusting*, the *prodigal*, the *careless*. No prince, indeed, had ever before him so nobly flung away the money of the people. He went along, like the man in Rabelais, eating his grapes when they were still unripe, and his corn when it was growing. He made money of everything—wasting the present, drawing upon the future. One might have fancied that he did not suppose he would live long in France. His great resource was the alteration of the coinage ; Philip the Fair and his son, Philip de Valois, had had free recourse to this form of bankruptcy. John cast them all in the shade, and he went beyond every bankruptcy, either royal or national, that could ever take place." In the course of one year no less than eighteen variations took place in

the value of the coinage ; in fact, the silver mark in a
few months varied from five livres five sols to eleven
livres, that is to say, at the rate of cent. for cent.

Notwithstanding all these arbitrary measures, the
public exchequer was empty, and, with the view of
procuring money, John decided upon appealing to
the nation. The States-General were summoned to
meet at Paris in 1365, but they produced no result ;
for, although in answer to the numerous complaints
made by the deputies, some promises were wrung
from the king, yet we do not find that they came to
any effect.

In the meanwhile, a third competitor to the throne
of France appeared in the person of Charles of
Navarre, surnamed *le Mauvais*, from his turbulence
and his spirit of intrigue. Grandson of Louis X. on
his mother's side, Charles *le Mauvais* might have
inherited the throne but for the Salic law. Till he
could see his hopes realized, he claimed Champagne
and Angoumois. · This last province having been bestowed upon the king's favourite, the Constable de
Lacerda, Charles had him murdered ; thereupon
John seized the fiefs which the King of Navarre had
in Normandy, and Charles went over to England
dreading lest something worse should happen to him.

The truce between France and England had
expired, and Edward was only too anxious to begin
again a war which had procured to him such advantages of every kind. He landed at Calais in August,
1355, and ravaged the province of Artois, whilst his
son, "The Black Prince," entered France by Bordeaux, and fared so successfully that he brought from

Languedoc a thousand waggon loads of booty. The inactivity of the French king during the raids of the English, and the inefficient manner in which he opposed their progress were scandalous, but no available funds existed to carry on the government, and a fresh appeal to the States-General was absolutely necessary. They met on December 2, 1355.

Peter de la Forest, Chancellor of Paris and Archbishop of Rouen, opened the sitting in the name of the king, and requested the deputies to see together what subsidy they could grant to the Crown, sufficient towards defraying the expenses of the war ; and, forasmuch as he had been given to understand that his subjects were very much aggrieved by the alteration of the coinage, he promised to establish a strong and durable coinage, if they would only allow him money enough to carry on the war. The deputies selected by the States to return an answer to the king were John de Craon, Archbishop of Reims ; Walter VI., Count de Brienne and Duke of Athens ; and Etienne Marcel, provost of the merchants of Paris, —speaking respectively in the name of the clergy, the nobility, and the commons. These three men informed King John that the States would grant him an army of thirty thousand men every year, of which they would bear the expense ; and, in order to procure the necessary money, it was decided, further, that a tax of eight *deniers* per *livre* should be paid by all Frenchmen without distinction of rank or profession, besides the salt tax (*gabelle*) which was to be levied throughout the kingdom. The yield of these contributions was estimated at 5,000,000 *livres*.

In return for these grants, the States-General, actuated by what seemed then an act of extreme boldness, obtained a pledge that the coinage should be restored to its nominal value, that the right of confiscation and seizure till then exercised by the king wherever he sojourned, should be abolished, and that *they* alone (the States-General) should have the right to collect and pay the war-tax by the means of agents appointed by themselves. " These measures," M. Duruy observes (" Histoire de France "), " amounted to a revolution, for the collecting of the taxes and the care of controlling the expenses are an essential part of the rights of sovereignty."

The notion of paying taxes was as hateful to the nobles as it was new and unheard of, and the two most conspicuous heads of the opposing party were the King of Navarre and his friend Count d'Harcourt. The king, hearing of this, exclaimed, " I am, and mean to be, the sole master in France," and caused the two malcontents to be arrested at Rouen, at a festival given to them and to a number of lords by the Dauphin Charles. The King of Navarre was thrown into prison, and the Count d'Harcourt was beheaded.

In the meanwhile, the Prince of Wales had taken the field at the head of two thousand men-at-arms, and six thousand archers ; he had crossed the Garonne and Dordogne, and laid waste the provinces of Auvergne, Rouergue, Limousin, and Berry. The King of France met him near Poitiers ; he had under his orders one of the most brilliant armies that France had ever raised. There were, besides his four sons, twenty-six dukes and counts, one hundred and forty knights-bannerets, and about fifty thousand soldiers, of which a large number were horsemen clothed in steel armour. John had arrived on the battlefield before the Prince of Wales, and had thus cut him off from the road to Bordeaux and from communications with the South of France. If he had only waited patiently, the English would have been starved, but John thought it most knightly to force a passage through the enemy.

There was only a narrow path by which to arrive at the army of the Prince of Wales ; the king sent there a detachment of mounted soldiers. "Then," says Froissart, "the battle began on all parts . . . and they set forth that were appointed to break the array of the archers ; they entered a-horseback into the way, where the great hedges were on both sides, set full of archers. As soon as the men-at-arms entered, the archers began to shoot on both sides, and did slay and hurt horses and knights, so that the horses when they felt the sharp arrows, they would in no wise go forward, but drew aback, and flung and took on so fiercely that many of them fell on their masters, so that for press they could not rise again, insomuch that the marshal's batayle could never come at the prince. Certain knights and squires that were well-horsed passed through the archers, and thought to approach to the prince, but they could not " (cap. 162).

The English then descended the hill. "The Lord Chandos said to the prince, 'Sir, take your horse and ride forth ; this journey is yours. God is this day in your hands ; get in to the French king's batayle, for there lieth all the sore of the matter. I think, verily, by his valiantness, he will not fly ; I know we shall have him by the grace of God and Saint George, so he be well fought withal ; and, sir, I heard you say that this day I should see you a good knight.' The Prince said, ' Let us go forth; ye shall not see me this day return back ;' and said, 'Advance, banner, in the name of God and of Saint George " (*ibid.*)

"When the Duke of Normandy's batayle saw the prince approach, they thought to save themselves, and so the duke and the king's children, the Earl of Poitiers and the Earl of Touraine, who were right young, believed their governors, and so departed from the field, and with them more than eight hundred spears that stroke no stroke that day " (*ibid.*)

This sudden and unlooked-for defection was terrible for the French. King John had committed gross blunders, first, by attacking the English prematurely ; and, next, by employing cavalry in a position where horses could not stand the shots of the archers ; but he did prodigies of valour, and Froissart bears witness to his personal courage. " On the French part," he says, " King John was on that day a full right good knight ; if the fourth part of his men had done their devoirs as well as he did, the journey had been. his by all likelihood ; " and, further on, " King John with his own hands did that day marvels in arms ; he had an axe in his hands, wherewith he defended himself, and fought in the breaking of the press." By his side was his son who won the surname of *the bold* (*le hardi*), and who kept saying, 'Father ! ware right ! Father ! ware left !'"

The rout was complete, and lasted till the gates of
Poitiers. "There were many slain and many beaten
down, horse and man; for they of Poitiers closed
their gates and would suffer none to enter; wherefore, in the street before the gate, there was horrible
murder, more hurt and beaten down; the Frenchmen
yielded themselves as far as they might know an
Englishman; there were divers English archers who
had four, five, or six prisoners. . . . Then there was
a great press to take the king, and such as knew him
cried, 'Sir, yield you, or else ye are but dead!' There
was a knight of Saint Omer, retained with wages with
the King of England, called Sir Denis of Morbecke,
who had served the Englishmen five years before,
because in his youth he had forfeited the realm of
France for a murder that he did at Saint Omer. It
happened so well for him that he was next to the
king, when they were about to take him; he stepped
forth into the press, and, by strength of his body and
arms, he came to the French king and said, in good
French, 'Sir, yield you!' The king beheld the knight,
and said, 'To whom shall I yield me? Where is my
cousin the Prince of Wales? If I might see him I
would speak with him.' Denis answered and said:
'Sir, he is not here; but yield you to me, and I shall
bring you to him.' 'Who be you?' quoth the king.
'Sir,' quoth he, 'I am Denis of Morbecke, a knight of
Artois; but I serve the King of England, because I
am banished the realm of France, and I have forfeited all that I had there.' Then the king gave him
his right gauntlet, saying, 'I yield me to you.' There
was a great press about him, so that the king could

FRONT ENTRANCE OF NOTRE DAME, AT POITIERS.

not go forwards with his young son, the Lord Philip, with him because of the press " (cap. 164).

Eleven thousand Frenchmen were left dead on the field of battle ; the English had only lost two thousand five hundred. They had three times as many prisoners as there were soldiers to keep them. Thirteen counts, one archbishop, seventy barons, and two thousand men-at-arms, besides a large number of common soldiers had surrendered, and the question now was how to dispose of them. They were dismissed on giving their word that they would come to Bordeaux at Christmas-tide, and pay the stipulated price for their ransom or remain captives. King John was treated more courteously by the Prince of Wales, who felt the importance of the prize which fortune had thus unexpectedly placed within his hands.

" The same day of the battle, at night, the prince made a supper in his lodging to the French king, and to the most part of the great lords that were prisoners ; . . . and always the prince served before the king as humbly as he could, and would not sit at the king's board, for any desire that the king could make ; but he said he was not sufficient to sit at the table with so great a prince as the king was ; but then he said to the king : "Sir, for God's sake, make no evil nor heavy cheer, though God this day did not consent to follow your will ; for, sir, surely the king, my father, shall bear you as much honour and friendship as he may do, and shall accord with you so reasonably, that you shall ever be friends together after '" (cap. 108).

The King of France was treated with the same courtesy during the whole of the journey from

Poitiers to London. "When the King of England
knew of their coming, he commanded them of London to prepare themselves and their city to receive
such a man as the French king was; then they of
London arrayed themselves by companies, and the
chief masters' clothing different from the others. At
St. Thomas of Canterbury the French king and the
prince made their offerings, and there tarried a day;
and then rode to Rochester, and there tarried that
day, and the next day to Dartford, and the fourth
day to London, where they were honourably received,
and so they were in every good town as they passed.
The French king rode through London on a white
courser, well apparelled, and the prince on a little
black hobby by him; thus he was conveyed along
the city till he came to the Savoy, the which house
pertained to the heritage of the Duke of Lancaster.
There the French king kept his house a long season.
. . . And after, by the commandment of Pope Innocent VI., there came into England the Lord Talley-
rand, Cardinal of Perigord, and the Lord Nicholas,
Cardinal d'Urgel; they treated of a peace between
the two kings, but they could bring nothing to effect;
but at last by good means they procured a truce.
between the two kings and all their assisters, to
endure till the feast of St. John the Baptist, in the
year of our Lord God 1359; and out of that truce
was excepted the Lord Philip of Navarre and his
allies the Countess of Montfort, and the Duchy of
Brittany. Anon after, the French king was removed
from the Savoy to the Castle of Windsor, and all his
household; and went a-hunting and a-hawking there-

about at his pleasure, and the Lord Philip, his son with him ; and all the other prisoners abode still in London, and went to see the king at their pleasure, and were received all only on their faiths " (cap. 173).

The behaviour of the nobles was beginning to excite great dissatisfaction amongst the common people, who accused them both of cowardice and of spending on themselves the money raised for the carrying on of the war. The princes of the royal family shared this want of confidence ; the Dauphin Charles had fled from the battle-field by his father's order, well and good. But why did he take away with him 800 lances ? Why did the Duke d'Orléans move off with his entire " batayle " before they had had the chance of fighting the enemy ?

It was in the midst of all this excitement that the Dauphin Charles, young and sickly, arrived in Paris on the 29th of September, took the reins of power as lieutenant for the king, and called a meeting of the States-General for Monday, October 17th.

Two very popular men—Etienne Marcel, Provost of the merchants, and Robert Lecoq, Bishop of Laon —took the lead in the opposition made by the people to the government of the Dauphin. They were both scandalized by the dilapidations which were going on around them, and the prelate, an ambitious man, who had expected to be appointed Chancellor of France, hated the royal family for not taking notice of his supposed claims, and made no secret of his sympathy for Charles de Navarre. Marcel carried out, with the Dauphin's consent, a plan for the better fortification of Paris, and managed to infuse into the States-General the spirit of patriotism by which he himself was animated. They aimed at nothing else but the direction of the government ; and when they pledged themselves to furnish the money necessary for the prosecution of the war, they, in their turn, imposed conditions which thoroughly frightened the Dauphin. Rather than find himself in subjection to the States-General, he preferred going without money, and, giving as a pretext the necessity in which he was of consulting the emperor, he broke up the assembly, and ordered the members to retire to their own homes. His real object was to appeal separately to all the large towns for help, and having signally failed, he issued, before starting for Metz, where he was to meet the emperor, a decree altering once more the value of the coinage. The result was a general rising ; and King John having annulled all that the States-General had done, the rising assumed the proportions of a revolution. It is then that Etienne Marcel, unable to obtain from the Dauphin any satisfactory answer to the complaints of the people, sought the assistance of Charles *le Mauvais*. What has been called the *great edict* (*la grande ordonnance*) of 1357 was a remarkable document, and its seventy-one articles contained plans of reforms which were very much needed ; but it was essentially *Parisian* in its origin, and as such did not excite much sympathy beyond the walls of the metropolis. However, Marcel was the real King of France, and in the almost universal disorder he seemed the only person who had any energy left. On the day after the decree had been issued ordering a fresh alteration in the coinage, he assembled all the trade corporations in arms, and, accompanied by them went to the hotel where the Dauphin resided. Then going up to the young prince's room, to ask him to provide at last for the defence of the realm, and to protect the people from the violence of the soldiery, "I would readily do it," answered the Dauphin, "if I could; but the keeping of the realm should belong to him who enjoys the rights and profits." Many bitter words were exchanged, and, finally, Marcel said to the prince, "Sir, you must not be astonished at any incident you shall see; but it is necessary that the thing should be done." Then, turning to some of those who had followed him: "Come," said he, "do quickly that for which you came here." The mob rushed immediately upon the Marshals of Champagne and of Normandy, the two principal advisers of the Dauphin, and murdered them so close to him that his dress was stained with blood. Charles, frightened, begged of Marcel to spare him. The Provost assured him that he ran no danger; however he put on the Dauphin's head his cap, which was red and blue—the colours of the city of Paris; and then, addressing the mob from the town-hall, he told then what had been done to the two marshals, those arrant traitors. The populace, crowding the Place de Grève, shouted.: "We own the fact, and we shall stand by you!" On his return to the palace, Marcel found the Dauphin overwhelmed with terror and with grief. "Do not be distressed, my Lord," said he; "what has happened is the will of the people."

Against this formidable movement of the Paris

bourgeoisie a reaction could not but take place. The other towns were far from sympathizing with it, and we need scarcely say that the nobles cordially hated it. Under the pretext of presiding over the States of Champagne held at Provins, the Dauphin left Paris, and was promised the support of the barons both belonging to the province and to Vermandois. He managed to raise seven hundred lances, and at their head laid waste the country, occupying in succession Meaux, Melun, Saint Maur, the bridge of Charenton, and stopping all the supplies arriving towards Paris by the Upper Seine and the Marne. On his side, Marcel had taken possession of the Louvre, fortified the metropolis, and provided all the streets with chains, which, when stretched from one side to the other, could stop the progress of the troops; he had also raised an army of mercenary soldiers.

The peasants were those who had to suffer most from the disturbed state of the country. The towns and castles were comparatively safe from the attacks of the *routiers;* the villages, on the contrary, could afford no resistance. The enemies, like a storm, passed on, plundering and robbing whatever came in their way; the French troops came next; they had to live, and as payment on their part was a matter of impossibility, they accomplished the ruin of those whom they were supposed to defend. The barons, too, must needs indemnify themselves for the losses they had sustained; they had to pay their own ransom and that of their families, to maintain a large band of men-at-arms, to keep stores and provisions of every kind. For all these requirements the peasants

were made answerable ; until one fine day, Jacques
Bonhomme (that was the common nickname given to
the French peasantry) could bear it no longer, and
hearing that the *bourgeoisie* had risen against the
nobles, he thought he would join in the fray.

> "Cessez, cessez, gens d'armes et pictons
> De piller et manger le Bonhomme,
> Qui de longtemps Jacques Bonhomme
> Se nomme."

This complaint, expressed in a rude poetical form, was
followed by deeds of the most brutal character. The
men of Beauvais, in Picardy, were the first to rise, and
after a while they gathered together both in Champagne and in Picardy to the number of one hundred
thousand, finding an unexpected and welcome ally in
Etienne Marcel, who was anxious to counteract the
power of the Dauphin. Taken in the first instance by
surprise, the nobles and barons soon recovered their
firmness, and began against the *Jacques* a war which
admitted of no mercy, and was relentlessly carried on.
In a few weeks the peasants were exterminated.

Deprived of his new allies, Marcel then tried to
secure the co-operation of the King of Navarre, whom
he had got out of prison, and for whom he had
obtained the title of Captain of the City of Paris.
But was it quite safe to trust a prince who had
powerfully help to slaughter the revolutionists and to
stamp out the *Jacquerie ?* Evidently no, for Charles
de Navarre was at the very time negotiating with the
Dauphin, who promised to satisfy all his claims, and,
further, to give him 400,000 florins if he would only
open to him the gates of Paris and surrender Etienne

Marcel into his hands. The Provost, driven to extremities, and anxious to save the revolutionary movement, determined upon substituting to the reigning family of France the representation of the younger branch, and accordingly he promised to Charles *le Mauvais*, that he would allow him access to the gate and bastile Saint Denis. The prince would thus make himself master of Paris, put to death all his enemies whose houses were specially marked with a distinctive sign, and get himself proclaimed king. The carrying out of the plot was fixed for the night between the 31st of July and the 1st of August.

"The same night that this should have been done God inspired certain burgesses of the city, such as were always of the Duke's party, such as John Maillart, and Simon his brother, and divers others, who by divine inspiration, as it ought to be supposed, were informed that Paris should be that night destroyed. They incontinent armed themselves, and showed the matter in other places, to have more aid ; and a little before midnight they came to the gate Saint Antoine, and there they found the Provost of the merchants with the keys of the gates in his hands. Then John Maillart said to the Provost, calling him by his name : 'Stephen, what do you here at this hour ?' The Provost answered and said : 'John, what would ye ? I am here to take heed to the town, whereof I have the governing.' 'By God,' said John, 'ye shall not go so : ye are not here at this hour for any good, and that may be seen by the keys of the gates that ye have in your hands. I think it be to betray the town.' Quoth the Provost, 'John, ye lie falsely.'

'Nay,' said John; 'Stephen, thou liest falsely like a traitor,' and therewith struck at him, and said to his company: 'Slay the traitors!' Then every man struck at them; the Provost would have fled, but John Maillart gave him a blow with an axe on the head, that he fell down to the earth, and yet he was his gossip; and left not till he was slain, and six of them that were there with him, and the others taken and put in prison.

"Then people began to stir in the streets, and John Maillart, and they of his accord, went to the gate of Saint Honoré, and there they found certain of the Provost's sect, and then they laid treason to them, but their excuses availed nothing.

"There were divers taken, and sent into divers places to prison, and such as would not be taken were slain without mercy. The same night they went and took divers in their beds, such as were culpable of the treason, by the confession of such as were taken.

"The next day John Maillart assembled the most part of the Commons in the market hall, and there he mounted on a stage, and showed generally the cause why he had slain the Provost of the merchants; and then, by the counsel of all the wise men, all such as were of the sect of the Provost were judged to the death, and so they were executed by divers torments of death. Thus done, John Maillart, who was then greatly in the grace of the Commons of Paris, and other of his adherents, sent Simon Maillart and two masters of the Parliament . . . to the Duke of Normandy, being at Charenton. They showed the Duke all the matter, and desired him to come to

Paris to aid and to counsel them of the city from thenceforth, saying that all his adversaries were dead. The Duke said, 'With right a good will,' and so he came to Paris, and with him Sir Arnold D'Andchen, the Lord of Roy, and other knights ; and he lodged at the Louvre." [1]

The situation of France was terrible, disorder reigned everywhere, and the usual accompaniments of war—famine and pestilence—were threatening the kingdom. Negotiations had been opened by King John with England, but they were of so humiliating a nature that the Dauphin refused to sanction them, and accordingly Edward invaded France once more (1359). He was himself beginning to get weary of this constant fighting, and the obstinate resistance he met with at every step he took, resistance made more obstinate by despair, discouraged him. There was no glory to be obtained, because there was no pitched battles ; no plunder to expect, because everything was either taken already, or concealed safely behind the walls of the fortresses.

The following episode has often been quoted, but it deserves to be recorded again as a touching and curious illustration of the way in which the war was now carried on. It is related by the chronicler, Jean de Venette.

"There is a strong place in a small village called Longueil, near Compiègne. The inhabitants, seeing that they would run into danger if the enemy were to take possession of that place in their neighbourhood, occupied it with the permission of the Abbot of

[1] Froissart, cap. 187.

Saint Corneille of Compiègne, to whom it belonged, and of the Regent. They provided themselves with arms and victuals, selected one of themselves as captain, and promised to the Lord Duke that they would defend their fortress to the last. Others came from the neighbouring villages. The captain was a tall, handsome man, by name Guillaume des Alouettes. He took as his servant another peasant, quite his match, a man of incredible strength of limbs, well-proportioned despite his stature, full of boldness and of vigour, and in his great body having a very low opinion of himself. He was called *le grand Ferré.* They therefore assembled in that place, two hundred in number, all agriculturists, or earning their livelihood by manual labour. The English, who held the castle of Creil, hearing what sort of men they were, went to Longueil full of contempt, and without precaution, saying: 'Let us drive away those rustics, and take possession of the place.' Two hundred of them had arrived unnoticed; finding the gates open, they walked boldly into the yard, when the unskilled soldiers of the garrison were still upstairs, looking out of the windows, and quite stupified at seeing the place full of armed men. The captain descended with some of his fellows, and began to strike; but soon surrounded by the English, he was killed. The *grand Ferré* and his companions said to one another: 'Let us come down, and sell our lives dearly, for we have no mercy to expect.' They assembled in good order, and sallying forth from several gates, they began to knock upon the English just as if they were engaged in their ordinary task of threshing the corn. The arms rose in the air, fell down upon the English, and every blow was mortal. The *grand Ferré*, brandishing his heavy axe, did not touch one but he cleft his heavy helmet or struck off his arms. Behold all the English taking to flight ; several jumped into the moat and were drowned. The *grand Ferré* killed their standard-bearer, and told one of his followers to carry the standard into the moat. His men showing him a number of English still between himself and the moat : ' Follow me,' said *le grand*, and he went forward, plying his axe right and left till the banner had been cast into the water. He had killed on that day, upwards of forty men. . . . On the morrow the English came in great numbers to attack Longueil ; but the people of the village no longer dreaded them, and they ran to meet them, the *grand Ferré* at their head. Several English noblemen were taken, and would have paid large ransoms if the peasants had, like the nobles, offered them the option ; but they killed them in order that they might do no more harm. On this occasion the *grand Ferré*, heated by his work, drank a good deal of cold water, and was seized with fever. He went to the village, reached his cottage, and took to his bed, not, however, without keeping by his side his good iron axe, which an ordinary man could not raise. Having heard that he was ill, the English sent one day twelve men to kill him. His wife seeing them come from a distance, ran to his bed saying : 'Ah ! my *Ferré*, here are the English ! I really believe that they are looking out for you. What is to be done?' He immediately forgetting his illness got up quickly, took his axe and went into his small yard.

'Ah! thieves!' said he; 'so you have come to take me in my bed? You have not caught me yet!' And in his wrath he killed five of them in a moment; the other seven took to flight. The victor went to bed again; but being very hot, he drank more cold water. Fever again seized him, and after a few days, the *grand Ferré* left this world, having received the sacraments of the Church, and was buried in the village cemetery."

This noble example and other similar ones did more than anything else to arouse patriotism in many faint hearts; even Charles *le Mauvais* yielded; he made his peace with the Regent, and declared that his only wish now was to prove himself a good Frenchman.

Meanwhile the negotiations which had begun came, after a long time, to a satisfactory result, and peace was signed at the hamlet of Brétigny, near Chartres, on the 8th of May, 1360. Guienne, Poitou, Saintonge, Angoumois, Limousin, Calais, Guines, Montreuil, and the whole of Ponthieu were abandoned to England; the King of France had, moreover, to pay a sum of 3,000,000 crowns (about 250,000,000 francs). He had been brought back to Calais, but recovered his liberty only on disbursing a first instalment of 500,000 crowns, and delivering into the hands of the English about one hundred hostages, including his second and his third son, his brother, twenty of the highest barons of France, and thirty-eight notable burgesses belonging to the principal cities of the kingdom. The money formed part of a sum of 600,000 gold florins given by Galeazzo Visconti as the price of the hand of the young princess, Isabel of France, whom he obtained as a wife foɪ nis son Giovanni Galeazzo.

It was with feelings of the bitterest sorrow that the inhabitants of the provinces ceded to England received the news of their no longer being French citizens, and in some places this sorrow led to deliberate acts of resistance. John, however, went through France, in order to take possession of the Duchy of Burgundy, which became his by right of inheritance, on account of the death of Philippe de Rouvres, and which he made over to his son Philip the Bold. Visiting the Pope at Avignon, he had been nearly persuaded by him to attempt another Crusade, when he heard that one of his sons, the Duke d'Anjou, had escaped from the hands of the English, with whom he had been left as hostage. Resolving most loyally to take his place, John returned to London and spent the winter of 1343 in festivities, which ended by killing him. He died April 8, 1364, at the early age of forty-four. He had created in 1351 the first *official* order of knighthood, the Order of the Star (*l'Étoile*) which served as a pattern for the Order of the Golden Fleece (*toison d'or*) instituted in 1439 by the Duke of Burgundy.

XI.

CHARLES V. THE WISE, AND FIRST PART OF THE REIGN OF CHARLES VI.

(1364-1392.)

CHARLES V. was twenty-seven years old when he succeeded his father. Delicate in his constitution, unable to stand any fatigue, so weak that many people suspected him to have been poisoned by Charles de Navarre, he seemed hardly the man to cope with the difficulties of the situation in which he was placed. His tastes, besides, were for study and literature ; he spent his time at the castle of Vincennes, or in Paris at the Hôtel Saint Pol, in the company of "solemn clerks" (*clercs solennels*), astrologers, and philosophers. Would such a king be able to conquer France from the English, and to hoist up the oriflamme ? Fortunately a whole school of captains had arisen who understood that war is a science, and that, although personal courage is indispensable, the knowledge of tactics and of strategy is not less so. Bertrand Duguesclin and Olivier de Clisson, Marshal Boucicault, Louis de Châlons, Le Bègue de Vilaines, the lords of Beaujeu, Pommiers et Reyneval, were the most distinguished of that band of soldiers, especially

Duguesclin and Boucicault, whose high deeds have been described to us in two works still reckoned amongst the monuments of mediæval literature. The "Livre des faicts du mareschal de Boucicault" (1368–1421) is the interesting record of a life full of adventures which read like the old *chansons de geste ;* the "Roumant de Bertrand du Glasquin," as the title sufficiently shows, must be considered less as a biography than as an epic, in which imagination has a large share ; and the purpose of which is to rouse up the courage of the "good French knights." A third work remains to be mentioned, connected with the history of the reign ; we mean Christine de Pisan's "Livre des faits et bonnes mœurs du Roi Charles V.," which brings before us in all their curious details the character, the manners, and the habits of a good and wise king.

Charles de Navarre had very soon forgotten the promise he had made of being *un bon Français* for the future, and he was once again threatening the realm ; but his attitude was no justification whatever of the treacherous way in which his two cities of Mantes and Meulan were taken. He resolved upon avenging himself signally, and announced his intention of preventing the coronation of the young king at Reims. With that view he had collected an army composed chiefly of English and Gascon mercenaries, commanded by Jean de Grailli, Captal of Buch. Charles V. did not wait till the force had begun to move ; he, too, collected some troops whom he placed under the orders of Duguesclin, just named by him Captain-General of Normandy, and on the day of his

CORONATION OF CHARLES V.

coronation (May 19th) he learnt that the enemy had been signally defeated at Cocherel, near Evreux. Jean de Grailli was taken prisoner, and the Navarrese compelled to come to terms, must needs remains satisfied with the barony of Montpellier in exchange for his Normandy fiefs.

The following portrait of Duguesclin is amusing.

> "Mais l'enfant dont je dis et dont je vais parlant,
> Je crois qu'il not si lait de Resnes à Dinant.
> Camus estoit et noir, malotru et massant (?)
> Li père et la mère si le héoient tant . . . ."

> "But the child whom I mention, and about whom I speak,
> I think there never was such an ugly one from Rennes to Dinan.
> He was flat-nosed, and black, ill-mannered, and (?)
> His father and mother hated him so much."

Such was the hero of Charles the Fifth's reign; after having played an important part in the war against Charles de Navarre, he took the command of the French forces, sent to the assistance of Charles de Blois, who was disputing the possession of Brittany with the Count de Montfort, assisted by the famous English captain, John Chandos. In a battle which took place at Auray (September 29, 1364), Charles de Blois was killed, and Duguesclin, made prisoner, had to pay the enormous sum of 100,000 livres to recover his liberty. The King of France thought it was high time that a war which had lasted upwards of twenty years should come to an end. He acknowledged John de Montfort as Duke of Brittany, and contrived that peace should be signed at Guérande between that baron and the widow of Charles de Blois (April 12, 1365).

STATUE OF DUGUESCLIN.

The next great task to which the King of France applied himself was to drive out of the country the numerous bands of adventurers which, under the name of *grandes compagnies*, were doing almost as much mischief as the followers of Jacques Bonhomme. It happened that about that time the Spanish prince, Henry of Transtamare, was engaged in a war with his brother, Don Pedro of Castile, one of the greatest and most cruel tyrants of the mediæval epoch. Charles V., to whom he had applied for assistance, was only too happy to find an opportunity of getting rid of the *grandes compagnies ;* he placed them at Transtamare's disposal, after having given to them as a leader Duguesclin, whose ransom he generously paid. Success favoured in the first instance Henry of Transtamare, but Don Pedro, having obtained the assistance of the Black Prince, defeated his brother, and Duguesclin became once more a prisoner of the English (April, 1367).

Don Pedro had promised to pay the English hand-somely for the assistance they had given him, but he was penniless himself, and the inhabitants of Guyenne were obliged to bear all the burden of a fruitless expedition. Thoroughly irritated, they felt all the more the insolence of their new masters, and finally entered a formal complaint against the Black Prince for not observing the conditions of the treaty of Brétigny. Summoned in consequence by the King of France, his suzerain, to appear and justify himself before the court of parliament in Paris, the prince sent to prison the two messengers who had delivered to him the order, and prepared for a fresh war. In

TOMB OF DUGUESCLIN.

the meanwhile the tragic death of Pedro the Cruel, stabbed by Henry of Transtamare, having put an end to hostilities in the south, Charles V. felt at liberty to concentrate all his energies upon the struggle with the English. The taking of Limoges (1370) was the Black Prince's last exploit, and it was marked by incidents of unwonted cruelty. He returned to Bordeaux, and finally died in England (1376).

The tide of affairs seemed beginning to turn in favour of the French. Charles V. renewed the old alliance with the Scotch; he secured the friendship of the Duke of Brabant and the Count of Hainault, and obtained the hand of the heiress of Flanders for his young brother Philip, Duke of Burgundy. It is interesting to compare the state of the English army with that of the French. The former had an admirable infantry, excellent archers, and a body of men-at-arms, who by their severe training and their knowledge of manœuvring were as good as regular cavalry. Around Charles V. was assembled a large *posse* of noblemen extremely brave, but ignorant of the most elementary rules of discipline. Under such conditions pitched battles were to be avoided, but small encounters might take place in the interval between two expeditions, and Duguesclin, now named Constable of France, distinguished himself in actions of that kind.

We are told that during the Breton war (1350) Robert de Beaumanoir, governor of the Castle of Josselin, sent a challenge to the English captain, Richard Bramborough, commanding the town of Ploermel. The two champions, each accompanied by twenty-nine knights, met on a heath near Josselin, and engaged in a desperate battle. Beaumanoir, wounded at the beginning of the fray, and very thirsty in consequence, asked for something to drink. " Drink your blood, Beaumanoir!" exclaimed one of his companions, Geoffrey Dubois, and went on striking right and left. Four Frenchmen, nine Englishmen (including Bramborough) were killed; all the others were severely wounded. The English surrendered to the French.

Now this was the kind of fight that Duguesclin most relished; he defeated at Pont Vallain Robert Knolles (1370), and routed another body of partisans near Chizey in Poitou (1373); the illustrious Chandos had been killed during the first campaign, and in 1372 the Captal de Buch was taken prisoner near Soubise. Evidently the English were losing ground in France; Poitiers and La Rochelle (1372) had been wrested from them, and, thoroughly wearied, they asked for a truce, which lasted till the death of Edward III. in 1377. Charles V. then broke it, and, having ineffectually tried to annex Brittany to the Crown, he was about to fight the Bretons, assisted by the English, when death carried him off at Vincennes (September 16, 1380).

We must now consider for a short time the King of France as an administrator and a protector of literature. His perseverance, his economy, his probity (he would not have recourse to the dangerous and immoral practice of altering the coinage), procured for him the " sobriquet " of *the wise*. He rendered the parliament permanent, curtailed the privileges of the nobles, and

introduced important reforms in the finances ; indirect
taxes (*aides*) were made permanent likewise, and
instead of allowing a salary to the members of the
parliament, he abandoned to them the fines they
might inflict upon condemned criminals and delin-
quents—a measure which was not calculated to
promote the cause of *indifferent* justice.

Charles V. was very fond of building ; he commenced the Bastile, repaired and enlarged the Paris
walls and the Louvre, and constructed the Hôtel
Saint Pol, the chapel of Vincennes, and the castles
of Beauté, Plaisance, and Melun. The idea of uniting
the Loire to the Seine, carried out two centuries later
by Henry IV., was originally his. To conclude this
enumeration, we shall give here the items of what
may be called the French budget for 1372. It is
taken from the great decree (*ordonnance*) for the same
year as reproduced in M. Duruy's " History of
France " :—

	FRANCS
For the payment of the gensd'armes	50.000
For the gensd'armes and cross-bow men of the new foundation	42,000
For the navy	8,000
For the king's *hostel*	6,000
To place in the king's coffers	5,000
Unforeseen expenses	10,000
Payment of the debt	10,000
	131,000

We must note that this is a monthly statement ; the
yearly expenses, therefore, amounted to 1,572,000
francs in gold crowns (about 130,000,000 francs
according to the present value of French money), and

out of this sum 72,000 francs, about 1-22nd, went for the personal expenses of the King, the Queen, and the Dauphin.

"Charles V.," says M. Michelet ("History of France"), " is perhaps the first king of that nation, .till then so light-hearted, who knew how to prepare from afar the success, and who understood the influence, distant and slow then, but even at that time real, of books over business. The prior, Honoré Bonnor, wrote by his order and under the odd title of ' L'arbre des Batailles,' the first essay on the rights of peace and of war. His advocate, Raoul de Presle, translated for him the Bible in the vulgar tongue. His old tutor, Nicholas Oresme, translated into French the other Bible of those days, namely, Aristotle. Oresme, Raoul de Presles, Philip de Maizières, worked together on those ponderous tomes—the 'Songe du Vergier,' the 'Songe du vieux Pélerin,' kinds of cyclopædic romances, where all the questions interesting at that time were discussed, and which prepared the abatement of the spiritual power and the confiscation of Church property. Similarly, during the sixteenth century, Pithou, Passerat, and a few others worked together on the ' Satire Ménippée.'"

Another book which should not be forgotten is the small political pamphlet entitled, " Le vray régime et gouvernement des Bergers et Bergères, composé par le rustique Jehan de Brie, le bon Berger." It is a matter of doubt whether it was not dictated in part to the author by Charles V. Under an allegorical form it is an appeal to concord and goodwill. Jean de Brie preaches from the well-known parable of the

sheepfold, and tells that the Good Shepherd scorns
to imitate Charles of Navarre, who tried to enter
into Paris by night ; he does not sell Christendom
secretly, like Clement IV., nor does he, after the
fashion of certain cunning and deceitful clerks, take
possession fraudently of prebends and rich benefices.

The remonstrances and counsels of Jean de Brie
were reasonable during the days of Charles V. ; how
much more so amidst the confusion, the misgovern-
ment, and general distress which marked the reign of
Charles VI.?

Although the eldest of the brothers of the late
king, Louis, Duke d'Anjou, had not been summoned
to wait upon him during his last moments, because
people dreaded his ambition, his greed, and his covetousness. Christine de Pisan describes him as "tall and
of a *pontifical* (stately) appearance ; most handsome
both of body and of countenance, very courageous,
and much desirous of lordships and of treasures."

The Duke d'Anjou had taken care to have the bed-
side of Charles V. watched by trusty followers, who
kept him well informed of all that took place and of
the progress of the king's malady. The fatal moment
had scarcely arrived, when he came to the palace,
and seized upon the Crown jewels and the treasury,
amounting, it is said, to nineteen millions. At the
same time he assumed the government of the state
contrary to the express will of Charles V., who had
entrusted the regency to his two other brothers, the
Dukes of Burgundy and of Berry, and to his brother-
in-law, the Duke of Bourbon.

The three princes above named were not in the

slightest degree willing to resign their claims, and they had their partisans and friends on whose co-operation they could rely in case of need. Besides, if the Duke d'Anjou had the advantage of being master of Paris, they had the far greater one of keeping under their guardianship the young King Charles, who was only twelve years of age, and who resided with them at Melun. What was to be done? A few lords, amongst whom was the Chancellor of France, Peter d'Orgemont, proposed that the difference should be submitted to a council composed of bishops, lords, members of the parliament, of the court of accounts, and burgesses of the principal towns (*bonnes villes*).

The meeting was a very stormy one; whilst the Duke d'Anjou maintained with much eloquence his rights of seniority, the Chancellor put forward the will of Charles V., and his express declaration on the subject of the regency. An appeal to brute force was imminent, when the Advocate-General, Desmarets, proposed that four arbitrators should be appointed, whose decision all would be bound to accept. The resolution arrived at was as follows: In the first place, the young king was to be crowned immediately, the Duke d'Anjou retaining the title of regent till the moment of the coronation, and sharing afterwards with the Dukes of Berry and Burgundy the tutelage of Charles VI. till his majority, fixed by his father to the age of fourteen. The Duke d'Anjou obtained besides what he most coveted—the jewels, plate, and money, the value of which would enable him to conquer the kingdom of Naples, to which he had been called by Joan, the late queen.

Charles VI. made a solemn entry into Reims on the occasion of his coronation ; he was accompanied by his four uncles, and by a large gathering of lords and prelates. After the ceremony a sumptuous banquet was held, during which an incident occurred which threatened to disturb the harmony re-established with so much difficulty. The prelates, according to custom, sat on the right of the king ; the Duke d'Anjou had selected the seat immediately on his left, but the Duke of Burgundy insisted upon occupying it, as being the premier peer of France, and the other competitor had to resign his pretensions not without expressing loudly his dissatisfaction. The banquet was served by the highest barons in the kingdom : the Lord of Coucy, the Constable Olivier de Clisson, Admiral John de Vienne, the Lord de la Trémoille ; they were mounted on their chargers and arrayed in cloth of gold. The festival was concluded by the performance of one of those " mysteries" or miracle-plays which constitute the dramatic literature of the Middle Ages.

On the return of the king to his capital, and after the excitement ordinary to the first few days of a new reign, the perils which threatened France became more and more evident. In the first place, a feudal reaction was manifesting itself against the acts of Charles V. ; his friends and advisers were dismissed, whilst the regents bestowed all their favour upon lords and barons who had long been kept excluded from the councils of the State. Then, the financial condition of the people was wretched, a rising seemed inevitable, and the Duke d'Anjou was reproached for not doing away with the *gabelle* and other excessive taxes which the late king had solemnly promised to abolish.

Upwards of three hundred men marched towards the palace to obtain an answer to their just complaints. The Duke d'Anjou, nothing daunted, got upon a table and, addressing the rioters, reminded them that the city of Paris was indebted to the Crown for all its privileges and its monuments ; the petitions of the citizens had always been courteously attended to, and on this occasion they would meet with the same consideration, provided order was re-established at once.

The salt tax being done away with according to the declaration, it became necessary for the regents to procure money by other means ; the Duke d'Anjou assembled no less than seven times in the course of one year (1381) the deputies of the three orders with a view of obtaining from them a grant of subsidies. It was all in vain ; people compared the successors of Philip the Fair with what tradition related about Saint Louis, the paternal nature of his government and his sense of justice. "The citizens of Paris," says the chronicler, Juvénal des Ursins, "assumed armours and war-dresses ; they elected captains of tens, fifties, and forties, laid chains through the streets, and had watches placed at the gates."

The Duke d'Anjou, without taking any notice of all this, resolved upon having a new tax of one-twelfth *denier* on all provisions. It was a difficult thing to find a man bold enough to announce the raising of that tax ; at last one individual undertook the duty, and riding in the market-place, he exclaimed, in a loud voice—" The king's plate has been stolen ; he who brings it back shall be duly rewarded ! " Having by this announcement gathered a crowd, he added, " To-morrow the tax shall be raised," then, putting spur to his horse, he rode off as fast as he could.

The next day one of the collectors ventured to ask one *sol* from an old woman who sold water-cress ; he was immediately knocked down and killed. So terrible was the alarm that the bishop, the principal citizens, and even the provost, whose business it was to maintain order, left Paris. The infuriated mob ran through the city armed with new leaden mallets (*maillets*) which they had taken in the arsenal ; they made a frightful slaughter of the tax collectors ; one of them had sought refuge in the church of Saint Jacques, and clung to a statue of the Virgin ; he was put to death on the very altar (March 1, 1382). They sacked the rich abbey of Saint Germain des Prés under the pretext that collectors and Jews had retired there.

From Vincennes, where they had withdrawn for safety, the princes watched the progress of the riot ; as soon as they saw that public feeling was declaring against the excesses committed by the *maillotins*, they applied to the university and the leading citizens, requesting them to act as mediators. It was agreed on both sides that the city of Paris should allow to the king a grant of one hundred thousand francs ; in return of this concession, Charles VI. was to abolish the new tax, and make a solemn entry in the capital (May, 1382).

It is not to be supposed that the sedition was confined to Paris ; at Rouen, at Orléans, at Châlons, and at Troyes, similar scenes occurred ; in Languedoc the peasants flew to arms under the name of *tuchins.*

As M. Michelet remarks (" Histoire de France," vi.) it seemed as if throughout the length and breadth of Europe a war was beginning, of the little against the great, the *proletariate* against the nobles. The " white hoods " of Flanders followed a citizen of Ghent ; the Florentine "ciompi" had for leader a wool-carder ; the people of Rouen compelled a draper to assume the supreme command ; in England Wat Tyler at the head of the mob obliged the king to grant freedom to the serfs.

It was generally felt that this revolutionary movement originated with the inhabitants of Ghent, who had been for many years struggling for their freedom against the counts of Flanders. "On the part of the counts," says Mr. Taylor (preface to " Philip van Arteveldt "), were Bruges, Oudenarde, Dendermonde, Lille, and Tournay ; and those on the part of Ghent were Damme, Ypres, Courtray, Grammont, Poperinghen, and Messines — a war which in its progress extended to the whole of Flanders, and excited a degree of interest in all the civilized countries of Europe for which the cause must be sought in the state of European communities at the time. It was believed that entire success on the part of Ghent would bring on a general rising almost throughout Christendom, of the commonalty against the feudal lords and men of substance. The incorporation of the citizens of Paris known by the name of "the army with mallets" (*maillotins*) was, according to the well-known chronicler of the period, "all by the example of them of Ghent." Nicolas le Flamand deterred them from pulling down the Louvre, by urging the expediency of waiting to see what success might attend the Flemish insurgents."

The princes were naturally anxious to crush the rebellion in its principal centre, and raised an army to assist the Count of Flanders in subduing the inhabitants of Ghent. On the 26th of November, 1382, the feudal army, commanded by the young king, Charles VI., and by his uncle the Duke of Burgundy, met at Roosebeke the troops of the Flemish *communes*, led by Philip van Arteveldt, son of the famous brewer of whom we have already spoken. The battle was fought on the next day, and in the midst of a thick fog the rebels displayed such courage that the French knights were driven back for a short time. Constable Olivier de Clisson, however, following the plan adopted by Duguesclin at Cocherel, turned round the enemy, cut off their retreat and made a frightful havoc of them. Arteveldt himself and twenty-five thousand of his men were killed ; the loss was very serious also on the side of the French.

Great was the consternation of the Parisians when the news of the battle of Roosebeke reached them. The royal army entered Paris as if it had been a city reduced to submission. The inhabitants fancied that by making a display of their strength they would obtain better conditions ; they paraded at the foot of Montmartre in a long array of armed men ; there was a company of crossbow men, one of soldiers

with swords and bucklers, one of *maillotins* amounting
by itself to twenty thousand men. This exhibition
only served to exasperate the princes. The gates of
the city were torn down and trampled under foot, the
soldiers were billeted upon the citizens, the street-
chains were removed and every one was ordered to
give up at once all kinds of weapons. One chronicler
tells us that the amount of arms thus left either at
the palace or at the Louvre, would have sufficed for
an army of eight hundred thousand men. Then
came the executions. A few of the ringleaders were
put to death. Finally, money had to be forthcoming :
all the rich *bourgeois* were taxed so heavily that some
of them paid more than they really possessed. When
nothing more could be squeezed out of the pockets of
the Parisians, an edict, solemnly proclaimed, re-established all the old taxes further increased. Complaint
was impossible ; there was no *commune*, no provost, no
magistrates, no city of Paris. Rouen, Reims, Châlons,
Orléans, Troyes, and Sens, were treated pretty
nearly in the same manner ; most of the money
thus iniquitously extorted went towards enriching
a few of the barons, and the public treasury very.
little profited by it.

Not only did those measures produce no effect,
but dissensions took place even amongst the king's
advisers. The old trusty councillors of Charles V.
remonstrated, endeavoured to enlighten the young
monarch on the conduct of his uncles, and advised
him to take the reins of government into his own
hands. Accordingly during the month of October,
1387, a great assembly of prelates and barons was

summoned at Reims; the Dukes of Berry and of Burgundy were present; the Duke d'Anjou had recently died in Italy. Charles VI. having asked the assembly to advise him as to the best way of remedying the evils from which the realm was suffering, Peter de Montaigu, Bishop of Laon, supported by the Archbishop of Reims, Olivier de Clisson, and other enemies of the regents, declared that his majesty being now twenty-one years old could govern by himself. The Dukes of Berry and Burgundy were furious; they left the court, but they made the Bishop of Laon pay for his boldness; he died of poison.

The departure of the king's uncles produced two good effects; in the first place, these princes could now attend to their respective dominions, re-establish order and commerce, drive away brigands and suspicious characters, &c. Next, the new advisers of the weak Charles VI., La Rivière, Clisson, and others, were men of steady judgment, and liberal principles, desirous of re-establishing the administration of justice, reducing the taxes and giving up all the rash and senseless undertakings planned by their predecessors. They were contemptuously nicknamed the *Marmousets*, because they had sprung chiefly from the people, and were of very humble extraction. If they had been able to retain office they would have no doubt done much for France, but a melancholy event upset all these hopes and brought fresh calamities to France.

Olivier de Clisson, one of the *Marmousets*, had managed to incur the hatred of two powerful noble-

CHARLES VI.

men—one being the Duke of Brittany himself, who
naturally was watched with suspicion by the Constable,
the sworn friend of the house of Anjou and Penthièvre.
Clisson longed for the moment when he would be
able to drive away to England the Duke of Brittany
and to rid France of the Montfort family. Another
nobleman, but not of quite so high an origin, was
Peter de Craon, a despicable character, retainer of the
late Duke d'Anjou, whose treasury he had robbed
and whose death he had caused. He promised to
the Duke of Brittany that he would rid him of his
enemy, and did so accordingly. One evening, Clisson
had just left the king when he was attacked by a
band of desperadoes at the head of which was Pierre
de Craon himself. He was not killed, but seriously
wounded, and Charles VI. promised that he would
avenge him in the most signal manner. An army
was assembled and the monarch who had only just recovered from a severe attack of fever determined, contrary to the advice of the physicians, upon commanding the royal forces in person. He would march into
Brittany, and put to death both John de Montfort
and Pierre de Craon, who had taken refuge at his
Court.

It was in summer (August 5, 1392) when the
army entered the forest of Le Mans. The heat was
intolerable. Suddenly a man, bareheaded and
wretchedly clothed, rushed forward and seizing hold
of the reins of the king's charger, exclaimed, " King,
do not move one step further, but return; you are
betrayed!" The man should have been arrested;
he was allowed to get away. Startled and terrified

by this strange incident, Charles VI. proceeded, when the lances carried by two pages riding near him happened to strike against each other, and at the noise he shouted: "Death to the traitors!" then drawing his sword he rushed upon his escort, killing and wounding several men, and threatening even his brother. Every one fled, but at last the unfortunate monarch was seized, disarmed, and brought back from Le Mans to Creil. The first thought which occurred to every one was that he had been either poisoned or "bewitched." The fact is that his debaucheries, his violent passions, and the intoxicating influence of royal power, had predisposed his weak head to an attack of madness which was now brought about by sudden excitement and by a sun-stroke.

XII.

SECOND PART OF THE REIGN OF CHARLES VI.
(1392–1422.)

SOME one having remarked to the Duke de Berry that the king was either "poisoned or bewitched," "Yes, by bad advice," was the answer. This was the death warrant of the *Marmousets*, so to say. Clisson hastened to retire to Brittany, Montaigu went off to Avignon; La Rivière, Novion, and Le Bègue de Vilaines were sent to the Bastile. Restored to power, the princes succeeded in governing France a little more deplorably than their predecessors had done. They concluded with England a truce of twenty-eight years (1395), and gave a daughter of Charles VI. in marriage to Richard II., but the death of that king nullified the advantages which might have resulted from the union.

The Crusade of 1396 is another rash and useless deed which brought into disrepute the new administration. The Turks had, during the last forty years, gradually secured a footing in Europe. They had crossed the Bosphorus, taken Adrianople, and conquered part of the valley of the Danube; they were now threatening Hungary. A Crusade was resolved upon, and the Count de Nevers, afterwards better

known as John the Fearless (Jean sans Peur), Duke of
Burgundy, took the command.   He was only twenty-
four years old, and thought, as well as all his followers,
that a Crusade was a kind of pleasure trip.   Despising
the wise advice of the King of Hungary, Sigismund,
they engaged the battle at Nicopolis with a total disregard of all the rules of tactics, and were signally
defeated.   The Sultan Bajazet ordered ten thousand
captives to be beheaded in his presence, excepting
from the massacre only the Count de Nevers and
twenty-four lords, who had to pay a heavy ransom.

Isabelle of Bavaria must not be forgotten amongst
the personages of this mournful drama.   She was not
fifteen years old when she left Germany to become
the bride of Charles VI.   Without relatives, without a
guide in the most corrupt Court in Europe, she adopted
the manners and habits of her *entourage*, and indulged
to the full her taste for luxury and pleasures.   Instead
of sobering her down, time merely developed her evil
habits.   From frivolity she sank down to debauchery,
and made use of her authority for the exclusive purpose of satisfying her passions and her revengeful
nature.

The Duke d'Orléans, husband of the beautiful and
accomplished Valentine Visconti, had been her lover.
She saw him massacred by some of the followers of
John the Fearless, Duke of Burgundy, who was jealous
of his popularity, and wished to retain the power in
his own hands.   We have all the particulars of this
terrible deed.   Since the attempted murder of Olivier
de Clisson it was quite evident that the closest verifi-
cation alone could guarantee that the victim was really

and unmistakably dead.   Accordingly a man carrying a lighted wisp of straw came forward and examined for himself if the intentions of the Duke of Burgundy had been carried out.   In this case no hesitation was possible ; the corpse was literally hacked to pieces ; the right arm cut through in two places, at the elbow and at the wrist ; the left wrist thrown to a distance, as if from the violence of the blow ; the head open from ear to ear ; the skull broken, and the brains scattered all over the pavement.   The Duke of Burgundy wanted, at first, to justify his action, but thinking that he might perhaps run the chance of being arrested, he fled to his possessions in Flanders, from whence he ordered it to be said, preached, and written, that by causing the Duke d'Orléans to be murdered he had merely anticipated the sinister designs of that prince.   He then marched (1408) against the inhabitants of Liège who had rebelled, and defeated them at Hasbain with the slaughter of twenty-five thousand of their men.   In the meanwhile a popular preacher, Jean Petit, undertook to justify the foul deed of John the Fearless. Mounting the pulpit he proved, by twelve arguments, in honour of the twelve apostles, that the Duke d'Orléans had deserved his fate.   1. Because he was suspected of heresy.   2. Because he armed at usurping the throne.   3. Because the State would have found in him a tyrant.   Strengthened by this extraordinary sermon, the Duke of Burgundy returned to Paris, and succeeded in wresting from the imbecile king letters of remission declaring that he, Charles VI., entertained no ill-will against the duke for having " put out of the world his brother, the Duke d'Orléans "

(Peace of Chartres, March, 1409). As for poor Valentine Visconti, it is no exaggeration to say that her husband's death killed her. She had taken as her motto: " Rien ne m'est plus, plus ne m'est rien," and died broken-hearted in 1408.

John the Fearless made himself extremely popular by opposing the levying of fresh taxes, promising a reduction of the old ones, and behaving most affably to " all sorts and conditions of men." He was especially courteous to the Parisians, restored to them all their old privileges, and even obtained for them the important right of possessing " noble fiefs," with all the advantages belonging to them. It was in the people of the market-place (*les gens des halles*), says an historian, that the strength of the Bourguignon faction resided in Paris. These concessions to the mob increased the displeasure of the Orleanists, and of all those who represented the old feudal party ; they took as their leader the Count d'Armagnac, father-in-law of one of the murdered duke's sons.

The situation of the kingdom was indeed deplorable; and did no protest arise, no cry of indignation, no appeals to the patriotism of true Frenchmen ? Yes ; three eloquent voices made themselves heard, three writers won their reputation by denouncing the crimes of some and the cowardice or want of energy of the rest.

Look at the condition of the people. Bears, lions, leopards, wolves, that is to say, the nobles combined to fleece the cattle. The ass, the cow, the ox, the goat, the sow, come in turns to bend the knee before the wild beasts of the forest ; the sheep ventures timidly to say that she has been already—

> " Quatre fois plumée
> Cest au-cy."

To these doleful and piteous moanings of the common
people a concert of sharp and threatening voices
answers—

> " Sà, de l'argent !   Sà, de l'argent ! "

" Money ! Money ! "   Such is the cry which all the
day long sounds in the ears of the famished people.
Every now and then, driven to frenzy, they rise, put
to death the collectors of the taxes, and then,
astonished at their own victory, they fall down again
under the yoke ; and hear the barons on one side, and
the king's lawyers on the other, pressing them—those,
sword in hand, these armed with a long piece of
parchment, and repeating, as before—

> "Sà, de l'argent !   Sà, de l'argent ! "

Sometimes Eustache Deschamps (such was the
name of that patriotic songster) directs his violent
invective against the foreign enemies of France, the
victors of Cressy and Poitiers—

> " Selon le Brut de l'isle des Géants
> Qui depuis fust Albion appelée
> Peuple mandit, tar dis (*tardily*) en Dieu créans..
> Sera l'isle de tout point désolée.
> Par leus orgueil vient la dure journée
>   Dont leur prophete Merlin,
> Pronostica leur douloureux fin,
> Quand il escript : *vie perdrez et terre.*
> Lors monstreront estrangiers et voisin,
> Où, temps jadis (*in former times*) estoit cy (*here was*) Angleterre."

Next to Eustache Deschamps, Alain Chartier takes
up his parable against his fellow citizens, and in the

"Quadriloge invectif" shows that all the four orders of the State are equally responsible for the grievous woes which God has sent upon the country. " Where is Nineveh, the great city around which it took three days to walk ? What has become of Babylon, cunningly built in order that it might last longer, and which is now a dwelling for reptiles?" Is France doomed to mix her dust with that of other nations? or is this only a terrible and transitory affliction ? " I have come to the conclusion that the hand of God is upon us." If God punishes, the French must be guilty.

We have already spoken of Christine de Pisan, that true patriot who, although Italian by birth, was more French at heart than many who boasted of their nationality. The letter in which she reminded Isabelle of Bavaria of her duties as a queen and a mother, is a monument of genuine eloquence. At every fresh misfortune which visits the house of France she utters a cry of alarm ; she styles herself "une povre voix criant dans ce royaume, désireuse de paix et du bien de tous." The weakest appeal may often remind men of their duties--

> "Si (*therefore*) ne veuillez mespriser mon ouvrage,
> Mon redoubté seigneur, humain et saige.
>
> . . . . .
>
> Car petite clochette grant voix sonne,
> Qui bien souvent les plus saiges réveille."

In spite of these cautions the civil war continued to rage with all its violence ; the Armagnacs prevailed in the west and the south, the Bourguignons in the north and the east. The former wore a white scarf, the latter a blue cap with the cross of Saint Andrew in white, a *fleur-de-lys* in the centre, and the motto : " Vive le Roy ! "

The Duke of Burgundy fortified himself in, Paris, armed the populace, and abandoned the power to a considerable extent to the co-operation of the butchers, who kept the rest of the population in awe, and had for their leaders the flayer (*écorcheur*) Caboche, a surgeon named Jean de Troyes, and Capeluche, the common hangman. The nobles and rich citizens were thoroughly frightened, and more than fifteen hundred of them, having the provost at their head, left Paris, and retired to Melun.

The excesses committed by the Burgundians brought about a reaction ; the Armagnacs returned to favour, and the rival leaders seemed on the point of being reconciled to each other, when news came that Henry V., King of England, had landed at Harfleur (August 14, 1415). Before entering upon a new war he had endeavoured to obtain by negotiations the whole of Normandy and the provinces ceded to him by the treaty of Brétigny, but finding his exorbitant pretensions indignantly refused, he besieged Harfleur, took it after a siege which lasted a whole month, and cost him fifteen thousand men ; then marching into Picardy, met the French army between the villages of Tramecourt and Azincourt. The French spent on horseback the night before the battle, and when the dawn came both men and horses were thoroughly worn out. The English, on their side, says a chronicler, sounded all night long their trumpets and different kinds of musical instruments, so much so that

HEAD-DRESS OF THE FIFTEENTH CENTURY.

17

the whole earth around re-echoed with the noise although they were sad, weary, and suffering from famine and other miseries. They made their peace with God confessing their sins, weeping, and partaking of our Lord's body, for they expected death the next day. And, indeed, it seemed hardly probable that twelve thousand Englishmen decimated by privations and illness could be capable of resisting fifty thousand fresh troops composed of the flower of French chivalry.

The battle began the next morning at eleven o'clock. The English archers discharged upon the feudal cavalry a shower of arrows which did terrible effect. The spot where that cavalry stood was soft and cut up by the horses, in such a manner that they could hardly move. Their armour, besides, was extremely heavy, and they were so closely packed together that they had great difficulty in moving their arms to strike the enemy, except those who were at the first rank. The English archers, lightly clad, seeing them thus discomfited, threw away their bows and arrows and seizing their swords, axes, and mallets tipped with lead, rushed amidst the French. They knocked them down as though they were heaps ; you might have thought they were striking so many anvils ; thus the noble Frenchmen fell upon the top of one another ; some were smothered to death ; others killed or taken prisoners.

Never was there a more complete, or more humiliating, defeat ; the proud French knights had been vanquished, not by English noblemen and gentlemen, but by merely archers on foot, by mercenaries five times less in numbers. Eight thousand *gentilshommes* remained on the battle-field, notwithstanding prodigies of valour ; amongst them were the Duke of Brabant, and the Count de Nevers, both brothers of the Duke of Burgundy, the Duke of Bar, the Duke d'Alençon,

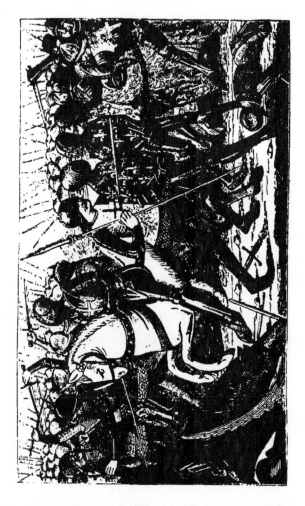

BATTLE OF AZINCOURT.

and the Constable d'Albret ; the Duke d'Orléans was severely wounded and remained for a long time amongst the dead.

The Duke of Burgundy on hearing of the disaster

at Azincourt, pretended to be very indignant, and marching towards Paris at the head of his army, announced loudly his intention of chastising the English, and of restoring the king to the full enjoyment of his power ; in reality his only desire was to reconquer his own authority. On arriving, however, he found not only that Armagnac (now created Constable of France and Superintendent-General of the finances) had forestalled him, but that an express order of the king prohibited him (John the Fearless) from entering the capital. Nothing daunted, the Duke of Burgundy issued a manifesto which secured to him the good-will of several important towns such as Reims, Châlons, Troyes, Auxerre, Amiens, and Rouen, and having succeeded in obtaining the help of a young man named Perrinet Leclerc, whose father was warden of the gate of Saint Germain, he entered Paris by night followed by his soldiers, and made a fresh appeal to the butchers and flayers. The massacre which followed was terrible ; the Constable d'Armagnac the Chancellor of France, the bishops of Saintes, Coutances, Evreux, Senlis, and Bayeux, the Abbot of Saint Corneille at Compiègne, two presidents in the Court of Parliament, and a crowd of noblemen citizens, and soldiers were put to the sword ; the total number of persons killed amounted to eight hundred some say to fifteen hundred. In vain did one of the staunchest *Bourguignons*, Villiers de l'Isle Adam and the Provost of Paris, endeavour to stop the fury of the hangman Capeluche and of his followers. "A fig for your justice and your pity !" they answered. " Cursed of God may those traitors the Armagnacs be ! They are English, they are dogs. They had already embroidered standards for the King of England and wanted to plant them on the gates of the city. They used to make us work for nothing, and when we asked what was our due, they would say to us : 'Scoundrels, have you not a penny wherewith to purchase a rope and hang yourselves?' In the devil's name, plead no more for them ; what you may say will be of no use." The Provost of Paris dare not resist those infuriated men. " Do what you please," said he, turning his head aside.

One month after these massacres, the Duke of Burgundy and Queen Isabelle returned to Paris (July 14, 1418); the national party seemed hopelessly destroyed, and whilst Charles, Duke of Touraine, and now Dauphin, through the death of his two elder brothers, had retired to Poitiers with the view of organizing resistance against the English and the *Bourguignons* combined, Henry V. was carrying on his triumphal progress through Normandy. Favoured by the avowed complicity of the Duke of Burgundy, he had taken Caën, Argentan, Alençon, Bayeux, and finally Rouen which capitulated on the 18th of January, 1419, after a long and stubborn resistance.

This last catastrophe led to a loud manifestation of the national spirit, and John the Fearless was, so to say, compelled to meet the Dauphin at a conference with view to a reconciliation. Corbeil was selected as the place of *rendezvous*, and a second interview was appointed to be held on the bridge of Montereau (September 10, 1419). Tanguy Duchâtel, who accompanied the Dauphin, had promised that no treachery was contemplated, and that the Duke of

Burgundy need entertain no suspicion ; however a cry
of alarm was raised, and Tanguy Duchâtel seizing a
battle-axe struck down the unfortunate duke who fell
on his knees and was immediately despatched.   The

CAPTURE OF TROYES.

excitement created in Paris by this act of undoubted
treachery can easily be imagined ; and although the
followers of the Dauphin certainly represented the
French party, Isabelle of Bavaria induced the new

Duke of Burgundy, Philip the Good, to conclude with Henry V. negotiations which ultimately led to the infamous treaty of Troyes (May 21, 1420) which handed over to England the crown of France and the whole kingdom. The wretched Charles VI., utterly in the power and under the control of an abandoned queen, and of the *Bourguignons*, signed, without being aware of it, the agreement which excluded his own son from the throne.

Henry V. was enthusiastically received in Paris. Misery had killed patriotism, and every one thought that peace was at last secured. The clergy, in procession, came to meet the two kings, and brought them the holy relics to kiss. They were then taken to Notre Dame where they prayed at the high altar. Charles VI. retired thence to the Hôtel Saint Pol ; the King of England took up his quarters in the fortress of the Louvre (December, 1420).

The task was not quite finished. Some time afterwards, the Duke of Burgundy and his mother appeared before the King of France, presiding as judge at the Hôtel Saint Pol, and asked of him vengeance for the " piteous death of the late Duke John of Burgundy." Henry V. was sitting on the same bench as Charles VI. Master Nicolas Raulin, pleading for the plaintiffs, asked that Charles, styling himself Dauphin, Tanguy Duchâtel, and all the murderers of the late duke should be led, torch in hand, through the squares of Paris in a cart to make *honourable amende.* The king's advocate spoke in the same sense, and the University delegates agreed thereto. The king sanctioned the prosecution, and Charles was summoned to appear within three days before the parliament. Having failed to do it, he was condemned, by default, to perpetual banishment, and declared to have lost all his rights to the crown of France (January 3, 1421).

The unfortunate prince, having retired behind the

THE OLD LOUVRE.

Loire, re-organized the national party and appealed to his sword. His troops defeated the English at Baugé in Anjou, but could not prevent the enemy from taking Meaux and several other places.

Things had come to this extremity when the

almost simultaneous death of the two kings gave to the treaty of Troyes an immediate application. Henry V. disappeared first (August 31, 1422). Six weeks later (October 21st) it was the turn of Charles VI. The poor demented monarch was attended at his last moments only by his chancellor, his chief chamberlain, and his confessor. No prince of the blood, not even the Duke of Burgundy, accompanied his remains to Saint Denis. An Englishman, the Duke of Bedford, had to do the last act of courtesy to the King of France. Before closing the tomb, the heralds-at-arms, holding their maces reversed, cried, "God grant peace to the soul of Charles VI., King of France, and God give long life to Henry VI., King of France and of England, our sovereign lord!"

Intelligent and far-seeing people knew pretty well that matters were not settled yet. Henry V. felt so, and he is reported to have predicted that his son would not retain possession of what had been so wonderfully conquered. As for the nation, crushed in their noblest sentiments, they began to think that the affairs of this world brought nothing but trouble and vexation of spirit, and that the care for our salvation is the one thing needful. About 1421 a book appeared, the title of which could not fail to attract notice, and which commended itself to all souls driven to despair. " L'internelle Consolation " has frequently been ascribed to Jean Charlier de Gerson, Chancellor of the University of Paris, and is certainly worthy of that truly excellent man. It is a translation of the " De imitatione Christi "—a translation superior to the original by its boldness, its feeling, and its *human* character. As for the "De imitatione" itself, it is the work neither of Thomas à Kempis, nor of Gerson ; it is the production of the age, and if many nationalities claim it, the fact simply shows that the meditations, counsels, and encouragements it contains express the feelings of a society living in the midst of the most terrible corruption.

The Dauphin Charles was at Meung-sur-Loire when the news reached him of his father's death. " Great sadness took possession of his heart," says the Chronicler Monstrelet ; " he wept very much, and put on immediately a black gown. The next day he attended mass clothed in a red gown, and then was raised the banner of France, and the Dauphin's herald-at-arms cried loudly and distinctly : ' Long life to Charles VII., King of France ! ' "

The affairs of the Church claim our attention here, for Charles VI. was obliged to interfere with them, and the University of Paris took an important part in the wranglings, quarrels, and controversies resulting from the schism. It was not likely that either a weak-headed king or rival princes contending for power would be able to restore peace to Christendom. Two national councils, however, summoned at Paris, and the first held under the third dynasty of kings, consulted about the best means of restoring peace. The only remedy was the convocation of a general council. It was held at Constance from 1414 to 1418, and ended in the deposition of the two rival Popes, John XXIII. and Benedict XIII., and the election of Martin V. (November 11, 1417). For the first time, then, and in order to prevent a new

schism, it was ruled that general councils should be
superior in authority to the Pope. Heretics were
also most severely dealt with, John Huss and
Jerome of Prague, for instance, being sentenced to
be burnt alive. Amongst the celebrated Frenchmen
who took an important part in the proceedings of
the council of Constance, we have already named
Gerson ; we must not forget Pierre d'Ailly, Cardinal-
bishop of Cambrai, author of a famous work entitled,
"Malleus Hæreticorum," and one of the most learned
divines of the day. The schism and its disastrous
results told even upon popular literature, and the
appointment of Cardinal Pietro di Luna as Pope at
Avignon inspired Eustache Deschamps, whom we
have had already occasion to mention. As a Frenchman and a Catholic he could not restrain his indignation, and composed a poem entitled, " Du Schisme de
l'Eglise qui est aujourd'hui moult troublée par la Lune."
The pun is a wretched one, no doubt, and the joke
in bad taste, but it is the honest, straightforward
expression of a true patriot. All the planets, all
the powers of heaven, says Deschamps, have had their
turn—

> " Mercure, Mars, Jupiter et Vénus,
> Et chalcun d'eux ensemble, le soulcil,
> Ont par longtemps régné, et Saturnus."

Now a fresh competitor arises, claiming absolute
power over the firmament ; the poet cannot conceal
his feelings of despair—

> " . . . . Tout périra : c'est mon opinion,
> Puisque je voy vouloir régner la Lune."

The protest of Eustache Deschamps availed naught

and Pietro di Luna was promoted under the name of
Benedict XIII.

We all remember the ingenious way in which
Montesquieu and Voltaire use fiction as a convenient
way of lashing the vices of their contemporaries and
denouncing the corruption which eats up society.
Honoré Bonnet, Prior of Salons in Provence, had
recourse to that style of composition, and in his
"Apparition de Maistre Jehan de Meung" he introduced the character of a Turk who takes upon
himself to lecture Christians, even popes and cardinals. Exempt of passions and of prejudices, completely disinterested in the things he sees around
him, during the course of a trip to Western Europe,
the stranger deplores the results of the schism ; he
feels that discussions on matters of faith arouse in
man all his worst passions—

> "Pour foy laisse père son fils
> Le frère son frère en péril,
> L'ami son ami mettre à mort."

As Luther was to do later on, our Saracen visits
Rome, and he plainly discovers there the source of all
the evils which afflict the Church. A general reform
is needed, and if the chair of St. Peter is not filled
by popular election, the faithful will decline to follow
unworthy leaders.

> "Mais je voy, le temps est venus,
> Qu'ils ne en seront plus créus ;
> Car li mondes voit per exprès
> Leurs oultrages et leurs excès."

One more person remains to be named in connection with the *French* expression of reform in matters

ecclesiastical, and that is Nicolas de Clémangis. A faithful churchman, as well as a staunch representative of the University of Paris, he denounced the corruption of the Church in a pamphlet ("De corruptione ecclesiæ") which, although written in Latin, is the utterance of a true Frenchman, and which brings before our eyes a faithful picture of France during the fifteenth century. Nicolas de Clémangis has often been regarded as a precursor of the reformers; he was really a Gallican of the school to which Bossuet afterwards belonged.

We see to what low estate France had sunk; it seemed as if she stood on the brink of a precipice, and the question was how she could recover her liberty, her unity, and her national existence.

XIII.

CHARLES VII.—END OF THE HUNDRED YEARS' WAR.

(1422–1461.)

THERE were two kings in France when the corpse of Charles VI. was lowered down into the grave at Saint Denis. The one, an infant nine months old, was grandson of the late monarch on his mother's side; his two uncles governed in his name, the Duke of Bedford, France; and the Duke of Gloucester, England. There seemed, at first, no opposition to Henry VI.; he had been acknowledged by the parliament, the university, the Duke of Burgundy, the Queen Isabelle of Bavaria, and the principal members of the nobility. His rule was obeyed in Paris, Ile de France, Picardy, Artois, Flanders, Champagne, and Normandy, that is to say, nearly all the provinces north of the Loire; in the South, Guienne owned his sway.

The other king, contemptuously designated as *the king of Bourges*, because he had been proclaimed in Berry, was the only surviving son of Charles VI., a young man of nineteen, graceful, but of a delicate constitution, a good scholar, timid, reserved, and too fond of pleasure. Touraine, Orléanais, Berry, Bour-

bonnais, Auvergne, Languedoc, Dauphiné, and Lyon-
nais were the only provinces which recognized his
authority. The reign of Charles VII. began in a
most disastrous manner, and the two successive
defeats endured by his troops, at Cravant (1423)
and at Verneuil (1424) seemed to prove that France
must now submit definitively to English rule.

The great advantage of Charles VII. was his
nationality ; the domination of foreigners might .be
endured, but it was detested by the majority of
Frenchmen, and the pride, the sternness with which
they exercised their authority became day by day
more hateful. A lively *chansonnier*, Olivier Basselin,
encouraged in spirited songs his countrymen to drive
the enemy out of the land :

> " Entre vous, genz de village,
> Qui aimez le roy Françoys,
> Prenez chacun bon courage,
> Pour combattre les Engloys.
> Prenez chascun une houe
> Pour mieux les desraciner.
>
> .   .   .   .   .   .
>
> Ne craignez point, allez battr
> Ces *godons* (*G-d d-n*), panches à poys (*paunches full of peas*),
> Car ung de nous en vault quatre,
> Au moins en vault-il bien troys."

Alain Chartier, another patriotic writer, exhorted
the clergy, the nobility, and the people to union as
the only resource for saving France. The Duke
d'Alençon made prisoner by the English at the
Battle of Verneuil, refused to purchase his liberty by
subscribing the clauses of the Treaty of Troyes. The
marriage of Charles VII. with Mary of Anjou had

attached to his cause not only that powerful family, but the house of Lorraine; the Count of Foix, Governor of Languedoc, declared that his conscience obliged him to recognize Charles VII. as the lawful king. The sword of constable given to Arthur de Richemont had had the effect of reconciling to the national cause Richemont's brother, John VI., Duke of Brittany. This was a most important result, for a number of valiant soldiers and distinguished captains belonging to that province followed, of course, in the same direction. Duguesclin's fellow-countrymen devoted to the service of France their courage and their heroism. By dismissing from his person, on Richemont's advice, Tanguy Duchâtel, and the other actors in the tragedy of the Bridge of Montereau, Charles VII. was paving the way towards his reconciliation with the Duke of Burgundy; Gloucester's imprudent conduct made this event more probable still. We must remember that if the English had become masters of Paris, and obtained the Treaty of Troyes, it was entirely owing to Philip the Good. The Duke of Bedford, Regent of France on behalf of Henry VI., knew this perfectly well, and accordingly made a point of keeping on the best terms with the Duke of Burgundy. Gloucester, on the contrary, by marrying Jacqueline, Countess of Holland, Hainault, and the neighbouring provinces, had become master of a district which Philip the Good was by no means disposed to see fall into the hands of a foreign prince.

These various circumstances all tended to strengthen the power of Charles VII. The provincial towns, on their part, were beginning to show signs of resistance to the English—Montargis, for instance, which commanded by La Faille, stood bravely a siege of three months. At the end of that time the garrison sent word to the king that they had neither provisions nor ammunition left. Dunois and La Hire started immediately at the head of sixteen hundred men intending to force their way into the town. As they were going along La Hire met a priest from whom he requested absolution. "Confess your sins, then," said the ecclesiastic. "I have no time to do so," was the answer, "for I am in a hurry to fall upon the English ; besides, I have done all that soldiers are wont to do." The chaplain having rather hesitatingly pronounced the sentence of absolution, La Hire knelt immediately by the wayside, and said aloud : "God, I pray Thee to do this day on La Hire's behalf what Thou wouldst that La Hire should do for Thee, supposing he was God and Thou wast La Hire." Having thus quieted his conscience, though in a somewhat uncanonical manner, he attacked the English and obliged them to raise the siege of Montargis.

Orléans was the city the possession of which must needs be of the highest consequence to the English, as being the key to Berry, Poitou, and Bourbonnais. Orléans once taken, nothing remained to "the king of Bourges" except Languedoc and Dauphiné. The next year, therefore (1428), the Duke of Bedford determined upon acting more vigorously than ever, and, at the head of an army of ten thousand men, part of whom had landed at Calais, under the command of Lord Salisbury, whilst the others belonged to the garrison of Normandy, he marched towards Orléans. On

18

his road he took Jargeau, Janville, Meung, Thoury, Beaugency, Marchenoir, and La Ferté Hubert. They arrived before the place on the 12th of October, 1428, and immediately set about building a series of forta- lices or small *bastiles*, the command of which was assigned to the most renowned captains, such as William de la Poole, Earl of Suffolk, Lord Talbot, and William Glasdale, who had sworn to put to death every man, woman, and child in Orléans. The su- preme direction was entrusted to the Earl of Salisbury.

The city must be saved at any cost ; Charles VII. appealed to the nobility and to the States-General. He obtained 100,000 crowns—a large sum indeed, considering the miserable condition to which France was reduced. The bravest *routiers*, Boussac, Dunois, Xaintrailles, La Hire placed themselves at the head of the garrison. The citizens, determined upon making a stout resistance, raised a municipal tax, and formed themselves into thirty-four companies, each of which undertook to defend one of the towers which stood out from the city walls. The suburbs were destroyed for fear of their getting into the power of the enemy. Artillery played a conspicuous part in the siege of Orléans ; that of the English was badly served, and excited the merriment of the besieged, who made fun of those eighty pound cannon balls which killed no one. The Orleanese, on the contrary, had excellent gunners, and each piece had its special part and particular duty. Some of the episodes connected with the siege are amusing. Here is one : At dinner time, one day, a lad, walking on the ramparts, found a

SIEGE OF ORLÉANS.

cannon ready loaded, and fired it. The ball killed the Earl of Salisbury, to whom William Glasdal: was at that very moment saying, " My lord, you see your city." The greater part of the winter thus passed. In February, however, a stratagem which might have saved Orléans was on the point of putting it in the possession of the English. The Count of Clermont, who was arriving to the assistance of the besieged with a powerful reinforcement, wished to carry off a convoy of herrings sent by the Duke of Bedford to the besiegers for the season of Lent. He unfortunately failed with the loss of between four and five hundred men. This " Battle of the Herrings " thoroughly disheartened the French. All their chief leaders gave up Orléans as hopelessly lost. The Count of Clermont retired, taking away with him the Chancellor, the Bishop of Orléans himself, La Hire, and two thousand men. An appeal was uselessly made to the Duke of Burgundy ; the Orleanese were themselves beginning to debate whether it was not better to live as subjects of the King of England than not to live at all. It was then that Joan of Arc appeared.

For some time an almost universal presentiment had spread that France was to be saved by a woman. The prophecies of Merlin said so, and to those prophecies the superstitious part of the population gave the utmost credence. Let us say a few words of the wonderful person whom heaven had destined to restore the nationality of France.

Joan was born at the small village of Domremy, in Lorraine, on the 6th of January, 1412. Her father's

JOAN OF ARC. (*Statue by Lefeuvre.*)

name was Jacques d'Arc, her mother's, Isabelle
Romée. It was a family of honest, hard-working
agriculturists, fearing God, and bringing up their
children with the utmost care. Joan grew up till the
age of thirteen surrounded by the best examples, at
spending her time in tending her father's flocks,
and, when indoors, in plying her distaff.

One summer's day, about the hour of noon, whilst
she was in the garden belonging to her father's cottage, she saw a brilliant light in the direction of the
church, and heard a voice saying to her, " Joan, be a
kind and good child ; go often to church." She was
thoroughly frightened. By and by she had visions;
the archangel Saint Michael, Saint Margaret, and
Saint Catherine conversed familiarly with her, and appeared to her accompanied by millions of angels.
" Joan," they said, " you must go to France." On one
occasion Saint Michael told her to go to the assistance
of the King of France, and restore to him his kingdom.
She answered, trembling : " My Lord, I am only a
poor girl, and I could neither ride nor take the command of men-at-arms." The voice continued : "You
must go to *maistre* Robert de Baudricourt, captain of
Vaucouleurs, and he will have you taken to the king ;
Saint Margaret and Saint Catherine will come to your
assistance."

For several years Joan resisted, frightened at the
idea of so new a mission, and disheartened by the
taunts of her father, who said to her that she had lost
her senses. One of her uncles, at last, allowing himself to be persuaded, accompanied her to Robert de
Baudricourt. The news of the distress of Orléans had

reached her, and her voices kept repeating : " Hasten! hasten ! " The captain of Vaucouleurs, in the first place, laughed at her. Nothing daunted, she exclaimed : " My lord captain, know that God, for some time, has made known unto me and ordered me on several occasions to go to the Dauphin who ought to be, and is, the true King of France ; he is to deliver unto me men-at-arms, with whom I shall raise the siege of Orléans, and take the king to Reims to be anointed." Baudricourt at last yielded. He gave Joan a sword and an escort, and dismissed her, without having much confidence in the success of her mission, saying : " Go, and happen what may ! "

On the 5th of March, 1429, about noon, Joan of Arc, dressed in military attire, entered the small town of Chinon, where Charles VII. happened to be. He gave her audience, but in order to put her to the test, he concealed himself amongst the lords and noblemen who formed his court. Led by her *voices*, she went straight up to him, and said : "God grant you a good life, noble prince." " I am not the king," answered Charles ; and, pointing to one of the lords present, who was richly dressed : " Here is the king." Joan, without allowing herself to be disconcerted, exclaimed : " In God's name, gentle prince, it is you who for a positive certainty are the king, and no one else.'' Charles then asked her her name, and what she wanted. "Gentle Dauphin,'' she answered, " my name is Joan the Maid (*La Pucelle*), and the King of heaven bids me tell you that you shall be anointed and crowned at Reims, and that you shall be lieutenant for the King of heaven, who is King of France." She then whispered to him a few words, at which Charles was very much astonished, and very joyous ; then, raising her voice, she added : " I tell you, in God's name, that you are the true heir of France, and son of the king."

Charles VII. was not yet completely satisfied, and he resolved to bring Joan of Arc before a committee of clergymen and theologians, who should put to her a variety of questions in order to test the validity of her mission, and to make quite sure of her orthodoxy. This tedious and puerile examination lasted some time, and having proved satisfactory, the next thing was to equip the " maiden " for her venturesome expedition. La Hire and Xaintrailles, two of the most distinguished generals on the royalist side, were to accompany her to Orléans at the head of a convoy of provisions and ammunition. She wanted a weapon, and her *voices* revealed to her that in the church of Saint Catherine of Fierbois there was behind the altar a sword of which the hilt was marked with five crosses. The indication proved perfectly correct, and from that day Joan of Arc never parted with that sword, although she did not use it, not willing, she said, to kill any person. She further procured a white standard.adorned with gold *fleurs-de-lys ;* on one side was the representation of the Almighty in a cloud, at His feet two angels, with the inscriptions—*Jésus, Marie ;* the other side gave the escutcheon of France supported by two angels. Another standard, of smaller size, which she caused to be made at the same time, represented an angel offering a lily to the blessed Virgin.

Joan of Arc's small army was a perfect contrast to the lawless, brutal, and fierce *écorcheurs* and *routiers* which at that time devastated not only France, but the whole of Europe. It was preceded by a group of priests singing hymns ; the main body consisted of adventurers and *ribauds* whom *La Pucelle's* influence had quite transformed. No swearing was allowed,

MEDAL OF JOAN OF ARC.

and this for La Hire had all the character of a downright privation. Pitying his distress she allowed him to swear " by his staff" (*par son bâton*).

The expedition arrived under the walls of Orléans on

the 29th of April, 1429. Dunois came to meet Joan, and introduced her into the town, with her convoy and her men-at-arms. The inhabitants received her with great demonstrations of enthusiasm.

The siege of Orléans had lasted seven months already; in ten days Joan of Arc raised it. One of the English *bastiles* was named Rouen, another Paris, and a third, London. How humiliating for the besiegers to have to abandon positions bearing such proud designations! But it must needs be done. Orléans once delivered, Joan of Arc went to join the king at Tours, and urged him to march at once with his army towards Reims, where the ceremony of consecration was to take place. " I shall not live much more than one year from hence; we must think of toiling hard, for there is much to be done." A start was made, and of the most brilliant kind; Jargeau, Meung-sur-Loire, and Beaugency were taken from the English. On the 18th of June a decisive victory was won at Patay, between Orléans and Châteaudun, in which Talbot and several English captains of distinction were taken prisoners. No serious obstacle now stood in the way of Charles VII. After a two days' siege Troyes was carried; a few days later the Bishop of Châlons brought to the king the keys of that city. Finally, on the 16th of July, 1429, Charles entered Reims, having by his side Joan of Arc, who carried her standard; the ceremony of the coronation was fixed for the 17th, which happened to be a Sunday.

The situation of the Duke of Bedford had become rather difficult. The national sentiment was thoroughly roused in France; not only had the English given up all hope of conquering the districts of the centre, they were beginning to lose their possessions in the northern provinces ; the towns of Crécy, Provins, Coulommiers, and Château-Thierry had driven away the foreign garrisons. Encouraged by this awakening of patriotism, the generals of Charles marched towards Paris, and attacked the gate of St. Honoré ; unsuccessful there, they fell back in the direction of Compiègne, which they took after a protracted siege. This was to be the last step in the career of the Maid of Orléans. She had lately been repeatedly warned by her *voices* that she was to be captured before the festival of St. John, but how and when she knew not. One day, after hearing mass and taking the holy communion, she said to those who surrounded her : " My children and dear friends, I warn you that I have been sold and betrayed. I shall soon be put to death ; I entreat and beseech you to pray God for me."

It was during a sally headed by **La Pucelle** that the fatal event took place. Either by mistake or by treason, the drawbridge was raised before she could re-enter the town, and she was seized by about twenty soldiers. She surrendered to a knight of the household of the Duke of Burgundy. In spite of an appeal made by the University of Paris, Joan was given up to the English for the sum of 10,000 livres, and a judge was appointed to try her. The person selected for that wretched task was a certain Pierre Cauchon, Bishop of Beauvais, a great champion of the English and of the Bourguignons. He had taken an active part in the excesses of the *Cabochians*, and had caused himself to be named judge to try the Armagnac clergy. For

this piece of zeal he had been rewarded with a bishopric
by the Duke of Burgundy, and now he was resolved
to curry favour with the English by putting Joan of
Arc to death. It was, to all intents and purposes, a
foregone conclusion ; the trial had taken place at
Rouen, the sentence that the unfortunate heroine
should be burnt alive was carried out on the 30th of
May, 1431. Twenty-four years later, at the request of
Charles VII., Pope Calixtus III. ordered the trial to

STATUE OF JOAN OF ARC.

be revised, and on the 7th of July, 1456, the rehabili-
tation of the Maid of Orléans was solemnly proclaimed.
The situation of the English had not improved by this
tragic event ; King Henry VI. was crowned indeed
at Paris (December 17, 1431), but this ceremony
created a great deal of dissatisfaction amongst the
people. Why was the officiating priest an Englishman, the Cardinal of Winchester, and not a French-

man? Why did not *one* single French lord attend? Why did not the usual acts of kindness and royal generosity follow upon the coronation, such as liberation of prisoners, remission of taxes, money gratuities? Then the Duke of Burgundy was getting weary of his foreign allies; he had had to put up with their haughtiness and their pretensions. Notwithstanding the signal services he had rendered them, he had never received from them the slightest assistance in his times of distress and of embarrassment. All these circumstances were cleverly turned to use by the Constable de Richemont, whose talents as a politician were fully equal to his courage; and the only thing which prevented Philip the Good from breaking off his alliance with the English was a kind of chivalrous *point d'honneur* he felt bound to respect.

Meanwhile a general conference took place at Arras with the view of considering the terms of a truce, or possibly a permanent peace. All the European states sent representatives—the Pope, the emperor, the kings of Navarre, Castile, Arragon, Portugal, Sicily, Naples, Cyprus, Poland, Denmark; the large towns, the University of Paris had their delegates. The King of France was represented by Constable de Richemont and eighteen lords; the King of England by the Cardinal of Winchester and a large number of barons; the Duke of Burgundy appeared in person.

The English were the first to state their pretensions. They wanted merely a *truce* and the marriage of Henry VI. with a daughter of Charles VII. The French ambassadors, however, declared that their mission was expressly to conclude a *peace*, and they insisted upon the King of England giving up his pretended rights to the French crown and to all the provinces which he occupied on the Continent. These terms were contemptuously rejected, and on the 1st of September the English delegates announced their intention of leaving the assembly and returning to England. The Pope's envoys took the opportunity of renewing their entreaties with the Duke of Burgundy, and this prince, already more than half disposed to give way, was determined by the news he received—(1) of the death of the Duke of Bedford at Chantereine, near Rouen ; (2) of the approaching end of the old queen, Isabelle of Bavaria. Considering himself as relieved, by this twofold event, from his former engagements, he signed the treaty of Arras (1436), independently of the English. The conditions were both onerous and humiliating for Charles VII., who had, in the first place, to disown the murder of John the Fearless, and to make a kind of *amende honorable ;* and, in the next, to give over to the Duke of Burgundy the countships of Auxerre, Mâcon, several towns on the Somme, besides 400,000 gold crowns. On the other hand, he new had Paris, and that was an ample compensation for the rest. The citizens called in the Constable de Richemont, and opened to him the gates of Saint Jacques on the 29th of May, 1436. Lord Willoughby and the fifteen thousand English soldiers who defended Paris shut themselves up within the Bastile. They would have been a rich booty if it had only been possible to reach them, for the number of noblemen who composed the main force of that army could not have got off without paying a heavy ransom; but Richemont could not undertake the siege of the fortress for want of ammunition, artillery, &c. He had therefore to accept the terms offered by the enemy, to wit, that they might retire with all their goods and effects, accompanied by those who had cast in their lot with them. On that condition they gave up the Bastile to the French, left Paris by the gate of Saint Antoine, embarked on the Seine, and retired to Rouen.

The first part of the reign of Charles VII. may be said to end here. His moral character had never been particularly severe, and to the end he indulged his passions very freely. His *liaison* with Agnès Sorel is a case in point, and although this episode has been ridiculously exaggerated, yet it has doubtless a foundation in fact. But whereas, up to the year 1436, he had shown himself careless, indolent, and neglectful of his duties, he now, thanks to age and experience combined, really played the part of a king, and sought the advice of good and trustworthy councillors. His wife, Marie d'Anjou, and his mother-in-law, Yolande, had always enjoyed much influence over him. Jean Bureau, Master of the Artillery, the banker (*argentier*) Jacques Cœur, Etienne Chevalier, who was secretary to the king, Guillaume Cousinot, Master of Requests, may be named amongst the most notable of his advisers. Pierre and Jean de Brézé, Xaintrailles, La Hire, Chabannes, and Dunois served him on the battle-field. Let us notice that all the persons we have just named belonged either to the *bourgeoisie* or to the *petite noblesse*; the Constable, Count de Richemont, was the only real nobleman in the king's council, and he had been equally active against the monarch's favourites and against the English.

The entry of Charles VII. in Paris took place with a great deal of pomp and ceremony. The king only remained three weeks there, and started for the southern provinces, where he had to encounter the English on several occasions. He wrested from them Marmande, Dax, Saint Sever, La Réole, Tartas, Blaye, and received the homage of some of the principal lords in Languedoc and Guienne. The previous year he had made a campaign in the Eastern districts, and distinguished himself at the siege of Pontoise.

The first year's truce (1444–49) had come to an end, and France was in a condition to resume hostilities with great chances of success. The royal forces invaded Normandy, and occupied the whole of that province after two campaigns, crowned by the battle of Formigny (1450). Dunois then marched into Guienne, and made himself master of Bordeaux and Bayonne (1451). Two years later the English, willing to retrieve their disasters, made a fresh attempt south of the Garonne, and succeeded at first; but the death of Talbot, killed at the battle of Castillon (1453), was a fatal blow struck at the invaders. Charles VII. entered Bordeaux in triumph on the 19th of October, 1453. The Hundred Years' War was thus finished, and the English retained in France merely Calais and two small towns in the neighbourhood.

The enemies thus subdued, the time had come at last for introducing into France a thorough system of reforms, and for reorganizing the administration of the kingdom. The state of the army required the king's earliest care, and the energy with which he went to work proved that he felt the gravity of the situation. His first attempt was made nearly twenty years before the battle of Castillon, and it resulted in a civil war. Charles VII. assembled the States-General at Orléans in October, 1439, and obtained from them a subsidy of 1,200,000 livres, which was to be raised by means of a permanent tax. The object of this subsidy was to pay a regular body of *gendarmerie*, thus placing the armed forces of the realm under the king's immediate authority, and crippling the power of the feudal lords. So bold a measure incensed, as may well be supposed, both the aristocracy and also the *écorcheurs*, who saw their occupation entirely gone. They rose against the king, and selected as their leader the Dauphin Louis, who was destined to be, when on the throne, the most energetic opponent of the system he now undertook to support. This rebellion was called the *Praguerie*, by allusion to the revolt of the Hussites of Prague, in Germany, and it brought together, by a singular contrast, both the *élite* of the nobility, such as the Dukes of Bourbon and of Alençon, the Counts of Dunois and of Vendôme, on the one side, and, on the other, the principal leaders of the *routiers*, Antoine and Jacques de Chabannes, for instance, the bastard of Bourbon, Jean de la Roche, and Jean Sanglier. Charles VII., however, had no difficulty in

suppressing this insurrection. He had on his side, at
once, all the middle classes, the *bourgeoisie* and
the common people. A few measures of severity
frightened the rebels, and when they saw the Count
de Saint Pol sewed in a sack and thrown into the
river, they understood that this was no joking matter.
The Dauphin thought better of the false step he had
taken, and the Duke of Burgundy felt the necessity
of keeping quiet. Two expeditions, the one in
Switzerland and the other of Lorraine, disposed of
the remainder of the *écorcheurs*, and the king was at
last able to carry out the scheme of reform sketched
out in the *Ordonnance d'Orléans*. In 1445 the French
army was reduced to fifteen companies of one hundred
lances, each lance including the man-at-arms, his page,
three archers, and one inferior retainer (*coutillier*), all
mounted. They did garrison duty in the principal
towns, and the most important of them having
only twenty or at the outside thirty lances, the
citizens were numerically stronger than the soldiers,
and therefore able to repress any disorder which
might arise. Strange to say, the old *routiers* were
very anxious to belong to those *compagnies d'ordonnance*, and vacancies were immediately filled. Charles
VII. had thus at his disposal a body of nine thousand
picked cavalry, and those *routiers* who could find no
occupation were compelled to return to their own
homes, under threat of severe punishment, if they
disturbed the public peace.

Three years later (1448) another royal decree provided for the organization of the French infantry.
Every one of the 16,000 parishes of which the king-

dom consisted was bound to supply a foot soldier
properly armed and accoutred, who was to undergo a
military, training every *fête*-day and serve the king,
whenever required to do so, for a pay of four francs a
month when on duty, besides being exempted from
certain of the taxes. These *francs-archers* could not
be expected to be at the outset accomplished soldiers,
and the witty poet Villon made great fun of them in
one of his amusing pieces—

" Ya-t-il homme, qui à quatre (=*avec ses quatre valets*)
   Dy-je, ya-t-il quatre qui veuillent
   Combatre à moy? si tost recueillent (=*qu'ils relèvent de suite*)
   Mon gantelet ; velà (=*voilà*) pour gaige !
   Par le sang-bieu ! je ne crains paige,
   S'il n'a point plus de quatorze ans.
   J'ay autresfoys tenu les rencz,
   Dieu mercy ! et gaigné le prix
   Contre cinq Angloys que je pris,
   Povres prisonniers desnuez (=*dépouillés de leurs armes et de leurs habits*)
   Si tost que je les euz ruez (=*jetés par terre*).
   Ce fut au siège d'Alençon. "

The *Franc-archer de Bagnolet*, who boasts of having
made five English soldiers prisoners at the siege of
Alençon, and who is almost frightened to death by a
scare-scrow, is a kind of French Falstaff, but we need.
not take him as a fair specimen of the body to which
he belonged ; in a few years he will become as brave
as Dunois himself, and his descendants will hold their
own on all the battle-fields of Europe.

Financial reforms were quite as urgent as military
ones. On the 25th of December, 1453, Charles VII.,
acting on the advice of Jacques Cœur, his *argentier*, or
Chancellor of the Exchequer, introduced an order which

PORTRAIT OF JACQUES CŒUR.

· provided for the better management of the finances
(1) by submitting to a mutual control the various
officers and boards or committees entrusted with the
assessment and collecting of the taxes; and (2) by giving
a permanent character to these taxes, so far at least
as the Langued'oil districts were concerned. Languedoc, Dauphiné, and the provinces south of the
Loire continued to vote the taxes in their provincial
assemblies (*états*), hence the name of *pays d'états*
which they had by opposition to the *pays d'élection*
where the subsidies were collected by the agents
(*élus*) of the government. This wise reform raised
the revenues of the state to 2,300,000 livres.

The institution of a parliament at Toulouse (1443),
and of another at Grenoble (1453), and the idea partly
carried out of compiling a code of the custom-laws
(*coutumes*) in use throughout the kingdom, are due likewise to Charles VII., and must not be forgotten. In
the meanwhile the taking of Constantinople by the
Turks (1453) excited great emotion throughout
Christendom, and it was thought that the Duke of
Burgundy would take the command of a new Crusade
against the infidels. The days of faith and Christian fervour, however, had passed away. During the˙
Middle Ages fasting and penance would have been
deemed the only fit preparation for so serious an
enterprise; now, instead of fasting, there was ban-
queting, and instead of penance there were jousts and
tournaments. On second thoughts it appeared that
Mahomet II. threatened only the German Empire ;
accordingly the idea of a Crusade which Philip the
Good had never seriously entertained, was given up.

The feudal system was in the last throes of agony, but its turbulent representative, the Duke of Burgundy, did his best to keep it alive and to raise up enemies against Charles VII. Amongst the nobles thus encouraged in their rebellious course were the Duke d'Alençon and the Count d'Armagnac. They were both arrested and condemned, the former to prison for life, the latter to exile (1456, 1455). The Dauphin Louis, sent by his father into the domains which belonged to him by virtue of his title, carried on his political intrigues with such energy and such impudence that Charles VII., besides sending against him Antoine de Chabannes with a body of troops, marched towards Lyons with a second army. Frightened by this promptness, Louis fled into the estates of the Duke of Burgundy, who received him with every possible honour, but refused him the military assistance he would fain have obtained against his father. Louis, however, succeeded so thoroughly in frightening Charles VII., that the wretched King of France, weakened, besides, by his indulgences and his excesses, fancied that the Dauphin wanted to poison him, and he starved himself to death (July 22, 1461).

The cowardly manner in which Joan of Arc was given up to the English, and the condemnation of the *argentier*, Jacques Cœur, are two actions which have done much harm to the reputation of Charles VII. Jacques Cœur had originally been a simple tradesman. Voyages on the further side of the Alps and in the Levant had revealed to him the secret of the prosperity which distinguished the great commercial cities of Italy. Following their example, he went to Syria and to Egypt, brought from thence all the produce of the East, and had a fleet of his own. Charles VII., who had known him at Bourges, named him his *argentier royal,* and for the space of twelve years he took a prominent part in all the most important affairs of the government. His motto was : "*à vaillant cœur rien d'impossible.*" Distinguished above all others by the clearness of his mind and his severe probity, he always contrived to face the financial difficulties by which he was surrounded, and drew from his own resources, when the national exchequer was empty. Thus he advanced to Charles VII. 200,000 crowns (24,000,000 francs of the present coinage) wherewith to conquer Normandy. "Sire," said he, " all that I possess belongs to you." The courtiers took him at his word, brought him before the judges on a calumnious charge of malversation, divided his fortune amongst themselves, and caused him to be kept a prisoner in a convent at Beaucaire. His late clerks, however, succeeded in getting him out by main force, and took him to Rome where he was most honourably received by the Pope (1455). He died in the next year from a wound received at Chios in a fight against the Turks. Another *financier,* Jean de, Xaincoings, had been, during the previous year, condemned quite as severely, and quite as unfairly. The death of Charles VII. caused throughout France a great deal of sorrow. Having started from Meung-sur-Loire, the royal cortège reached Paris on the 5th of August, and the funereal ceremony took place on the 8th, at Saint Denis. As the corpse was lowered into the grave, a herald-at-arms, lowering his mace, exclaimed

"God have in His holy keeping the soul of Charles VII., the most victorious king"; then, after a moment's silence, he added, "Long live the King!" and the crowd shouted out: "Long live King Louis!"

XIV.

LOUIS XI.
(1461-1483.)

IT seemed, at the accession of Louis XI., that the day for feudalism had come at last. Were not all the antecedents of Louis XI. a pledge that he would restore to the nobility their privileges, their influence, their political authority? Was he not the intimate friend of the Duke of Burgundy, than whom no prince was so completely identified with the feudal system? All these hopes were in the most unexpected manner doomed to be frustrated; after having lost the judicial power under Philip the Fair and his sons, and the military prestige during the Hundred Years' War, the nobles were now about to be shorn of their political greatness.

The houses or families with which the struggle must be carried on were those of Anjou, Brittany, and Burgundy. The first included, besides Anjou itself, Provence, Maine, and Lorraine, provinces too far apart from each other to be able to undertake a combined action against the king. Further, the chief of that house was at that time "good King René," a prince more engrossed by art and poetry

KING RENÉ.

JEANNE DE LAVAL.

than by politics. The population, under the rule of the Duke of Brittany had the decided advantage of being bound together by a community of traditions and laws, but they were too poor to venture upon a war which must necessarily involve a considerable expenditure, even supposing the issues were favourable to them.

Remained the formidable house of Burgundy, formidable in appearance, and ruling over territories which were as rich as they were extensive. Burgundy, Franche Comté, Picardy, Artois, Flanders, the countships of Auxerre and Mâcon, Bar-sur-Seine, Ponthieu, Bourbonnais, the towns on the Somme and all the cities of the Netherlands—such were the chief constituent parts of the duchy then governed by Philip the Good.

Besides those three houses we must take into account the *apanages* granted to the younger sons, and which represented distinct feudatory establishments (Bourbon, Alençon, Courtenai, Armagnac, &c.).

There is no doubt that if the numerous provinces composing the Duchy of Burgundy had been strongly knit together, the task of bringing them under submission would have been a most severe one ; but the chance of wars and of treaties had made them part of the same body, not national affinities ; they were not really united together, and Flanders, for instance, was only awaiting a favourable opportunity to recover its independence.

The King of France, who had now to cope with all these forces, has been so accurately described and appreciated by Commines, Sir Walter Scott, and M.

Victor Hugo, that rather than attempt to place before our readers a fresh portrait, we feel it safer to quote from the pages of one of these distinguished writers.

"Brave enough for several useful and political purposes," says the author of "Quentin Durward," "Louis had not a spark of that romantic valour, or of the pride generally associated with it, which fought on for the point of honour, when the point of utility had been long gained. Calm, crafty, and profoundly attentive to his own interest, he made every sacrifice, both of pride and passion, which could interfere with it. He was careful in disguising his real sentiments and purposes from all who approached him, and frequently used the expressions, 'that the king knew not how to reign who knew not how to dissemble ; and that, for himself, if he thought his very cap knew his secrets, he would throw it into the fire.' No man of his own, or of any other time, better understood how to avail himself of the frailties of others, and when to avoid giving any advantage by the untimely indulgences of his own."

"He was by nature vindictive and cruel, even to the extent of finding pleasure in the frequent executions which he commanded. But, as no touch of mercy ever induced him to spare, when he could with safety condemn, so no sentiment of vengeance ever stimulated him to a premature violence. He seldom sprung on his prey till it was fairly within his grasp, and till all hope of rescue was vain ; and his movements were so studiously disguised, that his success was generally what first announced to the world the object he had been manœuvring to attain."

"In like manner, the avarice of Louis gave way to apparent profusion, when it was necessary to bribe the favourite or minister of a rival prince for averting any impending attack, or to break up any alliance confederated against him. He was fond of license and pleasure; but neither beauty nor the chase, though both were ruling passions, ever withdrew him from the most regular attendance to public business and the affairs of his kingdom. His knowledge of mankind was profound, and he had sought it in the private walks of life, in which he often personally mingled; and, though naturally proud and haughty, he hesitated not, with an inattention to the arbitrary divisions of society which was then thought something portentously unnatural, to raise from the lowest rank men whom he employed on the most important duties, and knew so well how to choose them, that he was rarely disappointed in their qualities."

The whole life of Louis XI. was a perfect illustration of Sir Walter Scott's portrait of him; the ceremony of his coronation which took place as usual at Reims, August 18, 1461, drew together all the high barons who reckoned upon a speedy restoration of the feudal system. The Duke of Burgundy, surrounded by his vassals, took the lead as premier peer of the realm; but when he asked the king forgiveness for all those who might have offended him when he was Dauphin, Louis granted the request with the exception of eight persons whose names he would not let be known.

The entire administration of the state was altered; the advisers of Charles VII. were dismissed, and

replaced by men sprung from the lowest classes of
society; his physician, Fumée; his cook, Pierre des
Habilités; his barber, Olivier le Daim, nicknamed
Olivier le Diable; and Tristan L'Hermite, whom he
familiarly designated as his *confrère*, were the persons
honoured with his confidence. This measure created
a great deal of irritation, and several hasty and imprudent attempts at reform made about the same
time heightened the general discontent. The people
had expected a remission of taxes on account of the
coronation; instead of this they were raised from
1,800,000 livres to 3,000,000, and a riot having taken
place at Reims, Louis ordered several of the *bourgeois*
to be hung, and some to have their ears cut off. The
university of Paris, and the Parliaments were not
better treated; the power of the Church was reduced
and its privileges curtailed.

The nobles, equally disappointed and irritated, were
seeking an opportunity of making Louis XI. feel
their power, when the important purchase of the
cities of the Somme made by the king from the Duke
of Burgundy afforded them the pretext they required.
The son of Philip the Good, the Count de Charolais,
so celebrated afterwards under the name of Charles
the Bold, considered this bargain as unfairly forced
upon an old man taken by surprise; he, himself, had
private grievances against the king, and was eager to
try conclusions with him. Such was the origin of
what has been called "the league of the common
weal" (*ligne du Bien public*). Louis XI., by way of
counteracting it, published a manifesto addressed to
the citizens of the "good towns," and to all the

kingdom ; this document was favourably received in
Dauphiné, Auvergne, and Languedoc, and in most of
the large centres of population. The Paris *bourgeoisie*,
amongst others, prepared for a vigorous defence.   In
the meanwhile, the army of the League commanded
by the Count of Charolais, had mustered at Saint
Denis ; it consisted of about fourteen hundred men-at-
arms, and eight thousand archers. After having taken
possession of some of the neighbouring villages, the
count made a fruitless attempt to enter the capital,
and finally met the king's army at Montlhéry (July
16, 1465).   The battle was fought with much spirit
on both sides, but the royal troops re-entered Paris,
and Louis immediately began negotiations which led
to the treaties of Conflans (October 5th) with Charles
the Bold, and of Saint Maur (October 29th) with the
confederate princes.   By virtue of these two agree-
ments, the king made to his enemies the most extraordinary concessions, firmly resolved, at the same
time, upon setting them at nought on the very earliest
opportunity.   This was destined to happen soon ; a
quarrel broke out between the Duke of Brittany and
the Duke of Normandy, and Louis XI. immediately
invaded this latter province with the view of restoring
it once again to the authority of the Crown.   This
was a distinct violation of the treaty of Conflans, but
it was sanctioned by the States-General summoned at
Tours on the 1st of April, 1468 ; so the king, backed
by the nation, ventured at once to propose to the
King of England the invasion of Picardy, one of the
domains of Charles the Bold.   We say Charles the
Bold, for Philip the Good had died suddenly, and the

PHILIP THE GOOD AND CHARLES THE BOLD.

dangerous task of thwarting the views and defeating
the intrigues of the King of France now devolved
upon a rash and turbulent prince, " who," to use the
words of Sir Walter Scott, "rushed on danger, because
he loved it, and on difficulties because he despised
them. As Louis never sacrificed his interest to his
passion, so Charles, on the other hand, never sacrificed
his passion, nor even his humour, to any other consideration."

Meanwhile, what had been the result of the boasted
ligue du bien public? merely the enriching of certain
lords bent, as the historian Commines says, upon
getting out of the monarch all they could, and
plundering the kingdom. No wonder that Louis XI.
wanted to have his revenge, but Charles the Bold
hearing of the treacherous proposal made by him to
the King of England, wrote to him a most impertinent
letter, full of threats, and lacking the simplest
forms of courtesy, especially taking into consideration
the fact that it was addressed by a vassal to his liege
lord. What was to be done? Count Dammartin
and the rest of the officers were for violent measures.
" In God's name," they said, " if we are only allowed
to have our own way, we shall soon bring that
Duke of Burgundy to his senses ! The king makes
a sheep of himself, and bargains for his fleece and his
very skin, as if he had not wherewith to protect himself ! 'Sdeath ! in his place we had rather venture
the whole kingdom than allow ourselves to be led
about in this fashion ! "

Louis, however, as he was wont, preferred negotiating, and it was settled that an interview should take

place at Péronne, a town situated on Burgundian
territory. Was this a snare ? Some persons thought
so, but the king would now allow himself to be dis-
suaded, and went to meet the Duke of Burgundy,
who received him most cordially, embraced him, and
led him to the castle, where lodgings had been prepared for his reception. "Now," says Commines, "when
he came to Péronne, the king had forgotten that he
had some time before sent two ambassadors for the
purpose of exciting the inhabitants of Liège against
the duke. These ambassadors had so well succeeded
that a great revolt had taken place, and the Liegese
had already captured the city of Tongres."

The rage of the Duke of Burgundy can easily be
imagined ; at the very time when Louis came to treat
of the conditions of peace, was he thus plotting against
him, and sowing the seeds of rebellion amongst his
own subjects ? The first step he took was to make
quite sure that it would be impossible for his rival
to escape. When Louis XI., thus made prisoner,
began to consider that he was shut up in the same
tower, where in days gone by, the Count of Vermandois
had put to death Charles the Simple, he could not
help fearing lest the same destiny was in reserve for
him ; however, the Duke of Burgundy, though excited
by many of his advisers to use the most violent
measures against the king, was satisfied with making
a new treaty with him, obliging him to the humiliating
condition of helping to reduce the Liegese into submission. On these terms Louis recovered his liberty ;
he entered Liège wearing the cross of Saint Andrew
of Burgundy on his cap, and shouting *Vive Bourgogne*

as loud as he could, to the great amazement of the inhabitants. The whole affair having come to an end, he was allowed " to depart wherever he wished to go, after having spent the three most anxious weeks of his life."

The Péronne incident could not fail to excite French wit, and to supply food for that satirical spirit which has always been such a distinguishing feature amongst the Parisians; the picture shops were full of caricatures referring to Péronne, the little children went about the streets singing a *complainte* about Péronne ; magpies, jackdaws, and other talking birds cried out Péronne ! Péronne ! The magistrates had to interfere. The children were whipped ; the owners of satirical birds threatened with condign punishment ; finally, it was forbidden under penalty of being hung, to sing or compose satires, *virelais*, rondeaux, ballads, or libels casting opprobrium upon our lord the king.

Scarcely had he returned to France than Louis XI. sought for a convenient opportunity of tearing to shreds the treaty of Péronne, and resuming hostilities ; but, in the first place, he endeavoured to win over to his side the chief allies of Charles the Bold, and principally his own brother, Charles, Duke de Berry. These negotiations, however, had produced no result, when an unforeseen circumstance proved to Louis that he was betrayed by a person in whom he had placed all his confidence, namely, Cardinal Balue. The unfortunate prelate had to appear before the king, together with the Bishop of Verdun, his accomplice ; obliged to confess their secret machinations, they were shut up separately in iron cages—the cardinal at

Onzain, near Blois, and the bishop at the Bastile Saint Antoine. They remained prisoners for more than ten years.

This event hastened the reconciliation of Louis XI. with his brother ; the latter consented to an agreement which procured for him as an *apanage* Guienne, Agenois, Périgord, Quercy, Saintonge, and Aunis, with the title of Duke de Guienne. Charles was thus relegated to the South of France, and withdrawn from the influence of the Duke of Burgundy.

Urged on by the Count de Saint Pol, solemnly released by the States-General from all obligation to keep the treaty of Péronne, emboldened by the state of England, by the strength of his own armies, and his desire of vengeance, Louis now resolved upon renewing hostilities. In the first instance, he summoned Charles the Bold to appear before him at Ghent ; furious, disconcerted, warned besides by the Duke de Bourbon, my Lord of Burgundy assembled an army in all haste, and marched into Picardy ; Roye, Montdidier, Amiens, Saint Quentin, were taken by the French. Vainly did he write to France and to England for the purpose of bribing soldiers and politicians into his service. He re-crossed the Seine, burnt Picquigny to the ground, failed in his endeavour to take Amiens, was obliged to submit, and ended by signing a truce in April, 1471.

Charles the Bold, following the example of his rival, reckoned upon the power of intrigues to make up for his military failures in the north. He employed all his skill in detaching from the crown of France the most influential lords of the realm, especially the

Duke de Guienne. This prince had remained faithful to his brother so long as he thought that he was
heir apparent to the throne ; but Louis having had a
son by his second wife, Charlotte of Savoy, these
hopes were dashed to the ground, and henceforth the
little court of Bordeaux became the *rendezvous* of all
the disaffected ; the plan of a new league was even
freely discussed.   Louis XI. heard of it, and felt that
the kingdom was in the most critical position.   The
question of dismembering the monarchy and re-
establishing the feudal system still pre-occupied
Charles the Bold.   " I am so eager for the good of
the kingdom of France," said he, " that instead of one
king there, I should like to see half-a-dozen."
" English, Bretons, Bourguignons," exclaimed others
in his presence," are going to hunt the king, and if
he should undertake anything against the Duke de
Guienne, we shall set such a pack of hounds after
him that he won't know which way to escape."
   It is not surprising that Louis XI. should have been
accused of getting rid of his brother by poison, so
timely did the death of that prince occur for the
king's purposes (May 24, 1472), but there is nothing
whatever to prove the crime, and the reputation of a
somewhat unscrupulous politician is, in this particular
case, blameless.   Of course, Charles the Bold did not
scruple to charge the king with the crime of fratricide,
and he sent throughout his own domains, and to
several French towns, a manifesto, in which he
affirmed that the Duke de Guienne's death had been
" procured by poison, malefices, witchcraft, and
diabolical inventions."   Very few people credited

this, and Charles the Bold made of it a pretext to
invade Picardy, where he committed all sorts of
excesses. He then marched into Normandy, where he
reckoned upon meeting the Duke of Brittany ; but he
was stopped under the walls of Beauvais by a most
unlooked-for resistance on the part of the inhabitants.
Even the women took an important share in defending the town ; they had as their leader a young girl,
Jeanne Fouquet by name, and who subsequently
was called Jeanne *Hachette*, by allusion to the weapon
with which she defended herself. After a siege of
twenty-four days, Charles the Bold gave up the
attempt, and continued his march towards Normandy.

Louis XI. was watching closely all the movements
of his enemy ; he wrote to Dammartin the following
letter : " Keep well the city of Compiègne, it is a good
place ; dismantle those which cannot be held, in order
that the men-at-arms may not lose their time before
them. If it please God and our Lady, we shall soon
recover all. *Monsieur le Grand Maître*, I request you
to bethink yourself of the means of striking a good
blow on the Duke of Burgundy, if you can advanta-
geously do so. I hope, on my side, to do such dili-
gence, that you will see that if I have stayed a long
time here, I have not been idle ; I believe that, please
God, I shall soon have done, and I mean to go and
help you yonder."

In spite of his wish to hold his ground in Normandy,
Charles the Bold was soon obliged to return to Artois
and Picardy, where the constable had it all his own
way. Louis XI. took this opportunity of proposing a
general truce, and negotiations were begun ; they were

protracted, however, for nearly a year, and it was only at the end of 1473 that the rivals came to an understanding.

The Duke of Burgundy, thus free on the French side, attempted new conquests in the direction of Switzerland. This fresh enterprise was not attended with success ; defeated at Granson (March 3, 1476), and at Morat (June 22nd), he was killed in a battle under the walls of Nancy (January 5, 1477). The following quotation from Commines is interesting :

" By this every one may see into what a deplorable condition this poor duke had brought himself by his contempt of good counsel. Both armies being joined, the Duke of Burgundy's forces having been twice beaten before, and, by consequence, weak and dispirited, and ill provided besides, were quickly broken and entirely defeated : many saved themselves and got off ; the rest were either taken or killed, and, among them, the Duke of Burgundy himself was killed on the spot. One Monsieur Claude, of Baurmont, captain of the castle of Dier, in Lorraine, killed the Duke of Burgundy. Finding his army routed, he mounted a swift horse, and, endeavouring to swim a little river in order to make his escape, his horse fell with him and overset him : the duke cried out for quarter to this gentleman who was pursuing him ; but he, being deaf, and not hearing him, immediately killed and stripped him, not knowing who he was, and left him naked in the ditch, where his body was found the next day after the battle ; which the Duke of Lorraine (to his eternal honour) buried with great pomp and magnificence in St. George's Church, in the old town of Nancy, him-

GATE OF THE PALACE, NANCY.

self and all his nobility, in great mourning, attending
the corpse to the grave. The following epitaph was
sometime afterwards engraved on his tomb:

'Carolus hoc busto, Burgundæ gloria gentis
Conditur, Europæ qui fuit ante timor.'"

The death of Charles the Bold seemed the breaking
up of the feudal system : all the baronial houses gave
way in succession, and ruin struck down the proud
lords who had for so many years threatened the crown
of France. The Duke d'Alençon was amongst the
first. Condemned to death by Charles VII. for having
treated with the English, he had obtained that the
fatal sentence should be commuted for one of im-
prisonment for life. Released by Louis XI., he had then
joined in all the conspiracies against that monarch, and
rendered himself guilty of heinous crimes ; the king
ordered his arrest and his trial (1473-1474) ; he was
detained in prison till his death.

John V., Count d'Armagnac, deserved capital
punishment far more than the Duke d'Alençon ; he
was murdered in 1473. The Duke de Nemours, another
rebel, was beheaded in 1477. The Count de Saint Pol,
who had aimed at creating for himself an independent
sovereignty, and had deceived in turns the French, the
English, and the Bourguignons, endeavoured to deceive
Louis XI. ; this certainly was a bold attempt ; he paid
for it with his head on the Place de Grève, in Paris
(1475). The king's policy was to establish the pre-
eminence of the Crown at the expense of the aristocracy, and by dint of patience he completely
succeeded. He threatened with a lawsuit the old

Duke de Bourbon, and admitted into his own family
Pierre de Beaujeu, brother and heir of that lord, by
bestowing upon him the hand of his daughter Anne.
The house of Orléans was rendered dependent of the

CATHEDRAL OF REIMS.

Crown by the marriage of Duke Louis with Joan, the
king's second daughter. The house of Anjou sank
into the same state of submission, Louis XI. having

wrested from the old King René and from his nephew Charles a deed which recognized him, Louis, as heir of the countships of Maine, Anjou, and Provence. Brittany was kept in check, and magnificent offers were made to the most powerful and influential Breton noblemen. Thus Pierre de Rohan received the staff of Marshal of France, Gui de Laval was appointed to the important post of governor of Melun, and Pierre de Laval obtained the archbishopric of Reims.

Another question sprang from the death of Charles the Bold. As he had left only a daughter, Mary, what was to become of all the duke's vast domains? Suitors presented themselves from different sides, and Louis XI. vainly tried on behalf of his son, who was then only *eight years old;* the accepted candidate was Maximilian of Austria, and Olivier le Diable, who had been sent by the King of France, under the title of Count de Meulan, to enter an opposition, returned home discomfited. The marriage, settled on the 27th of May, 1477, may be considered as the origin of the desperate struggle between France and Austria.

By one of those nice distinctions with which he was so familiar, Louis XI. invaded Hainault, and took possession of Bouchain, Cambrai, Le Quesnoy, Avesnes, Thérouanne. Maximilian has assembled an army ; he met the French at Guinegate, a village near Thérouanne, and defeated them completely. This success, however, was not of much avail to him, for he had, with insufficient resources, to face the rebellion of the people of Ghent and of Guelders. Under these conditions a treaty with France could not be a difficulty ; it was signed at Arras (December 23, 1482) ; Louis XI.

obtained the most favourable conditions, amongst others the hand of Margaret, daughter of Maximilian, for the Dauphin Charles.

The wily king was not really old, but the anxieties through which he had to pass so frequently, his suspicious character, his struggles with the feudal lords, had impaired his health ; he never entirely recovered from an apoplectic stroke which he had in 1481 ; the idea of death continually beset him, and inspired him with the most superstitious terrors. He had obtained from the King of Naples for a holy man, François de Paule, permission to visit him at Plessis-lez-Tours, and he used frequently to kneel before him, entreating him to prolong his life. Sultan Bajazet sent him some relics which had been found at Constantinople ; he had caused the holy ampulla to be brought from Reims with the view of having his whole body anointed with the consecrated oil.

All was useless, and his physician, Jacques Coitier, made up his mind to inform him of what he most dreaded—the approach of death. " Sire," said he to him one day, " I must discharge a sad duty ; have no longer any hope either in the holy man of Calabria (François de Paule) or in any other remedy. It is certainly all over with you ; so, think of your conscience, for no remedy is available." The strength of the royal patient sank rapidly, and he breathed his last on the 30th of August, 1483, between seven and eight in the evening, repeating his habitual invocation : "Our Lady of Embrun, my good mistress, have mercy on me ! "

If we weigh equitably the actions of Louis XI., we

cannot help acknowledging that he was a great king,
and that he did much good to France.   His task was
to destroy a society which had served its time, and
was now only a hindrance to peace, order, and sound
government ; unfortunately the means he employed
were so often contrary to morality and characterized
by meanness, that sympathy was on the side of the
vanquished.   The rigorous measures commanded by
the best interests of the country seemed inspired by
personal revenge, and he allowed too much for
treachery and underhand intrigue.

We must not forget to mention a few important
reforms which Louis XI. introduced, and which are
not immediately connected with politics.   The principal, perhaps, is the organization of the postal service.
By a decree bearing date June 19, 1464, the king
established on all the high roads, at intervals of four
leagues, stations where horses of small size, properly
harnessed and fitted out, were kept in constant readiness for the service of the king.   The superintendents
or directors of these stations were known as *maîtres
tenant les chevaux courants pour le service du Roi.*
They were placed under the orders of a *conseiller
grand maître des coureurs de France.*   They were
directed to conduct in person, without delay, all messengers and other persons sent by the king and provided with regular passports.

Louis XI. created parliaments at Grenoble, Bordeaux, and Dijon ; he multiplied the appeals made to
the king's court against the sentences pronounced by
feudal tribunals ; he retained provincial assemblies
where they existed already, and created them where

they had not previously been formed ; he sanctioned the free election of magistrates, and granted to the *bourgeoisie* privileges which enabled them to hold their own against the barons. Thus, the command of the watch in the various towns belonged formerly to the aristocracy ; it might now be bought by the citizens or their representatives.

Commerce, industry, manufactures largely benefited by the encouragement they received from Louis XI. ; he had also conceived the idea of establishing throughout the kingdom uniformity of legislation, weights and measures ; and, although he was not destined to carry out this wise and useful measure, yet the mere thought of doing so proves his sagacity.

In conclusion, the reign of Louis XI. was for France an epoch of decided progress, and the political structure of the Middle Ages was now gone for ever.

XV.

CHARLES VIII. (1483–1498)—LOUIS XII. (1498–1515).

WHEN on his death-bed, Louis XI. sent for the lord of Beaujeu, his son-in-law, and said to him, "Go to Amboise and take care of the Dauphin; I have entrusted both him and the government of the kingdom to the guardianship of yourself and of my daughter, your wife. You know what recommendations I have made to him; see that these recommendations are strictly observed; bid him grant favour and trust to those who have served me well. You likewise know who are those against whom he should be on his guard, and whom you must not allow to approach him."

Charles VIII. was scarcely thirteen years old, and as the decree issued by Charles V. had fixed fourteen as the majority for the kings of France, the administration was left in the hands of the eldest daughter of Louis XI., Anne de Beaujeu, aged only twenty-three. The Chronicler Brantôme describes her as "the cleverest and ablest lady that ever was, and in every respect the true image and likeness of the king, Louis XI., her father." He himself was thoroughly

acquainted with the character of her whom he had
appointed to carry on his political system; he used
to say of her: "She is the least foolish woman in the
world; for there is no such person as a wise one."

Anne de Beaujeu knew full well that a reaction
was being organized against the old order of things,
and following in her father's steps, instead of offering
an open resistance, she applied herself to disarm the
malcontents by favours and promises. The Duke de
Bourbon, her brother-in-law, was named Constable of
France, and Lieutenant-general of the kingdom.
Louis, Duke d'Orléans, received the governorship of
Ile de France and of Champagne. Dunois was
appointed ruler over Dauphiné. Three subaltern
officers were sacrificed to public hatred; Olivier le
Daim and Doyac were sent to the gallows, and the
physician Jacques Coitier saved his head by paying
back fifty thousand crowns which he had received
from Louis XI.

Difficulties soon arose, however, springing, in the
first place, out of the summoning of the States-
General, and, in the second, out of the rivalry between
Anne de Beaujeu and the Duke d'Orléans. This
nobleman hoped that by convening the States he
might find an opportunity of rising again into power,
and the princess-regent was reluctantly obliged to
sanction the assembly. The States met at Tours on
the 15th of January, 1484, in the hall of the
archiepiscopal palace. Never had France been so
thoroughly represented; nearly three hundred
deputies took part in the proceedings; the three
orders of the State had sent their delegates to the

21

chief place of each *bailliage*, and even the peasants had recorded their votes.

After promising in the name of the regent reforms of the most satisfactory nature in every branch of the public service, the Chancellor of France, Guillaume de Rochefort, started the question about the composition of the council of State. It was stated that it should consist (1) of the princes of the blood royal, (2) of twelve members selected from the deputies to the States-General. The presidency was given to the Duke d'Orléans. This last measure was, perhaps, unavoidable, but created bickerings and jealousies which ended by a civil war.

The chatty chronicler Brantôme is worth quoting here : " I have heard say," he writes, " that from the beginning Madame de Beaujeu entertained for the Duke d'Orléans sentiments of affection, nay, of love ; so that if M. d'Orléans had only thought fit to under-- stand how matters went, he might have had a large share in the government of the kingdom, and I know this from good authority ; but he could not restrain himself, because he saw that she was too ambitious, and he wanted her to yield to him, as being the first prince of the royal family, and not him to her. Now she desired exactly the opposite, being bent upon holding the highest place and governing all. So there existed between the two strivings created by jealousy, love, and ambition."

Light, fickle, imprudent, but brave withal, the Duke d'Orléans had to oppose a princess remarkable for her sagacity, her discretion, and her cleverness ; he was doomed to fail. He then issued a protest

addressed to the Parliament, the University, and the
principal cities (*bonnes villes*) of the realm, com-
plaining of Madame de Beaujeu's interference with
all the details of government, and pledging himself
to restore to the young king full freedom of action.
This appeal not producing the desired effect, the
Duke d'Orléans had recourse to conspiracy and
rebellion. He was joined by the Duke de Bourbon,
the Counts de Dunois and D'Angoulême, and
especially the Duke of Brittany, that last representative of the great feudal houses, and the determined
adversary of Louis XI.

On her side the princess-regent had not been
inactive. She signed a treaty of alliance with the
Duke of Lorraine (September 29, 1484), the lord of
Rieux, and three other powerful vassals of the Duke
of Brittany (October 22nd), and the three great cities
of Flanders, namely, Ghent, Bruges, and Ypres
(October 25th). She then sent a body of men-at-arms
to arrest the Duke d'Orléans in Paris ; but warned in
time, he fled to the domains of one of his supporters,
the Duke d'Alençon, and from thence openly called
to arms all the barons of France. On the 13th of
December, 1486, he concluded a secret alliance with
the Emperor Maximilian, the King of Navarre, the
Dukes of Bourbon and of Brittany, the Counts of
Narbonne, Nevers, Commines, Dunois, Angoulême,
Albret, the Duke of Lorraine, &c. The pretext was—
enforcing obedience to the resolutions passed by the
States-General, and putting an end to the ambition
and coveteousness of the king's present advisers. On
the advice of Commines and of Georges d'Amboise

the confederates had entertained the bold thought
of seizing upon the king himself; but Madame de
Beaujeu—*la grande dame*, as she was familiarly and
justly designated—anticipated them.   In the first
place, she despatched a body of troops towards the
south of France ; they went as far as Bordeaux, and
reduced into submission the Count d'Angoulême, the
Sire d'Albret, and other powerful supporters of the
Duke d'Orléans.   Anjou and Maine were invaded,
whilst La Trémoille penetrated into Brittany and
destroyed the castles of Ancenis and Châteaubriant.
The two armies met at Saint Aubin du Cormier
(July 27, 1488), and the ultimate result was the
complete routing of the rebels.   The Duke d'Orléans
fought with the utmost bravery, but he was taken
prisoner, and shut up first at Lusignan, and next
in the fortress of Bourges.

Brittany was really the centre and focus of the
insurrection.   The duke, justly fearing the consequences of his ill-advised resistance, sent in his
submission to the king, pledging himself no longer
to abet the designs of his enemies, abandoning
certain cities as a guarantee of his sincerity, and
promising not to give away any of his daughters in
marriage except with the full consent of the King of
France.   Shortly after he died, and the Duchy of
Brittany passed into the hands of the princess Anne,
a child twelve years old.   It will be easily imagined
that a person thus circumstanced had plenty of
suitors : the most to be dreaded was the Emperor
Maximilian, very powerful already, and for whom
the possession of the Duchy of Brittany would have

been a source of influence highly prejudicial to France. It was asserted that he had gone so far as to form a matrimonial alliance with Anne by procuration, but this was no unsurmountable obstacle, and, at any rate, it must be set aside at any cost.

If we may trust contemporary historians, Charles VIII. was not of a very prepossessing appearance ; small in stature and badly proportioned, he had a large head, a big nose, prominent lips always half-open ; his utterance was full of hesitation, and a nervous irritation disfigured him. Deficient both in body and mind, his skill was concentrated upon athletic exercises, in which he displayed great proficiency. Well read, besides, in the old romances, he longed for an opportunity of imitating the high deeds of Charlemagne and of the mediæval *paladins*, and was constantly dreaming of expeditions to distant countries, possibly of a fresh Crusade.

Such, in a few words, is the portrait of Charles VIII. Anne of Brittany does not seem to have been much more attractive ; but she had mental qualities which made up for her physical drawbacks. She was clever, shrewd, and her intellect had been so cultivated that she understood Latin, and even somewhat of Greek. At any rate, the young King of France gained his point, and accomplished what the policy of Louis XI. most desired   The marriage contract was secretly signed in the Chapel of our Lady at Rennes on the 19th of November, 1491, and on the 16th of December following, the union was publicly and solemnly celebrated at Langeais. Charles was then one and twenty, and the bride nearly fifteen

years old. The new married couple made their official
entry in Paris on the 6th of February amongst a
large concourse of people gathered together from all
sides to greet them. This was the last political act
of Madame de Beaujeu. Her career as regent, so
prosperously and wisely conducted, had come to an
end. She retired into private life, and died in 1522.

By uniting to the Crown the domains of the house
of Anjou the kings of France had obtained pretentions upon the kingdom of Naples ; but was it prudent to put forth these pretensions ? Louis XI. did
not think so, and had never availed himself of his
undoubted rights. Madame de Beaujeu was of the
same opinion, and in her wisdom she had seen that if
the extension of France, and the strengthening of its
frontiers were needed, it should be in the direction of
Flanders in the north, not towards the Alps. Against
this opinion, maintained unanimously by Count de
Crévecœur and the old advisers of the Crown,
Charles VIII. opposed his own strong yearning after
chivalrous adventures, backed by the enthusiasm of the
younger members of the aristocracy, whose energy,
cramped at home for more than thirty years, wanted
to spend itself on foreign battlefields.

The situation of Italy at that time was critical ;
monarchy, theocracy, principalities, republics, every
form of government was represented in the peninsula,
and deep-seated corruption existed under the polish
of art and literature. Alexander VI. in Rome, Ferdinand at Naples, Pietro di Medici at Florence, Lodovico Sforza at Milan, were instances of what can be
done in the sphere of politics when vice is the moving

principle. Treachery had taken the place of courage, and men, who would have not dared to fight openly and to meet their enemies in a fair contest, had recourse to daggers and to poison. Instead of national armies were the *condottieri*, hired soldiers raised from the scum of Europe. Italian diplomacy, says a modern historian, was a school of crimes.

The temptation to invade Italy was all the stronger for Charles VIII. because he was invited over by some of the Italians themselves, Lodovico Sforza, the Duke of Savoy, the Neapolitan nobles, Savonarola, and the cardinals, enemies of the Pope Alexander VI. However, before starting for this expedition certain preliminaries had to be gone through which implied considerable outlay of money, and negotiations with powerful and ambitious neighbours. An English army had landed at Calais, the Emperor Maximilian was invading Artois, Ferdinand the Catholic, King of Spain was preparing to cross the Pyrenees. Bent upon his expedition to Italy, Charles VIII. had to purchase the neutrality of all these potentates. The English left France (treaty of Etaples, November 3 1492), on the promise of 745,000 gold crowns (40,000,000 francs), payable in fifteen years; Ferdinand the Catholic received back the provinces of Cerdagne and Rousillon (treaty of Narbonne, January 19, 1493); the Emperor Maximilian recovered Artois, Franche Comté, and Charolais (treaty of Senlis, May 23, 1493), which it had cost so much to Louis XI. to conquer. Having thus satisfied his ambitious neighbours, the King of France at last started in August, 1494, at the head of an army which Commines describes as most brilliant, but "little accustomed to discipline and obedience." It consisted of three thousand six hundred lances, six thousand Breton archers, an equal number of cross-bow men, eight hundred Gascons, eight thousand Swiss pikemen, and a good proportion of volunteers. The artillery struck the Italiàns with terror; forty siege and field pieces, and about one thousand smaller ones, served by twelve thousand men, and drawn by eight thousand horses. They had never seen such an array, and they themselves knew absolutely nothing of the working and managing of artillery.

The march of Charles VIII. through the Italian peninsula was like a triumphal progress; but his enemies had lost no time in the meanwhile, and when he believed himself firmly established in Naples, he received from Philippe de Commines the fatal news: (1) that of Lodovico Sforza's treachery; (2) of an alliance against him made by the Pope, the Emperor, the King of Spain, the Venetians, and the Duke of Milan. There was nothing to do but to return to France; leaving his cousin, Gilbert de Bourbon, Count de Montpensier, with a force of between eight and ten thousand men, to defend the kingdom of Naples, Charles VIII. began his retreat, and met with no obstacle till he arrived in the duchy of Parma; there he found the formidable army of the Italian league, thirty thousand men strong, at least, drawn up in battle array, near the village of Fornovo (July 5, 1495). The French fought their way through with complete success, although they were reduced to a force of ten thousand men, exhausted by a long march.

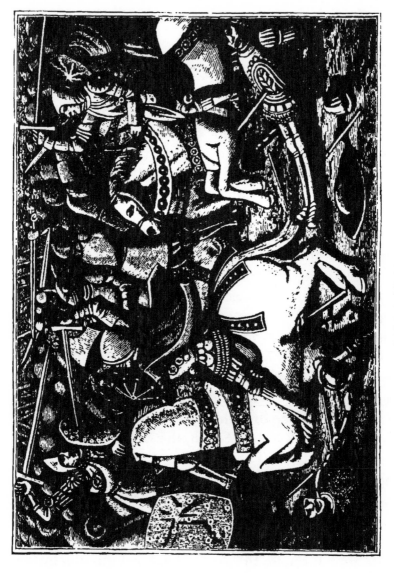

BATTLE OF FORNOVO.

On his return to France, Charles VIII. soon heard
that the Count de Montpensier had been driven out
of Naples, and a short time after, D'Aubigny came
back with the remains of the army of occupation ;
Gilbert de Bourbon had died of the plague at Atella.
The young king, forgetting the vicissitudes of his
Italian campaign, now resolved upon accomplishing
in the finances, the government of the State, and the
administration of justice, reforms which were very
much required, and the necessity of which he felt
more than any one else.   He was at Amboise, super-
intending some improvements carried on in the castle
by workmen whom he had brought with him from
Italy, when passing under a dark gallery he struck
his head against a door so violently that he died a
few hours afterwards (April 7, 1498).   " A prince,"
says Commines, " of indifferent ability, but so good
that it was impossible to find a better creature."
Louis XII., the new king, was the grand-nephew of
Charles V., and he had been obliged against his will
to marry Jeanne de France, daughter of Louis XI.
His great ambition was to take as his wife, Anne,
the rich heiress of the Duke of Brittany, and with
this view he petitioned the Pope for a divorce, on the
ground that his marriage with the Princess Jeanne
had been forced upon him.   " Right," to quote the
words of a modern historian, " had to yield to reasons
of State, and as Alexander VI., the reigning Pontiff,
desired to advance the fortunes of Cæsar, his favourite
son, he readily granted the required divorce.   Cæsar,
who brought the bull into France, was rewarded by
being made Duke of Valentinois, with a large pension,

a bride of the house of Albret, and ready promises of support in his Italian schemes, where he aimed at founding an independent principality for himself in the Romagna. All obstacles, including the poor Queen Jeanne, being thus easily removed, a splendid marriage followed. It was a piece of scandalous and cruel trafficking, but it was useful for France. Anne of Brittany, according to the terms of the contract with Charles VIII., in which it was written that, if the king died, she should marry his heir, now once more became Queen of France by marrying Louis XII. (1499)."[1]

The King of France had scarcely ascended the throne when he prepared to vindicate the rights on the kingdom of Naples, which his predecessors had transmitted to him, besides his own personal claims on the duchy of Milan, which he held from his grandmother, Valentine Visconti. The ruler of that province was still Lodovico Sforza, surnamed " Il Moro," from the fact that his cognizance was a mulberry tree; he had been the first to betray the Italian cause, and it was scarcely to be wondered at that he should remain isolated in the midst of his native country. Louis XII. sacrificed to the reigning passion for foreign conquests, but did not behave with the imprudence which had characterized Charles VIII. Without possessing superior qualities, he was cautious, considerate, and extremely kind. He began his reign by diminishing the taxes, and refusing the *don de joyeux avènement*, amounting to 300,000 livres, to which every man holding an office or privilege from

[1] Kitchin, " History of France," ii. 130.

the Crown had to contribute at the beginning of a
new reign, if he would secure his continued enjoyment of that privilege or office. He entertained no
grudge against La Trémoille and the other faithful
servants of *la grande dame*, who had beaten him at
Saint Aubin du Cormier ; but, on the contrary, said to
them, that the King of France had no business to
avenge wrongs done to the Duke d'Orléans.

The conquest of Milanese was speedily accomplished. Trivulzio, an Italian general who had joined
the service of Louis XII., no sooner presented himself with an army of nine thousand cavalry and thirteen thousand foot soldiers, than " Il Moro " fled, and
reached the Tyrol. Nothing but the maladministration
of Trivulzio gave him new chances ; he had been
expelled in October, 1499 ; on February 5, 1500, he
returned at the head of a motley band of Germans
and Swiss, and surprised Milan. A fresh army,
raised by Louis XII., came down the Alps, and met
the forces of Lodovico at Novara ; the mercenaries of
the Duke of Milan refused to fight, and a soldier of
the canton of Uri gave him up to the French. He
was sent to France, and retained prisoner in the
castle of Loches, where he died, after a captivity
which lasted some years. The Venetian ambassador,
Trevisano, who saw him soon after, wrote that, " He
plays at tennis and at cards, and he is fatter than he
ever was."

Leaving Lombardy, the French army started for
Naples (May 26, 1501) ; it numbered five thousand
four hundred cavalry, seven thousand infantry, and
thirty-six cannons. Thanks to the co-operation of

the Pope, Alexander VI., and of the King of Spain, Ferdinand the Catholic, the beginning of the campaign was attended with considerable success ; but the treachery of Ferdinand altered the position of affairs, and ruined for a time the French cause in Italy. " It is the second time," said Louis, " that the king of Spain has deceived me." " That's a lie," impudently answered Ferdinand ; " it is the tenth."

Louis made the greatest preparations to avenge himself upon Ferdinand, and to prevent the evil consequences which might arise from his defection. Three armies were sent in succession ; they all failed. Gonzalvo of Cordova, who led the Spanish forces, stopped the French on the banks of the Garigliano ; La Trémoille was prevented by illness from commanding, and his lieutenants were, first, the Marquis of Mantua, and next, the Marquis of Saluzzo. The rout of the French was complete ; artillery, baggage, and a great number of prisoners fell into the hands of the enemies. Bayard's heroism in defending the bridge of Garigliano was the only redeeming act on the part of the soldiers of Louis XII. The commander of Venosa, too, Louis d'Ars by name, refused to capitulate, and fought bravely his way back to France with the remains of the garrison.

Under favour of all these wars the Venetians had contrived to gain possession of Brescia, Cremona, and Bergamo. Louis XII. resolved to get these towns back again, and he succeeded in forming against the powerful republic, a league which was joined by the Pope, the Emperor Maximilian, and even Ferdinand the Catholic (League of Cambrai, 1508). The two armies

met at Agnadello in the province of Lodi (May 14, 1509) ; the French were commanded by Louis XII. in person, and by his two lieutenants Trivulzio and La Trémoille. At the head of the Venetians were Perigliano and Alviano. The king fought bravely, and exposed himself without hesitation to the attack of the enemy. " Let every one who is afraid," exclaimed he, "place himself behind me ; a king of France is not killed by cannon-shot." He did not lose many soldiers ; on the side of the Venetians it was estimated that between eight and ten thousand men perished. The results of this battle were considerable ; in a few days most of the towns of Upper Italy opened their gates, and Louis XI. recrossed the Alps, firmly believing that his conquest was secure.

After the league of Cambrai another league sprang up in direct opposition to it. and which was destined to put an end to the domination of the French in Italy. The papacy was held at that time by Julius II., a man of the most warlike disposition, who, far from shrinking from the employment of force, appeared on the field of battle clothed in a cuirass, and armed as a knight. His aim was to turn the *Barbarians* out of Italy, and with that view he formed *a holy league* (October 5, 1511) which was joined by Maximilian, Henry VIII. King of England, Ferdinand the Catholic, the Swiss and the Republic of Venice. The Spanish general Ramon de Cardona brought to the assistance of the pontifical troops twelve thousand men ; ten thousand Swiss commanded by the Cardinal of Sion, Matthew Schinner, descended from the Alps, and Louis XII. saw the frontiers of his kingdom

threatened on all sides.   In this crisis his nephew,
Gaston de Foix, Duke de Nemours, a young general
only twenty-two years of age, took the command of
the French forces in Italy, and for a short time maintained in the peninsula the prestige of the *fleur-de-lys.*
A furious battle took place under the walls of Ravenna
on the 11th of April, 1512.   "Since God created
heaven and earth," says a chronicler, "never was
seen a more cruel and harder fight than the one
which French and Spaniards engaged against each
other; they rested for a moment just to recover
breath, and then would begin again, shouting *France !*
and *Spain !* at the top of their voice.   The Spaniards,
at last, were completely routed and obliged to abandon
their camp, where, between two ditches, three or four
hundred men-at-arms were killed."   The battle was
won when Gaston de Foix, carried away by his ardour, rushed in pursuit of a troop of Spaniards in
full retreat; he had only twenty or thirty men about
him; he was immediately surrounded, and after
defending himself, "as Roland did at Roncevaux,"
he fell pierced with spear thrusts.

This fatal catastrophe rendered ineffectual the
victory of Ravenna.   France was threatened, and in
spite of a few successes both on land and on sea, Louis
XII. was reduced to negotiate.   The Swiss were
pacified with 400,000 gold crowns.   Maximilian had
penetrated by the northern frontier together with the
English; he met near Guinegate the French commanded by the Duke de Longueville, and who were
unaccountably panic-stricken.   Bayard, Longueville,
and other captains were taken prisoners, and the

MOUNT ST. MICHAEL.

22

derisive name of "Battle of the Spurs" commemorated
an engagement where no fighting had really taken
place.   Maximilian made his peace with France
(March, 1514), and Louis XII. pledged himself to the
Pope (Leo X.), never to put forth again any claim to
the duchy of Milan.   The English fleet, though far
superior in number to the French, had been defeated
by Hervé Primoguet off the British coast, and yet it
became necessary for the King of France to come to
terms with Henry VIII. also.   A separate treaty was
concluded in London, which secured to Henry the
possession of Tournay and a yearly pension of
100,000 crowns for the space of ten years.   Louis
XII., whom the death of Anne of Brittany had left
a widower, married the Princess Mary of England,
scarcely sixteen years old.   "For many reasons,"
says *Le Loyal Serviteur*, "the King of France did not
need to be married again, nor did he feel much
inclined to do so ; but seeing himself at war on all
sides, and knowing that he could not carry on these
wars without greatly over-taxing his people, he re-
sembled the pelican.   After Queen Mary had made
her entry into Paris, entry which was very triumphant,
and followed by sundry jousts and tournaments which
lasted more than six weeks, the king, for his wife's
sake, altered all his way of living.   Whereas he used
to dine at eight o'clock, he now must needs dine at
noon ; whereas he was wont to go to bed at six, he
now sat up till midnight."   This new *régime* told
upon the constitution of a prince who, since his great
illness in 1504, had never quite recovered.   He died
on the 1st of January, 1515, sincerely regretted by
the nation.

The administration of Louis XII., by its wise character and its excellent results, stands in strong and pleasing contrast with his foreign policy. He made up his mind to live and maintain his household within the limits of the income derived from his own domains, and by so doing he was enabled to reduce the taxes by nearly one-third. Gratuities, pensions, ruinous festivals were suppressed, and the strictest economy was established consistent with due regard to the exigencies of the public service. "My courtiers," he remarked one day, "may laugh at my avarice ; I had far rather they should do so than that the people should weep for my extravagance." A tax had been raised to supply the cost for an expedition against Genoa ; this war having been finished more quickly and more cheaply than was anticipated, Louis XII. remitted the surplus of the subsidy, remarking : "That money will bear more fruit in their hands than in mine." The soldiers and adventurers dare not plunder, and the peasants were protected against the unruliness of marauders and highwaymen. No mercy was shown to those who sought to put under contribution villages and homesteads ; those who were caught paid the penalty of their misdeeds by being sent to the gallows. Every encouragement was given to commerce, agriculture, and industry ; and we have the evidence of contemporary writers to show that "in twelve years' time the third part of the kingdom was cultivated, and that for every large merchant or trader who could formerly be found in Paris, Lyons, or Rouen, there were fifty during the reign of Louis XII. People thought much less then of

travelling to London, Rome, or Naples, than they did
in days past of going to Lyons or to Geneva." In-
comes of every kind rose to a wonderful amount,
and the collecting of the taxes and other sources of
the national revenues was accomplished much more
cheaply and easily than it had ever been before.
The States-General were convened once only during
the reign, namely, in 1506, and the deputies of the
bourgeoisie alone met for deliberation. One of their
acts was to bestow upon the king, through the
medium of their delegate, the glorious title of *Father
of the People.*

With the reign of Louis XII. must always be
associated the active, intelligent, and beneficent administration of Georges, Cardinal d'Amboise, who, for
the space of twenty-seven years was less the king's
confidential minister than his friend. Belonging to a
powerful family, born in 1460, D'Amboise obtained
the see of Montauban at the early age of fourteen ;
he attached himself to the fortunes of the Duke
d'Orléans, remained his faithful adviser so long as
Charles VIII. was on the throne, and received afterwards the promotion which he had so richly deserved
by his attachment and his devotedness. Appointed
successively to the archbishopric of Narbonne and
(1493) to that of Rouen, he was virtually the governor
of the province of Normandy, and inaugurated there
the reforms which, after the death of Charles VIII.,
he carried out in the whole kingdom. He really
loved the people, and in return he shared the re-
spectful affection which the people entertained for
their sovereign. He played under Louis XII. the

part which Suger did under Louis VII., and Sully, Richelieu, and Colbert enjoyed subsequently under Henry IV., Louis XIII., and Louis XIV. There is no doubt that critics might find, and have justly found, many serious faults in Georges d'Amboise's administration ; but, on the whole, it deserves to be remembered in history as excellent, and it became a proverbial expression to say : " Let Georges do what he pleases (*Laissez faire à Georges*)." Nor must we forget that he was an intelligent patron of the fine arts ; under his direction Roger Ango began the *palais de justice* of Rouen, and he built the *château* of Gaillon, which is a splendid monument of Renaissance architecture.

The creation of two new parliaments (Provence, 1501 ; Normandy, 1499), the reforms introduced into the administration of justice, the extension of the postal service, the compiling of the laws into one statute book pursued and carried on, and various other wise measures concurred to make of Louis XII. one of the most beloved and popular of French kings, and it is no mere formal phrase which *Le Loyal Serviteur* used when he said that he was buried at Saint Denis in the midst of the " deep cries and wailings and the profound regard of all his subjects."

XVI.

INTELLECTUAL LIFE OF THE FIFTEENTH CENTURY —LITERATURE, THE DRAMA, TRADE, INDUSTRY —CONCLUDING REMARKS.

THE intellectual life of the fifteenth century in France could not but be very poor in the midst of the terrible calamities which visited the country ; the *Esprit Gaulois* which runs so brilliantly and so amusingly through the old *fabliaux*, and the " Roman de Renart " seems to have quite disappeared, and the successors of the *Trouvères* remain silent. We have already named Eustache Deschamps and Olivier Bassilen amongst the French poets of the fifteenth century; we have given a word of praise to the vigorous and patriotic compositions of Alain Chartier and Christine de Pisan ; when we have added to our list Froissart, Charles d'Orléans, and Villon, we shall have exhausted the cycle of poets. Froissart is best known as *the* mediæval chronicler *par excellence*, but he began his literary career by writing sickly and sentimental ballads after the style of the " Roman de la Rose ; " the " Joli buisson de Jonèce " is one of his best pieces. It is sad to have to acknowledge that in all these pieces, and Froissart's poetical works are

numerous, the reader seeks in vain for the accents of
patriotism, for an expression of honest indignation at
the sight of the misfortunes from which France is
suffering. Poetry has become merely a *jeu d'esprit*,
an agreeable pastime, so much so, in fact, that even
Charles d'Orléans, whose father had been murdered,
who had lost a tenderly beloved wife, and who was
himself a captive in England, seldom rises to the
utterance of true feeling in his otherwise graceful and
harmonious poetry. As Charles d'Orléans was the
last songster of mediæval chivalry, so François Villon
appears as the last representative of the popular muse.
Before him, Rutebeuf had given the example of a deep
and natural vein of poetry; he walked in his footsteps
but surpassed him both by the scandals of his life and
the excellence of his compositions. Necessity, he
says, had driven him to commit actions of which he
felt thoroughly ashamed.

> " Nécessité fait gens mesprendre.
> Et faim saillir le loup des bois."

The excuse is a common one, and we remember how,
two centuries later, in Molière's " Fourberies de Scea-
pin," Argante asks the impudent servant whether it is
any justification for a man who has committed every
possible crime to say that *he has been urged on by
necessity.* At any rate, if Villon escaped the gallows,
it was thanks to the personal interference of Louis
XI., and he lived long enough to write that charming
" Ballade des Dames du temps jadis," the well-known
refrain of which

> " Mais où sont les neiges d'antan ? " (*ante annum*)

would have done honour to the most accomplished poet.

If we now turn to chroniclers, historians, and annalists, we find ourselves face to face, on the contrary, with a group of writers all more or less remarkable; and indeed the invasion of France by the English, the Civil Wars, the downfall of the house of Burgundy, are events which appealed in the most powerful manner to the talent of all those who had powers of observation and who could wield a pen. Enguerrand de Monstrelet, the continuator of Froissart, is extremely dull, we grant; but who would not appear dull when compared with the brilliant curate of Lestines? On the other hand, Monstrelet, we unhesitatingly say, is exact, accurate; he takes pains to procure the best information, and a modern critic who dismisses him with the contemptuous epithet of *registrar* (greffier), forgets that a registrar commits to paper what he actually sees, which after all is the principal, the indispensable quality of an historian. Froissart's chronicles take us from the year 1326 to the close of the fourteenth century; Monstrelet's narrative, divided into two books, describes the events which happened between 1400 and 1444.

After having named the two authors to whom we have just alluded, most critics go at once to Philip de Commines, and leave George Chastellain and Thomas Basin unnoticed; and yet Chastellain is in every way superior to Monstrelet; a thorough *Bourguignon* by his political sympathies, he aimed at combining with artistic colouring a due attention to details, and the faithful description of the

events which were going on under his eyes. His
principal work is the life of Philip the Good, unfortunately incomplete. If Monstrelet is tedious by
his dulness, Chastellain is wearisome from aiming at
grandiloquence. He had begun his literary career as
a poet, and the following lines are a fair specimen of
the bombast in which he was particularly fond of
indulging :

> " Muse, en musant en ta douce musette,
> Donne louange—et gloire célestine
> Au dieu Phébus, à la barbe roussette."

Chastellain's chronicle is written in the same style ;
monotonous in poetry, it becomes intolerable in prose.

Thomas Basin's experiences as an historian are
rather singular ; he was a great friend of Charles VII.
and, on the contrary, he managed to draw down upon
himself the hatred of Louis XI., who, on three different occasions, found him thwarting his political com-
binations. This was a crime which the astute king
could not forgive, and the unfortunate Basin, Bishop
of Lisieux, was driven from his see, persecuted in
the most odious manner, and obliged to leave his
native country. By way of revenge he composed in
Latin the biographies of Charles VII. and Louis XI.,
praising the former beyond what he deserved, and
painting the latter under the most repulsive colours.
These works, published as the production of a certain
Amelgard, are worth reading, because, notwithstanding the author's gross partiality, they contain a number of interesting and authentic details. It is only
quite recently that the name of Amelgard has been
discovered to be a mere fiction, and that Bishop

Basin has had his claims as a biographer duly restored.

We now come to *the* historian of the fifteenth century, the first really philosophic historian France can boast of, Philip de Commines, Sire d'Argenton,

PHILIP DE COMMINES.

the devoted friend and passionate admirer of Louis XI. Originally a servant of Charles the Bold, his methodical, astute, and scheming nature was incompatible with the capricious, rash, headstrong character of the Duke of Burgundy, whereas it suited that of the French monarch. Philip de Commines and Louis XI. complete each other, and are the perfect embodiment of the fifteenth century. The particular line of political conduct which has since been called Machiavellian was then prevalent at the court of all the European princes, and the Sire d'Argenton belonged essentially to the school of Machiavel. He therefore is very indulgent for the crimes of his master, and has an excuse for all his tricks, provided they are cleverly carried out ; nay, they seem to him more deserving of praise than of blame. His ideas of right and wrong were those of his contemporaries ; but he remains unequalled as an interpreter of events, and a judge of character ; no one has combined to a greater extent common sense and cleverness. If we look upon Commines as a mere writer, we find in his chronicles all the marks which characterize an epoch of transition. The genius of the Middle Ages and that of the Renaissance are blended together. A modern critic has observed that he did not know the classical languages, and the few Latin forms which are to be met with in his style come not from the study of books, but from the colloquial habits of those amongst whom he lived. He thus avoided the pedantry which spoils the chronicles of George Chastellain, and which makes the greater part of the fifteenth-century authors so painful to read. Finally, we must not forget that Commines was a shrewd politician ; carrying on the designs of Louis XI., he contributed to found the national unity of France, and would have made of Flanders a French province, if he had had his own way.

Besides chroniclers, a certain number of minor prose writers flourished about the same epoch. The fashion of meeting for the purpose of telling short stories and questionable anecdotes had penetrated into France from the other side of the Alps, and Boccaccio found imitators at the court of the dukes of Burgundy. The "Decameron" suggested the "Cent nouvelles nouvelles," which have been generally ascribed to Antoine de la Salle, author of a pretty little tale entitled "Le Roman du Petit Jehan de Saintré et de la Dame des belles cousines." It seems more probable, however, that several *collaborateurs* had a share in the work, and that Louis XI. contributed no less than eleven stories to the whole collection. It was compiled between 1456 and 1461, when Louis, the Dauphin, was undergoing a voluntary exile at Dijon.

We possess abundant evidence to show that literature was seriously encouraged in France since the reign of Charles V. Catalogues have been handed down to us proving that libraries existed in a number of baronial residences and the collection of the Louvre numbered 1174 works, a large amount for the fourteenth century.

The origin of the French drama belongs to this part of our subject. We have already glanced at it in a previous chapter; but it requires to be examined here somewhat in detail. Whether we study the theatre from its serious side, or consider it as a humorous picture of every-day life, whether we deal with tragedy or comedy, we find it persisting amidst revolutions and political disturbances, dynastic changes, civil and foreign warfare. In the squares and public places, in churches and chapels, in princely residences and baronial halls, everywhere the drama found its way, grave or comic as the case might be ; and it is not too much to say that the services of the Church formed a kind of dramatic exhibition, combining interest and edification. Without going back to the days of Hroswitha, the learned nun of Gandersheim, who, during the tenth century composed six Latin comedies after the style of Terence ; without seeking the origins of the French stage in the works of Rutebeuf, the "Jeu d'Aucassin et de Nicolete," and the "Dit de Marcol et de Salomon," we shall name first Jean Bodel and Adam de la Halle as the real fathers of the French theatre. The former, in the "Jeu de Saint Nicolas," gave, as we have seen, a definite and regular form to the serious drama ; whilst the "Jeu de la Feuillie" by the latter is nothing else but an amusing comedy. Both poets belonged to the thirteenth century.

The best critics have classified as follows the productions of mediæval dramatic literature :

a. The foremost rank belongs by right to the *mysteriés* or *miracle plays* performed by the *Confrères de la Passion*, a brotherhood or guild of pious artizans who devoted their leisure to the edification and entertainment of the faithful. This first attempt to organize a kind of theatre was strictly prohibited by the Provost of Paris in 1398, but the "brotherhood" appealed to the king, and obtained on the 4th of December, 1402, letters patent authorizing them to give representations in the metropolis. We cannot attempt to give a list of the mysteries which make up the *répertoire* of the

Confrères de la Passion ; let us name the principal—the
"Mystère de la Passion" by Arnoul Gréban, divided
into twenty *journées* and extending to 40,000 lines.

b. The *farces* or *pièces farcies,* so called from the
farcita epistola in macaronic Latin, may be mentioned
next ; they were satirical pieces, pictures of society
always most amusing and not unfrequently very objec-
tionable. The actors who thus undertook to denounce
the vices, foibles and ridicules of their neighbours were
a set of lawyers' clerks, known by the name of *Clercs
de la Basoche,* the *Basoche* (Basilica ? βάζω, οἶκος ?),
designating then the chief law court of Paris.   The
fraternity of the Basoche was sanctioned by Philip
the Fair as a regular corporation, and they obtained in
1303 the right of electing from amongst their body a
chief, who was styled *roi de la Basoche.*   Their performances contrasted most strongly with those of the
confrères de la Passion, and soon obtained an amount
of popularity which proved fatal to the serious drama.
The mysteries were both too edifying and too long,
and five hundred lines were the utmost that a
Parisian audience could put up with. A catalogue of
mediæval *farces* is as impossible as one of miracle
plays ; the best of them is the immortal *Farce de
Patelin,* the authorship of which is ascribed by some to
Pierre Blanchet, by others to Antoine de la Salle,
whom we have already named.

c. The *Enfants sans soucis* remain to be described.
Under the direction of a leader called *le prince des sots,*
they started as a dramatic company during the reign
of Charles VI. and performed comic pieces named
soties, which were similar to the farces in style and

character. The most distinguished amongst the *Prince des sots* was Pierre Gringore or rather Gringon, who lived during the latter part of the fifteenth century and the beginning of the sixteenth. The following amusing piece of poetry is a kind of advertisement or appeal to the play-going public :

> "Sotz lunatiques, sotz estourdis, sots sages,
> Sotz de villes, de chasteaux, de villages,
> Sotz rassotes, sotz nyais, sotz subtilz,
> Sotz amoureux, sotz privés, sotz sauvages,
> Sotz vieux, nouveaux, et sotz de toutes âges,
> Sotz barbares, estrangers et gentilz,
> Sotz raisonnables, sotz pervers, sotz restifz,
> Vostre prince, sans nulles intervalles,
> Le mardi gras, jouera ses jeux aux Halles."

After having thus given an idea of the mediæval drama, we need hardly tell our readers that at an epoch and in a country where the satirical vein was always tempted to go beyond proper limits, both the " Clercs de la Basoche " and the " Enfants sans soucis," had no scruple to turn into ridicule lords, kings; prelates, nay, even the Pope himself. Thus Gringore's " L'Homme obstiné" was directed against Julius II., the "Farce des frère Guillebert " attacked the monks. We have already alluded to the " Franc-archer de Bagnolet." The Basochians carried their freedom of speech so far that their performances were suppressed, and, in 1540, a royal edict was published threatening with the gallows any person or persons bold enough to venture upon any dramatic representations.

The introduction into France of the art of printing is so important an event that we must dwell upon it here at some length. Charles VII. had commissioned

(1458) one of the best engravers of the Paris mint, Nicolas Jenson, to go and study the mysteries of typography at Mentz. But whether Jenson dreaded the spite of Louis XI., who persecuted the late king's favourites, or from some other reason with which we are not acquainted, he went to Italy and settled at Venice. It was towards the end of 1469 that two distinguished members of the university of Paris, Guillaume Fichet and Jean Heynlin sent to Germany for three printers who had served as prentices at Mentz, namely, Ulrich Gering, Michael Triburger, and Martin Crantz. On their arrival in Paris they were provided with accommodation for themselves and their tools in the very buildings of the Sorbonne where they remained till the year 1473, when they moved to the Rue Saint Jacques, at the sign of the Golden Sun. They soon had many rivals in Paris, and the art of printing, encouraged by Louis XI., spread quickly from one end of France to the other. Presses were set up at Metz (1471), Lyons (1473), Angers (1477), Poitiers (1479), Caën (1480), Troyes (1483), Rennes (1484), Abbeville (1486), Besançon (1487), Toulouse (1488), Orléans (1490), Dijon and Angoulême (1491), Nantes (1493), Limoges (1495), Tours (1496), Avignon (1497), Perpignan (1500). It would be interesting to know what was the first printed book written *in French*, but this we cannot determine ; however, the earliest French printed book, bearing a *certain* date, is the "Recueil des histoires de Troye," composed by Raoul le Fure, chaplain to the Duke of Burgundy, Philip the Good ; we know that it was printed before 1467, but from what presses it was issued is a matter of doubt. The first French book printed in Paris and dated is the "Grandes Chroniques de France," issued in 1476 (1477, New Style) by Pâquier Bonhomme.

The cultivation of fine arts, which had been so splendidly carried on during the age of Saint Louis, was not neglected in the fourteenth century, and a number of beautiful specimens of ecclesiastical, political, and civil architecture could be named testifying to the skill and genius of French builders. As far as *churches* are concerned, the fifteenth century cannot boast, indeed, of many new monuments; the energy of the architects was rather reserved for the completion and perfecting of structures already begun, and of which only the indispensable portions were available for the necessities of public worship. Thus the nave of the Cathedral of Troyes, the Church of Saint Ouen at Rouen, the chief portal of Bayeux Cathedral, the Church of Tréguier, the Cathedral of Strasburg. It is curious to notice how certain local influences affected the erecting and ornamentation of churches, chapels, &c. Thus in Guienne, the English style is distinctly perceptible; in Provence, one may note the influence of the Papal Court of Avignon.

• Under the general title of *political* architecture we include town-halls, prisons, and fortresses. We have seen already that the northern provinces were the chief seats of municipal life; during the fifteenth century a perfect crop of guildhalls sprang, so to say, from the ground at Arras, Béthuné, Douai, Saint Quentin, Saint Omer, Noyon, Compiègne; we are only alluding, of course, to those built on French soil. Dreux,

Évreux, Orléans, and Saumur can also be named in connection with that part of our review. If we now turn to the subject of *prisons*, it will suffice to mention the famous Bastile of Paris, which has played so important a part in the history of France. Begun in 1369, by Hugues Aubriot, provost of the city, it was completed in the course of twenty years, and its originator, it is said, was .the first person confined within its walls.

Monuments of *civil* architecture abound: at Rouen, the Hôtel de Bourgtheroulde ; at Bourges, the Hôtel of Jacques Cœur ; at Tours, the Hôtel de Briçonnet ; in Paris, the Hôtels de Sens and de Cluny. Most of those elegant structures show us symptoms of the approaching Renaissance, by the combination of the severe Gothic style with a more graceful and ornate system of design and embellishment. Painting in its various applications to glass, wood, plaster, and MSS., should not be forgotten ; Colart de Laon and Jean Fouquet are two from a long list which we could easily have extended. The latter was one of the most accomplished miniaturists whom France could boast of. In the collection of the Paris National Library is to be found a MS. of Josephus translated into French. It was written in 1416 for the Duke de Berri who caused it to be illustrated, at the beginning with three large miniatures. The volume, unfinished, came into the possession of Jacques d'Armagnac, Duke de Nemours, who was beheaded in 1477 by order of Louis XI. This lord completed the decorations of the book by inserting eleven other paintings, each of which is a masterpiece ; from the Armagnac

family, the MS. passed into that of the Dukes de
Bourbon, and is now the property of the State.

Playing cards may fairly be regarded as a branch
of illumination, and as they are connected with the
reign of Charles VI. we shall mention them here. In
an account or memorandum of payments made up in
1392 by the treasurer, Charles Poupart, we find the
painter, Jacquemin Gringonneur, alluded to as having
received *fifty-six sols parisis* in payment for three
packs of cards in gold and colours with various devices. A seventeenth-century critic, Father Ménétrier,
has hastily concluded from that passage to the in-
vention of playing cards by Gringonneur; but, in the
first place, it may be observed that cards are mentioned
in the thirteenth chapter of Antoine de la Salle's
"Petit Jehan de Saintré," and, in the next, the description given by Poupart of the three packs supplied to
King Charles VI., clearly shows that playing cards
were in use before the days of Gringonneur; although
they may have been, and probably were, inferior in
make and in quality.

Nor is it more accurate to say, with the Abbé Bullet,
that if Gringonneur did not actually *invent* cards, they
are nevertheless of French origin (1376-1379), and
that from France they passed, in the first instance, into
Spain, then successively into Italy, England, and the
rest of Europe. The fact that *fleurs-de-lys* occur on
the costumes of the court cards, that the name of
Charlemagne has been given to the king of hearts,
and that the four knaves are called after four of the
most distinguished French mediæval *paladins* proves
nothing whatever in support of Bullet's hypothesis

because the Parisian artist who adapted the original images to the latitude of France and the court of Charles VI. could easily change the names of the figures and modify their costumes.

Industry and commerce rose to great prosperity during the fifteenth century, and we have evidence to show that articles of luxury were abundant in the houses, not only of princes, but of well-to-do *bourgeois·* Trades-guilds and corporations protected with great severity the rights, privileges, and constitution of the numerous industries which supplied at that time the wants of the population, and if the institution of these guilds resulted in creating privileged classes, and in excluding the very poor from trades where they might otherwise have exercised their skill, yet it secured perfection of work, honest dealing, and the total absence of those degrading frauds which result from over-competition. Another most important result in the system of corporations was that by limiting the number of tradesmen and mechanics, it furthered indirectly, but most effectually, the cause of agriculture, as it lessened the inducements which the rural populations might have had to flock to towns.

In thus tracing the progress of intellectual and social life during the fifteenth century, we must notice that gradually a new spirit had come over European civilization, and that new influences were at work substituting themselves to the traditions of the Middle Ages. Till then Rome had been regarded as the centre of the moral world, and for the solution of the manifold problems which affect the life of man all eyes were turned towards the Vatican. Now, however, that by the means of war, commercial intercourse, and diplomatic arrangements, frequent and easy intercourse was established between France and Italy, the *prestige* which had for so many ages surrounded Roman Catholicism had begun to wear away. What right, some inquirers boldly said, has the Pope to put forth his pretensions as the vicar of God on earth? Why should we feel bound to obey blindly the dictates of men who often lead the most scandalous lives, and whose conduct is actuated by the grossest ambition and the most unblushing rapacity? What intellectual benefit can we derive from a teaching the outcome of which is the scholastic nonsense of an Ockham or a Buridan?

The questions we have thus put are, every one must acknowledge, difficult to be answered, and well calculated to perplex the weak and the unlearned. Then the most casual observer could not help noticing that the Romish Church towards the close of the fifteenth century was like a house divided against itself. If the Popes were right, the corporations and small societies, which aimed at high spiritual life and devoted themselves to the works of practical piety, were wrong. Now, could this be admitted for a moment?

Whilst the whole of Europe was tossed about by uncertainty respecting the highest problems of our nature, the Renaissance movement dawned upon the world, and a fresh element was thus introduced into the apparently insoluble difficulty. Socrates, Aristotle, Plato, Epictetus, Seneca, Cicero began for the first time to be studied and appreciated; now the question would naturally suggest itself—Were all these men, patterns oi virtue and of wisdom, condemned to everlasting destruction from the fact that they were born beyond the influence of Christianity? Further, are not the principles which actuated them in their noble lives quite good enough for us, and need we go to other sources for direction and advice?

The field of discussion, we notice, had thus become considerably widened, and from challenging the authority of the Pope, men had arrived to call in question the authority of Christianity itself. It is on such a state of things as this that the epoch closed which we have undertaken to describe, so far as France is concerned. The Middle Ages had done their work, and it now remained for society to apply itself to the perplexing but noble task of borrowing from the past what was really worth retaining, and making of it a considerable element in the new order of things.

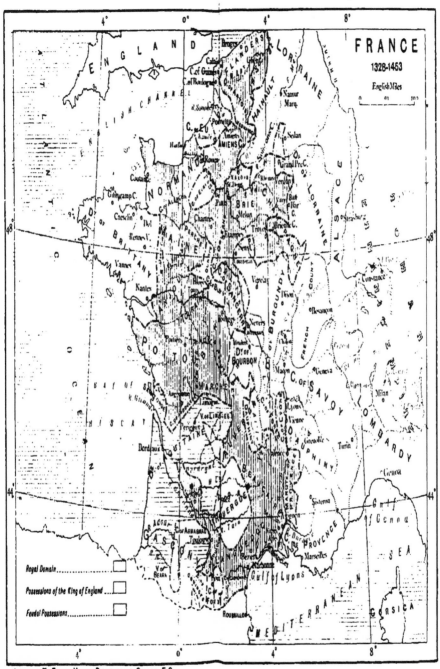

FRANCE
1328-1453

English Miles

Royal Domain
Possessions of the King of England
Feudal Possessions

LONDON: T. FISHER UNWIN, PATERNOSTER SQUARE, E.C.

GLOSSARY OF MEDIÆVAL WORDS.

A.

Aissi and *Aici* are two Provençal forms of *ici* = here ; adv.

Allodial from the Teutonic *al, lod* (hence the Low L. *allodium ;* Fr. *alleu*), hereditary property free from all dues.

Altre, for *autre* (L. *alter*).

Amatz, Provençal for *aimez* (L. *amatis*), love.

Araire, L. *ararium* from *ager aratorius,* a ploughed field. Mod. Fr. *arpent.*

Ardoir, L. *ardere,* to burn.

Art, he burns, consumes, from *ardoir.*

Avetz, L. *habetis,* you have.

Autrui, of other, or others. Used in Old French without a preposition.

B.

Baterie (de cuisine), kitchen range, utensils.

Bible, name given during the Middle Ages to all compositions of an ethical and didactic character.

Bochu, Picard pronounciation of the adjective *Bossu,* hunchback.

Buous, Provençal for *Bœufs,* oxen ; L. *Boves.*

C.

Capdel, capitaine, captain. *Capdel* is Provençal.

Castoiement, châtiment ; also *castiement* in O. F. [a book of] remonstrances, reproofs.

Cavaleisia, Provençal for tournaments. From the Low L. *caballus,* a horse.

Cendreus, base, cowards, a serf who is employed in making cinders (*cendres*) out of burnt wood.

Cervoisiers, those who sell *cervoise,* a kind of beer (*cervoise ; cervisia* in Pliny).

Chacier, chasse. To go in pursuit of.

Changier, changer.

Char, chair, flesh.

Cil, celui. From the L. *ecce, ille.*

Clamour, clameur.

Cor, cœur.

C'on for *qu'on,* whom one.

Cordouaniors, cordonniers, shoemakers ; literally, dealers in goods made of Cordova leather. Eng. *cordwainer.*

Coronies, couronnés, crowned [heads].

Coy, qui, who ; *decoy* = de qui, whose.

Créans, croyant, believer ; hence, *mécréant,* a miscreant.

Cuiche, couche ; je [me] *cuiche,* I lie down.

D.

Damage, dommage.

Déduire (se), to enjoy one's self. Synonym, *se divertir.*

Démenée, menée ; *démener*, to lead [out of the right way].

Demour, demeure. Que je demour, that I may remain.

Dère, précieuse. Eng. dear.

Desputizon, dispute, controverse.

Destrenchier, trancher. couper, décapiter.

Diex, Dieu.

Doloir, souffrir, from the L. *dolore.*

Dom, the Lord. L. *Dominus.*

E.

El, le.

Emperaieur, empereur.

Enfès, enfant.

Entremist, (s), undertook.

Estuet (m'), me faut, I must.

Exhauchier, exalt. Mod. Fr. *exhausser.*

F.

Fais, faix, fardeau, burden.

Faz, fais.

Féronnerie, the place where ironmongers have their stalls or shops.

Fou, feu.

Foux, fou.

Fremiers, fermiers.

G.

Gaaingner, Gagner.

Gente, gentil.

Gonfañon, also *Gonfalon*, flag, standard. From the Old High Ger. *Guntfano*, from *Gundja*, fight, and *fano*, banner.

H.

Hardement, hardiment.

Hauz, haut.

Héoient, Haïssaient. Thus Froissart : "Quand it remontroit un homme qu'il *h/oit.*"

Hom, Home, Homo, Homme.

Honte [faite à] Dieu (la).

I. J. K.

Istore, histoire.

Jor, jour.

Ki, qui.

L.

Lais, laisse, I leave.

Laist, laisse, leave off, desist.

Lez, près, from the L. *latus*, side. Eng. *near.* Thus again : *Plessis-lez-Tours*, Plessis near Tours.

Li, le, les, the.

Loer, louer.

M.

Mais, mieux. L. *magis.*

Mandic, mendiant.

Menacier, menacer.

Mengier, manger.

Mès, mais.

Mie, point. L. *mica*, crumb. "Ne le suis *mie*"=I am not so at all.

Miex, mieux.

Monges, moine. L. *monachus.*

Morveus, morveux. Eng. snotty.

N.

Nacaire. Eng. cymbals.

Nayx, naïf. L. *nativus.*

Nice, difficile.

Not (il), n'y eut.

O.

Orde, sale. Eng. dirty.

Orguelh, orgueil.

Ot, eut.

P.

Panches, panse. Eng. paunch

Payx, pays.

Pris, prix.

Prisier, priser. Eng. to esteem.

Pou, peu.
Puis, put, depuis.

Q.

Quant, ce que. L. *quantum*. Eng.
as much as.
Querquier, chercher.

R.

Regratiers. Eng. retail dealers.
Riens, chose. L. *Rem*.

S.

San, sens. Eng. sense.
Sayx, sain? L. *Sanus.*
S'en, sien. *S'en porteront* = There-
fore they will carry of it.
Sente, sentier. Eng. path.
Sermoneis, prêchez.

Set, sait.
Si, c'est pourquoi. Eng. therefore
Siatz (qui vous), soyez.
Solacier, donner du plaisir. Eng
to solace.
Solas, plaisir. Eng. solace.
Soume, somme.
Suelh, j'avais coutume.

T.

Tolu, enlevé. L. *tollere.*
Tot, tout.
Traïs, trahi.
Tristor, tristesse.

V.

Voir, vrai. L *verum.*
Volt, veut. L. *vult.*

INDEX.

24